S.95
N

Guatemala

ack

D1150551

The world is divided into two groups of people: the Christian anti-Communists, and the others.

John Foster Dulles, US Secretary of State under Eisenhower

The numerous bandits in gold braid who have used North American gold to subject [the country] to a reign of blood and squalor.

Miguel Angel Asturias, *El Señor Presidente.*

The president's rule of conduct is never to give grounds for hope, and everyone must be kicked and beaten until they realize the fact.

Ibid.

Cover photo: General Oscar Humberto Mejia Victores, Guatemalan Head of State

Garrison Guatemala

George Black

in collaboration with

Milton Jamail and
Norma Stoltz Chinchilla

Zed Books Ltd., 57 Caledonian Road, London N1 9BU
in association with
North American Congress on Latin America

Garrison Guatemala was first published by Zed Books Ltd.,
57 Caledonian Road, London N1 9BU, in assocation with the
North American Congress on Latin America, 151 West 19th
Street, New York 10011, in 1984.

Copyright © George Black, 1984

Copyedited by Mark Gourlay
Proofread by Miranda Davies
Cover design by Jan Brown
Map of Guatemala courtesy of Oxfam America
Printed by Biddles of Guildford

British Library Cataloguing in Publication Data

Black, George, 1949-
    Garrison Guatemala – (Latin American Series)
    1. Guatemala – Politics and government –
    1945-
    I. Title   II. Series
    972.81'052   JL1496

    ISBN 0-86232-186-7
    ISBN 0-86232-187-5 Pbk

US Distributor
Biblio Distribution Center, 81 Adams Drive, Totowa,
New Jersey 07512.

Contents

Select Bibliography   199

Maps

Tables

George Black, author of the now standard work on the Nicaraguan Revolution, *Triumph of the People* (Zed Press, London 1981), is at present a researcher on the staff of NACLA, the North American Congress on Latin America, in New York.

Milton Jamail is professor of Central American politics in the Department of Government of the University of Texas at Austin. He has travelled extensively in Central America since the 1960's.

Norma Stoltz Chinchilla is professor of sociology and women's studies at California State University, Long Beach. She is a member of the editorial board of *Latin American Perspectives.*

All three authors of *Garrison Guatemala* are active members of the Guatemala Scholars Network.

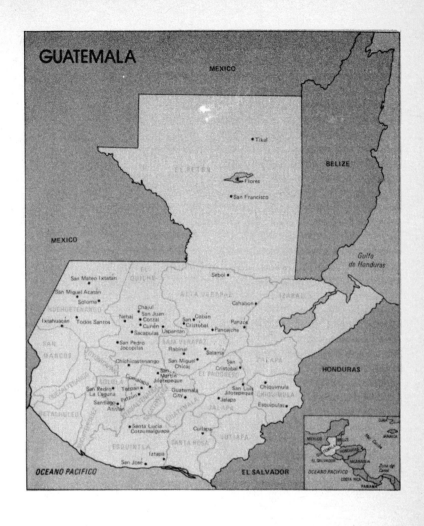

List of Abbreviations

AEU	*Asociatión de Estudiantes Universitarios*	Association of University Students
AGA	*Asociación Guatemalteca de Agricultores*	Guatemalan Agriculturalists Association
AGG	*Asociación de Gerentes de Guatemala*	Guatemalan Managers Association
CACIF	*Comité Coordinador de Asociaciones Agrícolas, Comerciales, Industriales y Financieras*	Co-ordinating Committee of Agricultural, Commercial, Industrial and Financial Associations
CAN	*Central Auténtica Nacionalista*	Authentic Nationalist Central
CAO	*Central Aranista Organizada*	Organized Aranist Central
CDP	*Comité de Pobladores*	Slum-dwellers Committee
CGUP	*Comité Guatemalteco de Unidad Patriótica*	Guatemalan Patriotic Unity Committee
CIC	*Coordinadora Institucional Comunal*	Institutional Communal Co-ordinating Committee
CLAT	*Confederación Latinoamericana de Trabajadores*	Latin American Workers Confederation
CNT	*Confederación Nacional de Trabajadores*	National Workers Confederation
CNUS	*Comité Nacional de Unidad Sindical*	National Trade Union Unity Committee
CONFREGUA	*Confederación de Religiosos de Guatemala*	Confederation of Guatemalan Religious
CRN	*Comité de Reconstrucción Nacional*	National Reconstruction Committee
CUC	*Comité de Unidad Campesina*	Peasant Unity Committee
EGP	*Ejército Guerrillero de los Pobres*	Guerrilla Army of the Poor
ESA	*Ejército Secreto Anti-Comunista*	Secret Anti-Communist Army
FAR	*Fuerzas Armadas Rebeldes*	Rebel Armed Forces
FDCR	*Frente Democrático Contra la Represión*	Democratic Front Against Repression

FERG	*Frente Estudiantil Revolucionario "Robín García"*	Revolutionary Student Front "Robin Garcia"
FGEI	*Frente Guerrillero "Edgar Ibarra"*	"Edgar Ibarra" Guerrilla Front
FIL	*Fuerzas Irregulares Locales*	Local Irregular Forces
FP-31	*Frente Patriótico 31 de Enero*	31 January Popular Front
FSLN	*Frente Sandinista de Liberación Nacional*	Sandinista National Liberation Front [Nicaragua]
FUN	*Frente de Unidad Nacional*	National Unity Front
FUR	*Frente Unido de la Revolución*	United Front of the Revolution
IGSS	*Instituto Guatemalteco de Seguro Social*	Guatemalan Social Security Institute
INTA	*Instituto Nacional de Transformación Agraria*	National Institute of Agrarian Transformation
IPM	*Instituto de Previsión Militar*	Military Social Welfare Institute
MLN	*Movimiento de Liberación Nacional*	National Liberation Movement
MONAP	*Movimiento Nacional de Pobladores*	National Slum-dwellers Movement
MRP	*Movimiento Revolucionario del Pueblo*	People's Revolutionary Movement
MR-13	*Movimiento Revolucionario 13 de Noviembre*	13 November Revolutionary Movement
NOA	*Nueva Organización Anti-Comunista*	New Anti-Communist Organization
NOR	*Núcleos Obreros Revolucionarios*	Revolutionary Workers Nuclei
ORPA	*Organizatión del Pueblo en Armas*	Organization of the People in Arms
PAAC	*Plan de Asistencia a las Areas de Conflicto*	Plan of Assistance to Conflict Areas
PDCG	*Partido Democracia Cristiana Guatemalteca*	Guatemalan Christian Democratic Party
PGT	*Partido Guatemalteco del Trabajo*	Guatemalan Labour Party
PID	*Partido Institucional Democrático*	Democratic Institutional Party
PMA	*Policía Militar Ambulante*	Mobile Military Police
PNR	*Partido Nacional Renovador*	National Renovation Party
PR	*Partido Revolucionario*	Revolutionary Party
PSC	*Partido Social Cristiano*	Social Christian Party
PSD	*Partido Socialista Democrático*	Democratic Socialist Party
UNO	*Unión Opositora*	Opposition Union
URD	*Unión Revolucionaria Democrática*	Democratic Revolutionary Union
URNG	*Unión Revolucionaria Nacional Guatemalteca*	Guatemalan National Revolutionary Unity

Introduction

Beneath the twin volcanos of Agua and Fuego — Water and Fire — lies the city of Antigua Guatemala. Here, in the old colonial capital of ruined white churches and convents, the devotees of the traditional order still gather together in the evenings to bemoan the horrors of encroaching communism in Central America, their worst nightmare that Guatemala will become a second Nicaragua. On occasion, after a few imported Scotches, they will lapse morosely into a verse or two of the *Horst Wessel Lied.* For the most part, they are likely to be coffee planters, afflicted with the same political flat-earthism that characterizes their oligarchical cousins in El Salvador. That blindness is, perhaps, the consequence of farming a crop which defines itself exclusively in relation to the outside world and its markets and pays no heed to the need for reforms at home.

On the rare occasions when Guatemala breaks out of its international isolation and appears on television screens in Europe or the United States, it is the attitudes of this rabid élite that most viewers remember with shock: the ex-president who dismisses the country's Mayan Indian majority as "robots and kamikazes"; the politician who vindicates organized rightist violence as akin to melody — which is after all merely organized sound.

At a political rally of this man's party — the far-right National Liberation Movement, or MLN, the hall is strident with pugnacious middle-aged ladies who cry for "Death to Communism!" The floor is strewn with sawdust and palm leaves. The sawdust seems a sensible precaution against the lurching, incoherent drunks who swarm to these meetings; the palm leaves may have some deeper religious significance for these murderous fanatics, who would equate all change with international Marxist conspiracy, invoke Christ as their saviour and liberator, the ultimate beneficiary of their mission to keep out Moscow and Havana.

In the dominant political culture of Guatemala, these barbarities are no paradox; the MLN is — and has long been — Guatemala's largest and best organised political party. This is a country where an obscure dictator with dreams of civilization erected Greek temples of Minerva out of cement and corrugated iron; where the grimmest and most sordid cow-towns bear the names of El Progreso and La Libertad. General Angel Aníbal Guevara, the dull-witted defence minister who carried out the Army's four-yearly ritual of

1

fraud as its presidential candidate in 1982, would announce with pride that he had been born in the town of La Democracia.

Atrocities in the name of freedom have been commonplace in Guatemala since 1954; they have been sanctified by the United States in Central America's most strategically important country since the days when Nicaragua and El Salvador were little more than names on dusty, neglected files in a State Department basement. In 1954, the Arbenz government — duly elected and genuinely popular — fell victim to cold war ideology at its zenith. In the five years that followed, the United States, organizers of that *coup d'état* would pump $110 million in direct aid into its laboratory experiment in counter-revolution.

The consequences make brief headlines: some 8,000 peasants — among them a handful of guerrillas — killed in a rush of violence in the late 1960s; as many again (some say more) in a six-month bloodbath under a born-again Christian president in 1982. Again, no paradox; this time, the killing is done in the name of love and salvation. Guatemalan opposition politicians, churchpeople, human rights activists, who make it their business to keep the gruesome tally day after day, year after year, calculate that 30 years of military rule has cost the lives of 85,000 Guatemalans.

But as we have learned in El Salvador, if we have learned anything, the recital of these statistics ultimately numbs. In both countries, the United States Embassy, relying on accounts in the officially controlled press, compiles body counts which undercut the figures of the human rights monitors. Embassy spokesmen vaunt their figures as proof that the human rights community are "guerrilla sympathisers", or that a client regime's record is improving, that it is "responding to quiet diplomacy". But whether a Central American government kills 5,000 or 10,000, 40,000 or 85,000 of its own citizens, lies ultimately in the sphere of political chess and not of truth. For the truth about Guatemala is eminently simple: Guatemala has been ruled for three decades by governments which must murder large numbers of their own citizens simply in order to survive. The price is international criticism, even pariah status, but that price is offset by the fact of survival; perhaps not for ever, but at least until tomorrow; and tomorrow is as far as the Guatemalan ruling class has ever looked.

Statistics do have their use, especially those that can provide a meaningful index of how people live. The Guatemalan economy grew, certainly, for long stretches of military rule. Its indices of sustained growth over the 1960s and 1970s are impressive by any Latin American standards; so too were those of Anastasio Somoza's Nicaragua. The similarities went further: in both countries, the refusal to contemplate any redistribution of this augmented national wealth, or even the provision of minimal social facilities, stored up the seeds of future political disaster.

Varied by a few percentage points, the raw facts on Guatemala could apply to most Central American republics — only Costa Rica's resilient parliamentary democracy would escape condemnation. A population of 7.3 million, of whom three in five live in rural areas, enjoyed a per capita income of $1,020 in 1979, a little higher than the inhabitants of El Salvador, Honduras and Nicaragua. But as always the average figure is a poor guide to the reality: the wealthiest 5% of the population concentrates a full 60% of the national income, leaving the remainder with an average of $408 per annum. By the time the calculation reaches the landless Indian peasant, we are dealing with annual incomes of well under $100.

This economy could guarantee work to only 55% of its active population; it managed to give literacy to even less — just 47%. As for potable water supply, the figure dropped even further; only two in five have access. Broaden the survey to cover hospital beds or sewage disposal facilities and the figures become even more alarming. Predictably enough, these cold facts translate into an infant population decimated by easily preventable disease, primarily diarrhoea and parasites. Out of every thousand live births, 89 babies can be expected to die before they reach their first birthday, more than in El Salvador; those who survive cannot expect to reach 60.

Access to land is of course the key. Guatemala's stunning rural beauty is deceptive; the delicate tracery of patchwork fields of green and darker green suspended on near-vertical slopes under cloud-wreathed volcanic peaks belie a catastrophic land tenure system. Of all the taboos in Guatemalan ruling-class circles, none is more absolute than agrarian reform. After all, the anti-communist demonology of 1954 was centred on the abrupt reversal of Arbenz's agrarian nationalism.

Equality of land tenure is measured by something called the Gini Index, which one arrives at by tabulating two variables — farm size and amount of land. "In a perfectly equal distribution," states a publication of the US Agency for International Development, "the Gini Index would equal 0. The higher the Index (100 is the theoretical maximum), the greater the concentration of land in larger farms." Guatemala, in 1979, scored 85.05 on the Gini Index, the highest figure for any Central American country. Fifteen years earlier, in 1964, its score had been 82.42. Inequality of land tenure, like income disparity, has actually increased as Guatemala has nominally become richer. By 1981, average wages were not sufficient to cover the vital needs of a family of five at 1964 prices, according to INCAP, the Nutrition Institute of Central America and Panama.

In the lowland departments of Escuintla, Suchitepéquez, Retalhuleu, the Gini Index becomes astronomical — 91.97% . . . 93.58% . . . 90.75%. These torrid coastal flatlands, mile after monotonous mile of cotton and waving sugar-cane, are the kernel of Guatemala's export-oriented economy. Those who produce that wealth descend each year in cattle-trucks from the cool highlands to pick the export crops for a miserable wage. And as the estates have swelled, so the plantation labourers' own subsistence farms have contracted. More statistics: in all Guatemala, there are some 600,000 farms; of these, farms of less than 7 hectares — 17.3 acres — account for 89.5% of all farms, but only 16.3% of the cultivable farmland. The smallest farms, those with less than 1.4 hectares, or 3.5 acres, represent 54.2% of all farm units but take up a mere 4.1% of farmland. At the other end of the scale, large estates of more than 900 hectares (2,223 acres) — of which there are only

3

482 in the whole country, one-seventh of one percent of all farms — occupy a colossal 21.6% of all available farmland. For their owners, Guatemala's true agrarian elite, a life of landscaped gardens, swimming pools, weekends at the country club or in Miami; while seven out of eight Guatemalan farms are inadequate to support the basic consumption needs of a family of five.

The deepening levels of mass immiseration over the decades of military rule have had their political counterpart; a progressive removal of the vestiges of democratic process. The counter-revolution was founded on destroying a real, functional democracy, the only interlude of its kind which Guatemala has known in a long dark night of authoritarian rule, where the shades of grey are not signals of dawn but merely the nuances of counter-revolutionary terror, updated and revised. As the 1970s wore on and political choices grew more stark and polarized, the concessionary framework of parliamentary elections that the generals had set in place to rationalize their power shrank; the circle of government accountability drew ever smaller. As fraud and manipulation became the publicly recognized norm, the elaborate constructs of legitimacy only revealed how deeply illegitimate the system of military rule had become. The list of those allowed to play the electoral game shortened year by year, and those who groped towards their political rights in the extra-parliamentary arena could expect to be murdered, disappeared, driven underground or into exile as enemies of the state. These decades of counter-revolutionary and military power are the subject of the first part of this book, chapters 1 to 3.

While immiseration may be the seed-bed, ultimately, of all revolution, it alone will not produce revolt: too much of the Third World still testifies mutely to this truth. Other factors must first intrude, as they have in Guatemala: the invariably violent and authoritarian response of a narrowly based élite to its political failure, and the dual process for most Guatemalans of being economically strangled and politically suffocated at the same time. The opposition movement which came to confront military rule arose from those simultaneous threats to survival. This much for the reasons behind its existence; the theme of the second section of this book, chapters 4 and 5, is the history which has woven the threads of indigenous revolt, visionary Christianity, revolutionary Marxism and nostalgia for aborted democracy into a single fabric, and the forms which this revolt has taken, in all their startling originality.

It is hard to think of a single fundamental human right which has been respected in Guatemala, apart from the untrammelled right of free enterprise. The charitable might have added the right of the people to elect their authorities, albeit in a travestied manner. But by 1982 the crisis of political domination had become so acute that even this right was jettisoned. The third and final part of this study, chapters 6 to 8, looks in some detail at the period of rule of General Efraín Ríos Montt, when for the first time in 19 years the Guatemalan military broke its own political mould and resorted to a *coup d'état,* thereby admitting for the first time that their own pivotal unity was under threat.'

By this time, the conflict between a militant revolutionary movement and a beleaguered government could no longer be treated as a purely local matter. The stakes of the new cold war geopolitics were too high for the United States to tolerate a neutralist regime in Guatemala. From the overthrow of Arbenz in 1954 to the advent of James Earl Carter in 1976, the Guatemalan military received a blank cheque from Washington. Monsters thus created are difficult to control, as Carter discovered, and human rights policies — far from reining them in — will only feed their messianic violence. In the sacred name of anti-communism, the Guatemalan military butchered its opponents, of whatever political stripe. In doing so, it consciously, even wilfully, accepted the consequences of becoming an international outcast. Removing plausible pro-US alternatives, it rested secure in its ultimate ability to blackmail its paymasters. It is Washington's creation of a cold war monstrosity that explains the apparent paradox: that a military establishment umbilically tied to Washington can yet exercise its autonomy with such ruthless intransigence.

The despairing ambition of Ríos Montt's 17 months in power was destined to fail, perhaps from the very outset, for the prescriptions he offered were essentially domestic. To be sure, he would have fallen even had he not antagonized the United States, for the young officers behind his rule never rallied a stable coalition of forces behind their vision. But in retrospect, the Ríos Montt regime highlights the disjuncture of Guatemala's crisis in the context of regional upheaval.

The limited options available to the Guatemalan élite in its attempts to paper over its domestic crisis were hard to reconcile with the demands for pliant Central American surrogates issuing from the Reagan Administration. As a US ally, Ríos Montt proved impossible to sell, bully or rehabilitate. Whatever his domestic successes or failures — and by the end he had antagonized most of the military and the private sector — this aloofness from Washington's strategic game plan also made the Ríos Montt experiment unworkable.

To override its defiant xenophobia and offer Washington a more obliging face, the Guatemalan military was obliged to resort to alternatives which promised less in the way of internal readjustments. During the incessant months of coup rumours which plagued Ríos Montt's tenure in the National Palace, and from the plethora of aspirant colonels and generals, it seemed improbable that he would in the end be replaced by his Defence Minister, General Oscar Humberto Mejía Víctores. This was the man who —according to US Congressman Clarence Long — looked as if his collar were about to ignite each time the issue of human rights came up. Yet Mejía Víctores it was who ousted Ríos Montt just three days after the manuscript of this book was set aside.

Mapping in book form the slow dissolves and the abrupt jump-cuts of a country in crisis is no easy task; what seems today's headlines can all too easily become tomorrow's footnoted curiosity. But that is the peril of writing instantaneous history, and it is a risk which must be taken. A month later, and the logic of Mejía Víctores' assumption of power becomes clearer. Though unlikely to offer anything on the domestic front beyond a return to unbridled hard-right excesses, his arrival was quite consonant with developments at the regional level. One day before the coup, Mejía Víctores met in Honduras and on board the US aircraft carrier *Ranger* with General Fred Woerne, second ranking officer of US Southern Command in Panama, and with Generals Eugenio Vides Casanova, Defence Minister of El Salvador, and Gustavo Alvarez Martínez, chief of the Honduran armed forces. Later, it transpired that US military attaché Major William Ricardo had been present in the National Palace, complete with walkie-talkie, when the coup took place.

Though the State Department shrugged off the first event as "a courtesy call" and the second as "a routine investigation of a disturbance", the drift was clear. In his inaugural address, Mejía Víctores was more than co-operative: Guatemala would "struggle by every means possible to eradicate the Marxist-Leninist subversion threatening our liberty and sovereignty". On regional security, he was no less forthright: "The Contadora Group has nothing to do with Central America . . . The Nicaraguan government represents a threat not only to Guatemala, but to the entire continent."

Within two months, CONDECA — the Central American Defence Council, defunct since the fall of Somoza in 1979 — was reactivated, with Guatemala again at its heart. This is not to say that Mejía Víctores' ascent to power was a crude made-in-USA coup. There were more than enough pressing domestic reasons for the army to act. Nor is Mejía Víctores any lover of Washington; he shares the vehement nationalism of the radical right which characterized his predecessors. No — a deal was surely struck, and the Guatemalan army will exact its price for entering into the regional military jigsaw.

In the historic Balkanization of Central America, Guatemala has been the regional metropolis. If it has managed to stay clear of the Central American conflagration and US intervention thus far, it is largely because Washington has deemed it unnecessary to become more directly involved. But it will surely do so when the delicate foreign policy equation rules out all other options — that equation which weighs up "threatened national interest" against acceptable political cost. By any set of criteria, Guatemala is the prize of Central America, the place where the Free World would argue with most passion for making its stand. Guatemala has oil and nickel where El Salvador and Nicaragua have none; it shares a long and porous land border with Mexico's vast petroleum wealth; direct US corporate invest-ments are higher than elsewhere in the region. So the argument for the defence of Guatemala is ready made, especially in these times of the resurrection of the Truman doctrine. Only the need has so far been lacking. for until now, Washington has trusted the Guatemalan army to keep control; this is no "nineteenth century constabulary", as one US official derisively called its Salvadorean counterpart, but an efficient counterinsurgency force which has been modelled on the North American pattern.

That control, of course, could snap; already, it is stretched thin. It is more likely that the fast-deteriorating regional situation will call on Guatemala to shoulder its Central American responsibilities, easier now that it has rejoined tripartite military alliance with its anti-communist neighbours, El Salvador and Honduras. All this remains in the realm of speculation. But a year which has witnessed the refusal to call off the search for a military victory by the United States in El Salvador, the conversion of Honduras into a base of military operations against Nicaragua's revolution, and US battle fleets off the coasts of Central America, leaves little room for optimism and even less to the imagination.

This book does not try to answer the question of how the Central American war will end; it seeks only to portray one of the complex social formations which go to make up the regional crisis; the country where the decisive battles for the region may well eventually be fought. In doing so, it has relied heavily — as any such effort must — on the advice and support of many people. The Guatemalans and other Central Americans who contributed insights and criticisms must remain anonymous, for reasons which they will readily understand. But this introduction cannot pass without registering a debt of gratitude to Jonathan Fried, Richard Lapper, Deborah Levenson, Marcy Mersky, Allan Nairn, Anne Nelson, Reggie Norton, Nancy Peckenham, Jean-Marie Simon and Noel Thomas, each of whom offered not only their knowledge but also their special affection for Guatemala. Thanks also to my fellow researchers and other colleagues of the North American Congress on Latin America (NACLA) for their patience in helping this project to completion.

George Black
New York City

Jean-Marie Simon

Man in graveyard

PART ONE

A Monopoly of Power

1. Counter-revolution as a Way of Life

February 1982. A bright orange cartoon tank, piloted by a hybrid of Mickey Mouse and Mr Magoo, rumbles across Guatemalan television screens. In its path appears a hammer and sickle, dripping red with blood. The tank commander takes up position, aims, fires — exploding the target into a thousand pieces as a deep, sonorous voice intones the military's message: "Guatemalans, only by force of arms will we destroy the threat of international communism."

Alejandro Maldonado, candidate of a centre-right coalition backed by the Christian Democrats, would have added a hesitant word about the social origins of revolt. But, lacking support within the all-powerful military establishment, his views counted for little. His Christian Democrat allies, battered by the officially sponsored attacks of the death squads, scarcely dared to campaign outside the capital, Guatemala City.

Otherwise, all four candidates in the upcoming presidential elections concurred with the view of the government-promoted television campaign ad. For 28 years, since CIA-sponsored invaders aborted a decade-long experiment in reform, Guatemala's élite have equated any notions of change with the machinations of international communist conspiracy. By the time of the March 1982 elections, only this virulent anti-communist glue bound together the savagely divided parties of the Right.

Successive US administrations, both Republican and Democratic, have vigorously promoted their model of economic growth without an accompanying redistribution of wealth. It is a model held together with sustained and sophisticated counterinsurgency, which has necessarily thrust the Guatemalan military into the epicentre of power.

During the Carter years, the wild excesses of the Guatemalan Right were shunned. Today, their beleaguered rhetoric strikes a responsive chord among influential sectors of the Reagan Administration, who have resurrected the cold war assumptions of the Eisenhower-Dulles era — a simpler age when the United States snuffed out Latin American radicalism at will.

Jean-Marie Simon

Worker with sugar sacks

The Democratic Experiment

Ché Guevara called it "the democracy that gave way".[1] In 1954, the Guatemalan bourgeoisie and the Eisenhower Administration coincided in their vision of the popularly elected government of Colonel Jacobo Arbenz Guzmán as Trojan Horse of a Soviet takeover of Central America.

The democratic interlude of 1944-54 came in response to a living anachronism — the primitive despotism of the Guatemalan coffee barons. Incarnated in the long dictatorships of Manuel Estrada Cabrera (1898-1920) and General Jorge Ubico (1931-44), oligarchical rule had submerged Guatemala in an economic system utterly dependent on a single crop — coffee — and on a market over which it had no control — the world market.

Ubico, a firm admirer of Hitler's Third Reich, took power as the global depression sent its worst shock-waves through Guatemala's vulnerable economy. As strongman of the coffee planters, he ran a personalized police state which suffocated both political activity and economic growth. US monopolies were meekly allowed to seize control of key infrastructure. Precapitalist relations, including forced labour obligations, remained the norm in the predominantly Indian countryside. The tiny middle class itched for a share of state power and the chance to modernize the moribund economy.

The needs of the US war economy, and the post-war boom which would follow, gave an opening to those who aspired to modernization. Throughout Central America, old dictatorships were confronted with new challenges. Between 1944 and 1948, upheavals in the isthmus dislodged archaic despots in Costa Rica, El Salvador and Honduras. The *caudillos* were swept away — Tiburcio Carías, who had ruled Honduras with an iron hand on behalf of the fruit companies since 1933; the theosophist general, Maximiliano Hernández Martínez, who had crushed peasant revolt in El Salvador in 1932 at the cost of 30,000 dead. Only Nicaragua's Somoza regime, more politically adroit, stood firm against the flames of bourgeois revolt, buying off Conservative opponents with two pacts, in 1948 and 1950, which guaranteed free economic operation in exchange for relinquishing political ambitions.

Everywhere, the narrowly based agrarian élites suffered a relative decline in their political power. The readjustment brought electoral democracy and a fledgeling welfare state to Costa Rica, the upsurge of a Liberal Party tied to modernizing groups in Honduras. El Salvador saw four years of contention resolved by a 1948 coup, led by military officers who favoured a partial modernization of the economy.

But nowhere did the change run so deep as in Guatemala. There, Ubico refused to accede to pressures to broaden the social base of his regime or to diversify production in the face of slumping coffee output. With the contraction of state revenues, unemployment and mass discontent were added to the frustrations of the middle class. Amid a wave of strikes in

May-June 1944, and faced with the withdrawal of United States support from his erratic regime, Ubico resigned. For a few short months, the obscure General Federico Ponce Vaides, an Ubico loyalist, tried to hold the fort. But by 20 October, a military uprising with worker and student backing had placed power in the hands of a three-man revolutionary junta.

There followed an explicit attempt to create a modern capitalist society. The "revolution" brought a heady period of economic expansion and democratic organizing. A dozen new political parties blossomed, led in the main by enthusiastic young middle class professionals.[2] In the first flush of euphoria, all sectors opposed to Ubico united behind philosophy teacher Juan José Arévalo, who was elected president in 1945 with more than 80% of the vote. Suffrage was extended, though it still excluded illiterate women, and the vote was scrupulously clean.

Arévalo's term of office brought what he called "spiritual socialism". In practice, this was capitalist development shot through with a strong dose of nationalism, but stopping short of major structural reforms — the root of social problems, according to the Arévalo philosophy, was not so much the redistribution of wealth as the state of human consciousness. His regime stimulated private investment in industry, diversified agricultural production, devoted a third of its budget to social sector expenditure and placed the first restraints on the activities of foreign economic enclaves.

Though Arévalo's goals were modest, the seeds of polarization were already sown. The old coffee barons, though formally displaced from government, maintained political leverage through their continued control of the country's key export crop, but new industrialists and sugar and cotton planters emerged as competitors. Furthermore, a series of laws between 1944 and 1954 granted the armed forces legal autonomy and increased their bargaining power within the state. Colonel Francisco Javier Arana, a former member of the 1944 junta, carved out his niche as plotter-in-chief of an officer class, of largely petty bourgeois origins, which was willing to modernize the economy while remaining quite immune to the contagion of serious social reforms. The "revolution" served as an incubating period for their later rise to power.[4]

In the course of his five-year term, Arévalo had to dismantle 32 military conspiracies against his regime.[5] Seeing a US hand behind many of the plots, he eventually declared American Ambassador Richard C. Patterson *persona non grata.*[6]

The Revolution Deepens

Arévalo's elected successor was the young army officer Jacobo Arbenz Guzmán. Though his victory in 1950 was convincing, the share of the vote received by his Revolutionary Party dropped to 63%, a hint of deepening resistance to reform from both traditional landed interests and the *nouveaux riches* capitalists whose interests in sugar, cotton, cattle and small industry had blossomed since 1944. Arbenz's opponents, of both groups, were alarmed by mounting working-class mobilization, new agrarian reform proposals and the assertión of nationalist rights over the excesses of foreign enclave capital.

With the new economic freedoms, strong working class and peasant organizations mushroomed. As they grew in self-confidence, their demands became progressively more radical. The Guatemalan Labour Party (PGT) — Guatemala's communist party — was legalized by Arbenz in 1951. The PGT, seeing socialism as a distant dream, enthusiastically gave its backing to Arbenz's programme of reforms. PGT congressional strength was limited — communists held only four out of 56 deputies' seats — but its activists took up key positions in agrarian reform and played an energetic role in mobilizing the 300,000 people who took advantage of the 1947 Labour Code to form trade unions and peasant leagues. Though the PGT in no sense set the tone for government policies, both the Guatemalan bourgeoisie and a US State Department deep in the throes of Truman Doctrine thinking were appalled that Arbenz accorded the party the status of a legitimate domestic political force, rather than the instrument of Kremlin machinations for world dominance.

> "Agrarian reform is incompatible with the existence of a constitutional state." Gert Rosenthal, Secretary for Economic Planning, 1970.

Arbenz's agrarian reform law of June 1952, which he dubbed "the most important pragmatic point of my government", was designed to create an internal market as the precondition for industrialization, and was moderate in tone. Only uncultivated portions of farms larger than 223 acres in size were to be touched. Even so, this restricted plan of expropriation brought benefit to 100,000 peasant families, who were granted 1.5 million acres of farmland.[7] What really panicked old and new cash crop growers, however, were the radical *methods* through which the reform was carried out. The takeovers rested less on legislation from above than on mass mobilization from below.

If the big farmers were angry, the United States monopolies were outraged. Arévalo had already taken on the three major US monopolies — the United Fruit Company UFCo: its affiliate, International Railways of Central America, and the utility company, Electric Bond and Share. Arévalo's focus (largely unsuccessful) had been the companies' refusal to submit to arbitration of wage disputes. But Arbenz pressed nationalist demands one notch higher.

Relying on the free market as well as outright expropriation, he built a state hydroelectric plant, a new Atlantic seaport and a highway to link the capital with the Caribbean coast. All the new infrastructure was in direct competition with existing US-owned facilities. And as the centrepiece of his agrarian reform programme, he announced the decision to expropriate 387,000 acres of idle UFCo lands, stipulating that compensation would only be paid on the declared taxable value. Where the Guatemalan government offered $3.00 per acre compensation, United Fruit — registering its claim directly through the US State Department — demanded $75.00. A head-on collision with the US government now meshed with internal class conflict.

The direct threat to US corporate interests was unacceptable; pointing to a shipment of Czech arms to Arbenz as his anti-communist rationale, President Eisenhower attacked. His hit-men were the Dulles brothers — Secretary of State John Foster and CIA Director Allen — both of whom had long-standing business links with United Fruit.[8] The operation which they devised was in many respects the blueprint for similar activity against Nicaragua's Sandinista government almost three decades later. While one brother mounted a diplomatic offensive to isolate Arbenz within the Organization of American States and United Nations, counting on the domestic support of an acquiescent press eager to demonstrate the "Red Menace", the other launched a covert action programme based in Honduras.

The Aborted Revolution

Extraordinary in retrospect is that a handful of renegade soldiers, anti-communist fanatics and cowboy employees of the CIA's Flying Tigers — never numbering more than 200 men — should manage to topple a ten-year old, popularly supported government with a minimum of bloodshed.

The Achilles' heels of the revolution are clear enough: though socialism was not necessarily imminent in 1954, the mass movement did threaten to overstep the limits of the populist consensus marked out by the revolution's leaders. Arbenz might well have used his "umbilical link" with the movement to consolidate a reform programme and stave off socialist transformation. But though the modernizing bourgeoisie had used working-class and peasant support as a bulwark against the more antediluvian landowners, it now proved more dedicated to securing its own economic status than to nationalist economic development.[9] When the crunch came, most of the new growers, urban industrialists and traders and state bureaucrats were easily seduced into alliance with the United States and the revitalized oligarchs.[10]

Furthermore, the Arbenz regime had proved unable — or unwilling — to transform mass sympathies into any more structured defence of the threatened democracy. As the invading army of self-styled *liberacionistas* inched its way into Guatemala from its Honduran base camps, peasant supporters of the revolution declared their willingness to fight. But the military high command had finally shown its true colours in a secret memorandum to Arbenz: arming the peasants is out of the question; purge the government of "communist and hostile elements", and the Army will support you.[11] When, to his credit, Arbenz refused to capitulate to the latter part of the armed forces' ultimatum, the officers withdrew their support and watched the unarmed regime collapse.

Among the peasant forces who had assembled to demand arms, there were those who wept openly on hearing of Arbenz's resignation.[12] The defeat was a devastating psychological blow to the mass movement, abandoned by a state which they had trusted faithfully to the last. Just as the 1932 slaughter has left its indelible mark on those who fight today in El Salvador, the 1954 reversal of democratic reform is embedded in the collective consciousness of Guatemalans. For Guatemalan revolutionaries, the continuing war is at once to recover aborted history and to complete unfinished business.

The Oligarchy Takes Revenge

Guatemala's tragedy was that its internal crisis, and its clash with imperialism, came at a moment when US power could be deployed unfettered against real or imagined enemies in its self-defined spheres of influence, whether in Iran, Greece or Central America.

The "liberator" of Guatemala, Colonel Carlos Castillo Armas — hand-picked by the Central Intelligence Agency for his malleability — flew into the capital on 3 July, 1954, aboard the private aircraft of the abrasive US Ambassador, John E. Peurifoy.[13] In pro-consular fashion, Peurifoy immediately furnished lists of radical opponents to be eliminated, as he had done on his previous posting to troublesome Greece. The regime meanwhile, with the assistance of the CIA, set up a National Committee for Defence against Communism. The bloodletting began promptly, with strong racial as well as ideological overtones. On 6 July, the daily *El Imparcial* reported "a fight between 400 Communist Indians and anti-communist Ladinos* of San Juan Sacatepequez, in which 17 Indians were killed and as many again wounded."[14]

"We were born fighting against communism; we live and we shall die fighting", declared Castillo Armas' National Liberation Movement (MLN), the political expression of the new order.[15] The party and its ferocious ideology recieved the blessing of the Roman Catholic Church hierarchy. (It had been a Pastoral Letter from the archbishop on 4 April, 1954, denouncing communism, which more than any other single event had galvanized right-wing opposition to Arbenz.) Castillo Armas and Ambassador Peurifoy were blessed by the Papal Nuncio as they descended the aircraft steps at La Aurora airport, and the "liberator" named the Black Christ of Esquipulas —Guatemala's most revered religious symbol — as

---

* While the term Ladino typically refers to those of mixed Indian and Spanish blood, Indians who have advanced their economic status or abandoned the visible symbols of their culture — costume, religious practices — may also consider themselves ladinos.

"Supreme Commander of the Liberation Forces".[16] The hierarchy followed up by encouraging a flood of missionaries into the country to preach anti-communism, henceforth the official ideology of the state.

> "I am a Fascist, and I have tried to model my party after the Spanish Falange."
> MLN leader Mario Sandoval Alarcón.

Duly sanctified by the Church, the *liberacionistas* set about dismantling ten years of reforms. Expropriated lands were returned to their previous owners and the agrarian reform was reversed, crushing any ideas of expanding the domestic market. Popular organizations were outlawed, their main leaders killed or driven into exile, and the revolutionary constitution was abrogated.

Drawing its initial social base from the recalcitrant coffee plantation owners, the *liberacionista* movement also built up an intimidating network of local mayors, municipal bureaucrats, medium-sized peasant producers and military commissioners* in the eastern, mainly Ladino departments of Jalapa, Zacapa, Jutiapa and Chiquimula. The MLN would eventually boast 10,000 active members from this base, outstripping any political party in Guatemalan history.[17]

Anti-National Development

Nonetheless, the reversal of reforms could not entail handing back political power lock, stock and barrel to the coffee barons. Guatemala could no longer rely exclusively on the earnings which their exports could yield. Neither could the halting modernization of the agro-exporting and industrial economy be ignored. Newly flourishing groups had sizeable investments in cotton, banking and industry. Rubber gathering, sugar processing and cattle raising all responded to the new postwar requirements of the US market. The economy, then, *would* expand and modernize; a new ruling alliance would be forged. In return for sharing the power they had once monopolized, the rural oligarchs were given guarantees that their land would not be touched by confiscatory reforms. Since 1954, no government — military or civilian — has breached that agreement.

Nor could Castillo Armas remain blind to the agressive new expansion of transnational capital. Having orchestrated the 1954 coup, US planners now designed a development package for the counter-revolution. Guatemala was to be a continental guinea-pig:

---

* With both coercive and administrative powers, the military commissioners — often ex-soldiers — handle local army recruitment and enlistment of government spies.

> Every nation in Latin America is watching to see how far the U.S. intends to go in helping Guatemala — the first nation ever to return from Communism — in solving the acute economic and social problems it now faces, commented one U.S. diplomat.[18]

The new strategy embodied a number of Arbenz's own modernizing ideas: agricultural export expansion, stimuli to domestic private industrial investment. But they were to be stripped of their nationalist content. The inflow of foreign investment would be encouraged. State involvement in the economy would diminish, subsidies to the private sector would be increased and direct taxation would be reined in.

In 1955, Castillo Armas drew up Guatemala's first petroleum code to attract foreign oil companies. Two years later, the Bank of America — largest of Guatemala's foreign banks — opened its local operations.[19] US economic planners began to grasp the investment potential in integrating the small élite markets of the five Central American republics. And Guatemala, with the region's largest economy and population, as well as its best transport infrastructure, would be the key to their plans. The permanent suspension of agrarian reform and the free penetration of foreign capital became articles of faith.[20] New infrastructure — highway systems, transport and communications, electrification — took pride of place in the generation of new wealth, financed by the US Agency for International Development (AID), the World Bank and the Inter-American Development Bank.

The marriage of convenience between the old and new capitalist classes, united in their anti-communist fervour, was not without friction. In a social context of bitter counter-revolutionary extremes, the dynamic new sectors — committed to economic modernization and the "American Way of Life" — were as profoundly anti-communist as the seigneurial diehards of the coffee oligarchy, an attitude nurtured by the aggressive cold war rhetoric of their US patrons. The Guatemalan economy too was shaped from the United States, and this meant that power depended on which group controlled relations with foreign capital. Old-fashioned coffee conservatives clashed with assertive financiers and industrialists, import traders and emergent cotton millionaires, in the search for clientelistic privileges from the transnational corporations.[21]

The murder of Castillo Armas in an obscure internecine squabble in 1957, an event mourned by Eisenhower as "a great loss to Guatemala and the world", robbed the counter-revolution of its *caudillo* and rallying-point, and in the process exposed divergent ambitions within the private sector.[22] These antagonisms had to be dealt with, though opening up the arena to broader consensus politics was by definition out of the question. Riding to power on a surge of acute social polarities, the *liberacionistas* branded the entire mass movement as potential enemies of the state, who had gained a threatening taste for democracy and organization. Whoever was to follow Castillo Armas into the National Palace had, then, to be proficient as both arbitrator and repressor. A lasting schema of political management was needed.

The Armed Forces to Centre Stage

For the United States, the final element in the strategic equation now came into play. Who but the armed forces could be called on to play this dual role, given the power vacuum which existed at the level of effective political parties? The MLN, which had held power up to now, was an exception, but its regressive fantasies left it ill-equipped to inherit the helm of US-conceived development plans for a modern state in the 1960s.

Not that the State Department and Pentagon had matters all their own way at the outset. The military's initial direct intervention into politics only served to fuel the tensions within the right wing. In the chaotic interlude following the death of Castillo Armas, the military annulled the results of the 1958 elections amid cries of fraud from the MLN, which considered itself —probably with good reason — as the rightful winner. In a fresh vote, the Army high command imposed its own hand-picked candidate, the former Ubico aide General Miguel Ydígoras Fuentes. Though Ydígoras would in time play along with the United States, Washington was initially mistrustful of an officer so overtly tied to the Ubico era.

Nor was the military united behind Ydígoras. Though he enhanced the legal autonomy of the armed forces at the expense of the civilian political parties, a substantial portion of the officer corps felt that his administration only damaged the prestige of the military institution. Young officers were angered by the rampant corruption within the Army under Ydígoras, and frustrated by its ineptitude as a fighting force. By 1960, the United States military mission had gained a foothold in the country through the introduction of civic action programmes in the wake of the Cuban revolution. They soon put their influence to good effect by proposing that Guatemalan territory should be used by anti-Castro Cuban exiles in training for the Bay of Pigs invasion in 1961. The nationalist sentiments of the young officer corps were particularly incensed by this docile surrender of Guatemalan sovereignty to the dictates of US military advisers. Backed by perhaps half the officer corps, the young officers attempted a nationalist coup on 13 November, 1960 — the first and last outburst of serious reformist tendencies within the Guatemalan Army.[23]

As he antagonized members of his own military establishment, Ydígoras also crossed swords with civilian opponents. The old agrarian bourgeoisie and the MLN looked with disfavour on the legal reforms which he instituted as the basis for industrialization. Worker and student riots shook the country in March and April 1962, and with them came the first stirrings of guerrilla resistance, led by the same disaffected young officers who had atempted the abortive November 1960 coup. Washington now concluded that this new outbreak of popular opposition was no local matter; a collapse of domestic stability in "showcase" Guatemala, only two years after the Cuban revolution had shaken hemispheric power relations to their roots, was to be treated as a menace of continental proportions.

Militarizing Guatemala

Throughout Central America, the early 1960s were years of US-financed changes in the local armed forces. Somoza's Nicaragua and military-ruled Guatemala, threatened by Central America's strongest guerrilla movement, were the major recipients of aid. The United States would train, equip, finance and professionalize the Guatemalan Army and security forces, ever augmenting their size, coercive powers and role as rulers of the state. The conception of their combat function would shift too: no longer would the primary goal be defence against external aggression. Instead, the watch-word would become counterinsurgency, national security and the suppression of internal dissent.

From 1950 until 1977, when the Carter Administration effectively halted weapons sales and training programmes, the United States would send $17.8 million in Foreign Military Sales (FMS), $16.1 million in Military Assistance Programs (MAP) and $6.5 million for International Military Education and Training (IMET). Under the IMET programme, 3,073 cadets would pass through US military training facilities. An additional $4.4 million in police training and supplies from 1957 to 1974 would beef up internal security under the Office of Public Safety's AID-administered programme. All told, the United States government would spend close to $45 million to help build up the most effective military machine in Central America.[24]

By 1963, the United States' ambivalent feelings about Ydígoras were resolved; a secret meeting in January of that year, chaired by President John F. Kennedy, approved an army plot to overthrow Ydígoras.[25] His crime? To allow the return of ex-president Arévalo from his Mexican exile to run in the 1963 elections — a race he might plausibly have won if the Army had allowed the voting to go ahead. Instead, on 30 March, a group of military conspirators struck, cancelling the elections and installing former defence minister General Enrique Peralta Azurdia as head of a new military regime. Designed to resolve the contradictions between fractions of the ruling class and to stifle the challenge from below, the coup opened a new era in Guatemalan history. The Army declared that its aim was to "avoid an imminent civil war and the establishment of a communist regime".[26] Proclaiming the need to cleanse the political system, the coup-makers called it *Operación Honestidad.*

The coup of 1963 also set a precedent for the coups which swept through the countries of the Southern Cone over the next 12 years: Brazil (1964); Bolivia (1971); Uruguay (1973); Chile (1973); and Argentina (1976). Each was a messianic interruption of the political process by the armed forces, whose agenda was the salvation of Western Christian Civilization and whose stay in power was to be indefinite.[27]

Peralta Azurdia's consolidation of military power brought a new Army-dictated constitution in 1965. Where some of the Southern Cone dictator-ships outlawed political party activity altogether — as the Ríos Montt regime would in Guatemala in 1982 — Peralta Azurdia laid the groundwork for a "limited democracy" with closely circumscribed political party activity and an institutionalized ritual of elections. Any threatening opposition outside an Army-decreed spectrum was constitutionally neutralized or explicitly banned:

> The formation of parties or entities which adhere to the communist ideology is forbidden, as are those which through their doctrinal tendency, means of action or international links attack the sovereignty of the state.[28]

The final clause restricted such "exotic ideologies" as social democracy and Christian Democracy, at that time a fast-growing new current.[29]

Yet Peralta Azurdia was perversely nationalistic, and his handling of the Army was outmoded and based on nepotism: on both counts he caused headaches for the Pentagon strategists who would bend the Guatemalan military to their will. After 1963, the guerrilla movement grew rapidly, gaining the upper hand over an Army and police force as yet unprepared for unconventional warfare. While US counterinsurgency experts on the scene were eager to import newly-acquired Vietnam skills into Guatemala, Peralta Azurdia allowed no expansion of existing military assistance programmes and no initiation of new programmes. Indeed, it was not the reactionary general who opened the floodgates of military aid, but his ostensibly progressive civilian successor, Julio César Méndez Montenegro.

Bolstering "Democracy"

Part and parcel of the military's notion of "limited democracy" was a four-yearly charade of elections to lend the regime a veneer of legitimacy. Elections were duly called for 1966. Three parties competed, all officially endorsed — the MLN, the Revolutionary Party (PR) and the Democratic Institutional Party (PID). The PID had been formed a year earlier as the "party of the armed forces".[30] The PR, meanwhile, was a shell of the party set up to guide the 1944-54 "revolution", and its activists were by now deeply compromised with the counter-revolution. Nevertheless, the party of Arévalo and Arbenz was the only established grouping still to hold shreds of legitimacy with the mass of the electorate.

In the event, 43.7% of the voters abstained anyway.[31] Those who did vote largely favoured Méndez Montenegro, candidate of the PR, despite the obstacles strewn in his path by hardliners in the military.

In accepting victory, Méndez depicted himself demagogically as head of the "Third Government of the Revolution". The question was whether the Army would allow him to take office. By this time, after three years of lackadaisical direction by Peralta Azurdia, the Army was in deep trouble against the guerrillas. Washington too demanded a radical solution to the insurgency, and found itself in a dilemma over Méndez' candidacy. The strategies of the Alliance for Progress called for reform-minded civilian politicians, and Méndez was just such a man; but, for the Pentagon, a high risk was involved in transferring any real power away from the Guatemalan military. The contradiction between counterinsurgency imperatives and reformist rhetoric was swiftly resolved: Méndez would be granted the presidential sash, but would not be allowed to wield real power — that would go to the high command, who would have *carte blanche* to wage war against the guerrillas. The subservience of the civilian political parties to the Army, and the impossibility of their claiming any degree of autonomy from the United States, ensured that the new president would accept these terms. With a US mediated military-civilian pact in its pocket, Washington insisted that the armed forces respect the results of the 1966 elections.

Méndez invited North American military advisers into Guatemala the day after his inauguration, entrusting to them the conduct of a counter-insurgency campaign crafted on the heady confidence of Vietnam before the traumatic reverses of the Tet offensive. In the eastern mountains, operations under Colonel Carlos Arana Osorio, known as the "Butcher of Zacapa", virtually wiped out the guerrillas in a two-year campaign. In the process, as many as 8,000 peasants would die. Victims of aerial bombing, napalm and death-squad killings they were the price of eradicating a guerrilla movement which never numbered more than 500 regular combatants.[32]

The theatre of war — the arid eastern departments of Izabal and Zacapa, inhabited mainly by small and medium-scale Ladino peasant farmers — became savagely polarized. Here, the MLN was the only established political force of the Right. Central government structures were weak, other civilian parties lacking any authority. Though the guerrillas received a degree of civilian support, many peasants were fearful that the Left's advance represented a threat to their property rights. The MLN's aggressive anti-communist recruitment campaign, allowing little space for neutrality, brought the party broad support and created the potential for a genuinely mass-based fascist movement. "I am a fascist," party leader and *caudillo* Mario Sandoval Alarcón would admit with pride, "and I have modelled my party on the Spanish Falange."

The main thrust of Operation Guatemala was in the rural war zone, but a simultaneous internal security drive in the cities, with the pretext of saving embattled electoral democracy from the international communist threat, allowed the police to dismember opposition newspapers, the University of San Carlos and political organizations. Even Méndez Montenegro's own Revolutionary Party was not immune, and saw many of its activists murdered.

Méndez faced two coup attempts from the right wing of the military, yet he meekly endorsed the transfer of power from the National Palace to the barracks. "The Revolutionary Party," he stated, "has decided to support the Army . . . in order to maintain peace and tranquillity, to strengthen our mutual relationship."[33] Eager to professionalize the armed forces, Méndez opened the *Centro de Estudios Militares,* where the officer corps attended high-level courses on economic management and government. He also reinstated the military rank of general, dropped during the revolution of 1944-54.

Having accepted subordination to the military, would Méndez' reformist inclinations hold out against the civilian right wing? Again, the answer was no. Where Méndez had promised agrarian reform, the Uruguayan writer Eduardo Galeano noted drily, he limited himself to signing an authorization that landowners could bear arms. Despite its ostensible commitment to the developmentalist goals of the Alliance for Progress, the United States did little to bolster Méndez' proposals for economic reforms. One major debate hinged on the overhaul of Guatemala's taxation system, historically one of the most regressive in the world. (Central government revenues fluctuated between a mere 8.5% and 9.5% of the gross domestic product.)[34] Bowing to pressures from the private sector, which denounced the proposed fiscal policies as "communist", Méndez sacked his progressive finance minister Alberto Fuentes Mohr in 1968.[35]

Again, United States influence at a crucial juncture proved decisive. Liberal officials at AID and the State Department were appalled by the intransigence of the Right on economic affairs, and by the brutal excesses of Arana's counterinsurgency campaign, but backed down when confronted by the reality that the Army was fast becoming, under US tutelage, the only credible political force in the country. A vociferous US business community, spearheaded by the luminaries of the local American Chamber of Commerce (AMCHAM), added its hostility to any idea of reform, asserting that an iron hand was needed to keep strategic Guatemala safe for American investments. Washington's retreat on the tax issue convinced the private sector that intransigence was the best course: sooner or later, whatever its moral qualms, the United States would inevitably be browbeaten into support for the Right. That capacity for blackmail has continued to characterize the Guatemalan Right and its Salvadorean counterpart throughout the escalating Central American crisis.

There was sound economic logic, too, in the hard line. The Central American Common Market (CACM), set up in 1961 to integrate the small élite markets of the five republics and rationalize economic competition, designated Guatemala as its base of operations, tied to the demands of world markets. What need was there then to create a domestic market through structural reforms? The middle class grew; the rich got richer; mass pauperisation worsened. And the military kept the show on the road.

For the ruling élite, the show was profitable. The very success of the economy, helped along by Guatemala's favoured position within the CACM — where it grew at the expense of weaker member nations — told them they were right. From 1960 until the onset of the oil crisis in 1973, inflation was almost unknown, averaging less than 0.5% throughout the 1960s.[36] Guatemala enjoyed one of the lowest foreign debts in Latin America; balance of payments problems were negligible; and the International Monetary Fund selected the quetzal — long pegged to the US dollar — as one of its stable reserve currencies.

It all added up to a boom. But the ruling élite was so narrowly based, its face so set against growth with redistribution, its machinery of mediation so poorly developed, that the routine conflicts facing any capitalist society were perceived as a mortal threat to the existing order, requiring the military as vigilant guardians and managers of the political system.

Another problem loomed, however: many military officers had themselves taken on a lean and hungry look. The decade of the 1970s would witness their transformation from custodians of the wealth of others to an economic power in their own right. The man who oversaw their transformation was Carlos Arana Osorio, the Butcher of Zacapa.

Notes

1   Speech to Latin American Youth Conference, Havana, 1960, cited in Régis Debray, *The Revolution on Trial* (Harmondsworth, Penguin books, 1974) p.271.

2   Miguel Pérez Ruíz, *Guatemala, un País que se construye en la guerra,* in *Le Monde Diplomatique en Español*, October 1979.

3   See Susanne Jonas and David Tobis (eds.), *Guatemala* (Berkeley, California, North American Congress on Latin America, 1974), pp. 46-7; Stephen Kinzer and Stephen Schlesinger, *Bitter Fruit: The Untold Story of the American Coup in Guatemala* (New York, Doubleday and Co., 1982), pp.37-42.

4   Gabriel Aguilera Peralta, "Estado militar y lucha revolucionaria", paper presented to first regional seminar of the Instituto de Investigaciones Económicas y Sociales (INIES), Managua, Nicaragua, June 1982; René Poitevin, *El proceso de industrialización en Guatemala* (San José, Costa Rica, EDUCA, 1977), pp.155-7.

5   Pérez Ruíz, *Guatemala.*

6   Debray, *The Revolution on Trial,* p.272.

7   Thomas and Marjorie Melville, *Guatemala: Another Vietnam?* (Harmondsworth, Penguin Books, 1971), p.61; Jonas and Tobis, *Guatemala,* p.49.

8   Richard H. Immerman, *The CIA in Guatemala: The Foreign Policy of Intervention* (Austin, University of Texas Press, 1982), p.124. Despite the title of Immerman's book, it dwells less on the machinations of the CIA and the United Fruit Company than does Kinzer and Schlesinger's *Bitter Fruit.* Immerman offers a more considered academic study of Guatemala's importance to the ideology of the cold war.

9   Fuerzas Armadas Rebeldes (FAR), *Guatemala en Lucha,* no.3, 1982.

10 Aguilera, *Estado militar.*

11 Edelberto Torres-Rivas, "Crisis y coyuntura política: La caída de Arbenz y los contratiempos de la revolución burguesa", *Política y Sociedad* no.4, (Guatemala City), July-December 1977, p.66.

12 Melville and Melville: *Guatemala,* p.102.

13 According to a *Time* magazine correspondent, cited in Kinzer and Schlesinger, *Bitter Fruit,* p.122.

14 Cited in Melville and Melville, *Guatemala,* p.121.

15 *Inforpress* (Guatemala City), 3 December, 1981. On the founding principles and ideology of the MLN, see *El Plan de Tegucigalpa, al alcance de todos los patriotas* (Tegucigalpa, Honduras, 1953).

16 *Brecha* (Mexico City), no.5 (July-August 1981).

17 *El Día* (Mexico City), 6 March, 1982.

18 Former US Ambassador to Mexico, William O'Dwyer, cited in Jonas and Tobis, *Guatemala,* p.76.

19 Ibid., pp.79-80; Allan Nairn, "The Subsidization of Terror: The Bank of America in Guatemala", *COHA Research Memorandum,* 8 February, 1982.

20   On the Central American Common Market, see David Tobis, "The Central American Common Market — The Integration of Underdevelopment", *NACLA Newsletter,* Vol. III, no.9 (January 1970); Julio Carranza Valles, *El Mercado Común Centroamericano — un caso de integración dependiente* (Havana Centro de Estudios sobre América, 1981), Enrique Delgado, *Evolución del Mercado Común Centro-americano y desarrollo equilibrado* (San José, Costa Rica, EDUCA, 1981).

21   See interview with Manuel Colom Argueta, *Latin America Political Report,* 6 April, 1979.

22   Blanche Wiesen Cook, *The Declassified Eisenhower: A Divided Legacy* (New York, Doubleday & Co., 1981), p.289; Immerman: *The CIA in Guatemala,* p.200.

23   Gabriel Aguilera, "Terror and Violence as Weapons of Counterinsurgency in Guatemala", *Latin American Perspectives,* nos. 25-26 (Spring and Summer, 1980), pp.91-113.

24   US Department of Defence, Defence Security Agency, *Foreign Military Sales and Military Assistance Facts,* 1980; US Department of Defence, *Congressional Presentation Document: Security Assistance Fiscal Year 1982;* US Office of Public Safety (OPS), *Termination Phase-Out Study of the Public Safety Project: Guatemala,* 1974. For full details, see Delia Miller, Roland Seeman and Cynthia Arnson, *Background Information on Guatemala, the Armed Forces and U.S. Military Assistance* (Washington DC, Institute for Policy Studies, 1981).

25   Kinzer and Schlesinger, *Bitter Fruit,* p.243.

26   Melville and Melville, *Guatemala,* p.173.

27   See Mario Esteban Carranza, *Fuerzas Armadas y estado de excepción en América Latina* (Mexico City, Siglo XXI, 1978), pp.7-67.

28   *Constitución de la República de Guatemala,* 1965, article 27.

29   See, "Posición del PSD respecto al proceso electoral en 1982", *Agencia Latinoamerica de Información (ALAI),* (Montreal, Canada), 4 December, 1981.

30   On the changing nature of the Partido Revolucionario in the 1960s, see Poitevin, *El proceso de industrialización,* p.191.

31   Aguilera, *Estado militar.*

32   Susanne Jonas Bodenheimer, "Guatemala: The Politics of Violence", *NACLA's Latin American and Empire Report,* Vol.VI, no.2 (February 1972), p.25.

33   Melville and Melville, *Guatemala,* p.223.

34   World Bank, *Guatemala: Economic and Social Position and Prospects,* (Washington DC, 1978), p.50.

35   Jonas and Tobis, *Guatemala,* pp.105-6.

36   World Bank, *Guatemala,* pp i and 25.

Bag lady and Bank of America

Jean-Marie Simon

2. The Decade of the Generals

Three generals ruled Guatemala during the 1970s: Carlos Arana Osorio (1970-4), Kjell Laugerud García (1974-8), and Romeo Lucas García (1978-82). Arana, popular wisdom has it, was the cunning old fox, Laugerud the insipid reformer, Lucas the psychotic tyrant. But these epithets, reducing the decade's waves of terror and intervals of reform to the whims of a leader's personality, mask the logic and continuity of the military regimes. After 12 years of their rule, a deep political crisis engulfed Guatemala's ruling class.

Capitalist modernization in the 1960s had segmented the bourgeoisie into agrarian, industrial, financial and commercial fractions, the rhythm of their formation dictated above all by the needs of transnational capital. Conflicts between the most entrenched coffee planters, represented by the MLN, and the newer, more dynamic groups were often rancorous. But otherwise, cotton growers and bankers, traders and cattle ranchers, did not allow sectoral competition to undermine the relative harmony which prevailed between them until the middle of the 1970s — as long, that is, as the economic boom lasted.

More important than these internecine disputes of the rich was the changing relationship between the armed forces and the bourgeoisie as a whole. Starting with Arana, the military developed its own economic interests. Brought into government originally as coercive protector of the established order, its senior officers used state power as a launching pad into agro-exporting, industry, finance and real estate. In the process, they became Guatemala's strongest political force. At the same time, internal cohesion came from the cult of loyalty to the military caste, and squashed any tendency within the ranks towards reformist experiments of the kind being demonstrated by the Velasco regime in Peru between 1968 and 1975.

Military rule neutralized still further the ineffectual parties, and the armed forces filled the vacuum with their own quasi-party structures. A clique of high-ranking officers functioned as a central committee in all but name. The Army chief of staff held veto power over cabinet appointments.

Though the armed forces encroached on many key areas of the economy

Franja Transversal del Norte

and the state through ever more Mafia-like methods, the bourgeoisie was not at first unhappy with the alliance. The military's extreme *laissez-faire* approach to economic management, combined with sustained growth rates and the denial of political reforms, provided most of the bourgeoisie with a tranquil business environment and a large enough cake, even if the slice which the military allotted itself did increase dramatically. With blind complacency, the ruling class believed that its economic growth model was eternal. If the political system remained unchanged, the Garden of Eden would bring forth its fruits in abundance.

But, like the Garden of Eden, this was ultimately a fantasy world. The fires of class conflict were stoked by the suffocating repression of the mass movement in the 1970s and the refusal to open up the political system. Rapid capitalist development brought profound changes in class structure, and the expansion of agro-exporting fuelled rural inequalities. As the end of the decade approached, the Guatemalan private sector found itself wholly unprepared for the sudden slump in cash-crop prices — particularly coffee — and the brutal impact of world recession. State violence, escalating into naked terror during the periods 1966-8, 1970-3 and 1978-82, proved the only means for defending the status quo.

Increasingly, that terror would hit the centre of the political spectrum. Christian Democrats and social democrats were fair game for the death squads if they threatened to become more than an ineffectual adornment to the military version of "pluralism". The fast-growing middle class — never allowed more than crumbs from the rich men's table — stood alienated from the military regime.[1]

Pacification and Growth

Widespread distaste for the brutality of his counterinsurgency campaign of 1966-8 had put Carlos Arana Osorio in mothballs for a year as Guatemalan Ambassador to Nicaragua. But after cementing strong ties, both commercial and political, with Nicaraguan dictator Anastasio Somoza Debayle, he was recalled to be the military's candidate in the 1970 presidential elections. Washington duly signalled its pleasure at Arana's election by dispatching $32.2 million in economic aid during 1972, the second highest annual figure ever to Guatemala.

Defeat of the guerrillas had done nothing to mitigate social tensions, and the bourgeoisie made it clear to Arana that pacification was top of their agenda. So did the US corporations that had invested in Guatemala over the previous decade. With over $200 million in direct investments, the US transnationals far outweighed national industrial capital — most industries employing more than 50 workers were foreign-owned.

In the peak years of regional integration, from 1960 to 1968, the influx of foreign capital to Guatemala had trebled, most going into oil and nickel extraction, industry and commerce. Without ever losing their *economic* predominance, the traditional agrarian interests saw their political role supplanted by military men making independent fortunes in industry, commerce and finance, and acting as junior partners to the foreign petroleum companies.[3]

Largest of the new operators was the giant Canadian nickel corporation, INCO. Its Guatemalan plant, EXMIBAL — in which the US Hanna Mining Company held a 20% stake — expanded sharply as world prices for nickel, a vital component for jet engines and aerospace technology, rose fivefold during the late 1960s. Granted a ten-year tax exemption by the Guatemalan government in 1968, INCO's initial investment of $50 million in 1960 soared to $180 million by 1969.[4]

On a different scale, 32 nationally owned companies were bought out by US investors at a cost of $24 million.[5] Guatemala was transformed into the hub of regional economic planning — headquarters for the AID Central American mission, the Central American Economic Integration System (SIECA) and the Central American Monetary Council.

By the time of Arana's inauguration, winds of change were blowing through the economy. The limited import-substitution industrialization of the Central American Common Market period was grinding to a halt, and after the 1969 war between Honduras and El Salvador, regional trade was in disarray. Richard Nixon's arrival in the White House in January 1969, backed by Cuban exile and Sunbelt investors, paved the way for their invasion of Central America. Their instincts were well-suited to rapid-profit speculation in tourism, real estate and new forms of agribusiness export (fruit, flowers and vegetables, destined mainly for the US market; and later cardamom, a high yield crop aimed at export to the Middle East, particularly Saudi Arabia).[6]

> "When a law is needed, it is considered a matter of ordinary business to discuss how much is to be allotted as gifts to [Guatemalan] Congressmen. It is routine." Miami banker, 1974.

Control of state power gave Arana — never the most fastidious of operators — a unique platform from which to build alliances with businessmen and conservative politicians from the power centres of Florida, Texas and California. At the same time, a parallel nexus of relationships grew up between leading Sunbelt figures and the Somoza clan in Nicaragua. Partnership with foreign capital, always attractive and lucrative, took on overtly criminal proportions in both countries. Corruption became the norm in government. Said one Miami businessman in 1974: "When a law is needed, it is considered a matter of ordinary business to discuss how much is to be allotted as gifts to [Guatemalan] congressmen. It is routine."

Though corruption was nothing new in Guatemala, the Arana regime raised it to new heights. Not only did corruption take place on a vast scale — indeed, Guatemala would come to rival cocaine-ridden Bolivia in the amount of government income siphoned off through corruption — but there was a qualitative difference in the systematic use of the state apparatus for the enrichment of the bloc in power — senior military officers and their closest civilian and bureaucratic allies. Arana himself set the tone: the 1973 Federal Budget granted him $12,000 a month in presidential "expenses" and allocated him a further $1.6 million a year in confidential discretionary funds.[7]

Arana's abrasive style did not endear him to economic competitors, but Guatemala's first Five Year Development Plan (1971-5) held out hopes to them that enough wealth would be generated to go around. Arana's authoritarian design to modernize the economy argued that not even the solid growth rates of the 1960s were adequate. A booming country, his economic team decided, should aim for sustained annual growth rates of 7.8% throughout the 1970s.

The New Infrastructure

To provide energy and communications for the large, foreign-based corporations, and to open up the virgin farmlands of the north, large-scale infrastructural projects got underway with the huge Chixoy hydroelectric project in 1974. Big construction contracts opened the door for lucrative kickbacks to the state agencies that dispensed them.

The second Development Plan (1976-9) gave even greater impetus to infrastructural projects under the government of Arana's successor, General Kjell Laugerud García. All would depend on a huge inflow of US and multilateral bank capital. Three hydroelectric plants alone — Chixoy and Chulac in the highlands and Aguacapa on the south coast — cost well over $1 billion. Add to this a 1.2 million barrel-per-day capacity oil pipeline from the Mexican border to the Caribbean, a small oil refinery at Pantín in the department of Baja Verapaz, a new Pacific port complex at San José and a $1 billion national highway system, and the concept was awesome.

The heart of the infrastructural development programme was the so-called *Franja Transversal del Norte* (Northern Transverse Strip), a vast swathe of territory stretching from the Mexican border to Guatemala's narrow Caribbean outlet at the port of Puerto Barrios. The 3,500 square miles of the *Franja* are a magnet for transnational investors: oil is here, part of the same field which runs through the southern states of Mexico. So too is nickel, along the shores of Lake Izabal. "The reason we're here," explains H.L. Megan, general manager of the Shenandoah Oil corporation of Fort Worth, Texas, "is because we're optimistic about making money." With good reason, for the transnationals were prime beneficiaries of the new, cost-cutting hydroelectric plants located in the *Franja*.

But more important, the region proved a playground for the new military-civilian class that ruled Guatemala after 1970. Here, in virgin territory, the regime set about creating a new geographical power base, far away from the traditional centres of agrarian power, for the most rapid and violent forms of capital accumulation. Reported an official of the National Institute of Agrarian Transformation (INTA) :

> The government gave away or sold land titles to outsiders, it went to politicians, the rich, the military. They all grabbed what they could. There are large untouchable estates we call "The Zone of the Generals".

Though they made fortunes from livestock, agriculture and forestry on the new frontier, their avarice made enemies of all other bourgeois groups. At the same time, it provoked frontal class conflict with the local peasant population. On both counts, the development of the *Franja* enmeshed the regime ever deeper in political crisis.

The Chixoy dam remained the pearl of the programme: after an initial injection of $7.8 million from the Central American Economic Integration Bank (BCIE) in November 1974, international cash flowed into a project whose 300,000 KW generating capacity made it the largest in the region. The World Bank supplied $145 million in 1975 and the Inter-American Development Bank (IDB) $105 million in the following year — that bank's largest ever single loan. United States voting representatives eagerly argued the case for both loans.[8]

As well as the access to infrastructure, the transnational corporations gained direct financial benefits. Legislation put through in 1975 gave them 100% tax exemption on profits for five years, and a one-year exemption from import taxes on machinery, plant, fuel and spare parts.[9]

By the end of the 1970s, 193 US companies had taken advantage of the "favourable investment climate" to set up Guatemalan operations; 52 of them were agribusiness concerns.[10] Direct investment amounted to $260 million, the largest figure in Central America, and 33 of the world's top 100 firms on the *Fortune* listing had established local operations.[11] This was in marked contrast to El Salvador, where only six are present.

The Army's Political Model

While Arana kept his bargain with foreign capital, he also redrew the rules of the political game at home. Bodies began to appear along the roadsides in a renewed wave of terror. In January 1971 alone, 483 people disappeared; not only nameless peasants and workers, to be hastily buried in graves marked "XX", but even nationally known figures — intellectuals, trade union officials, moderate party leaders — who had explicitly agreed to playing by the military's political rule-book. The gunning down in 1971 of Adolfo Mijango López, wheelchair-bound leader of the social democratic Revolutionary Democratic Union (URD) set the tone. Revolutionary opposition was clearly unacceptable, but the political process would from now on exclude anyone whose views were to the left of what the armed forces deemed the centre.[12]

Mother and child   Anne Nelson

> "In Guatemala, it is useless to think of governing, except as the result of a political decision by the Army." Christian Democrat leader Danilo Barillas, 1975.

The military took full control of the electoral machinery, and narrowed down the spectrum of "tolerable" opponents. And by opening new agencies such as the Army Bank to rationalize its economic holdings, the military showed that its ascent to riches under Arana was no short-term whim. Instead, it served notice that it intended to remain in power, shaping a system under which its economic and political status could never be challenged. Opponents, even those prepared to act out the intermittent farce of rigged elections, recognized the realities of the situation. In 1975, after a coalition backed by his party had been blatantly defrauded of electoral victory, Christian Democrat leader Danilo Barillas admitted to a reporter that "in Guatemala, it is useless to think of governing, except as the result of a political decision by the Army".

Down the Slippery Slope
Any ruling group, no matter how disdainful of public accountability, has to find ways of legitimizing its power. The creeping political crisis of the Guatemalan bourgeoisie in the 1970s lay in its failure to construct and hold together a viable social base.

Arana, Laugerud and Lucas García each took office at the head of a different right-wing coalition, patching together a transient alliance with one or other civilian group. None of the three was ever a purely military dictatorship. Each of them offered promises of change: Arana said he would provide "Bread and Peace"; Laugerud "gradual civic reform"; Lucas depicted himself in his electoral campaign as the "Centre-Left Soldier"; none could deliver. From 1970, through the frauds of 1974 and 1978, to the final collapse of the political model in 1982, the ritual of elections, which only the Right could contest and only the army candidate could win, degenerated into farce. Each new presidency burned more and more of its bridges to left, right and centre, until the armed forces stood bereft of all civilian support. The military continued to use a list of 72,000 proscribed political opponents drawn up after the 1954 counter-revolution, adding new names to it constantly.

General Kjell Laugerud García, a career officer of Norwegian extraction, took office in 1974. He was an Arana protégé, and the outgoing president had vowed that he intended to use "all the might that goes with holding power" to ensure the election victory of his hand-picked successor.[13] It was a crucial conjuncture. The previous two years had been difficult ones for the region's military regimes, and they took the threat seriously. In several countries, new bourgeois opposition groupings had coalesced around reformist electoral platforms, and working-class mobilization was on the upsurge. New guerrilla movements were flexing their muscles, their cadre a heterogeneous mix of disillusioned Christian Democrats, dissident communists and radicalized Roman Catholic activists. Rejecting electoral strategies as a mirage, they vehemently opposed the local communist parties' enrolment in bourgeois-dominated coalitions.

In Nicaragua, the catastrophic earthquake of December 1972 was followed within months by a major strike in the building industry, led by the Nicaraguan Moscow-line Socialist Party (PSN). Actions by banana workers and hospital employees followed. In parallel to this, centrist opponents of *Somocismo* merged into the UDEL coalition under the direction of liberal newspaper publisher Pedro Joaquín Chamorro. By the end of 1974, the Sandinista National Liberation Front (FSLN) had audaciously seized the initiative by successfully holding major regime figures hostage in the centre of Managua. Somoza's response was to clamp a three-year state of siege on the country and further centralize his own political control.

In El Salvador, the military defrauded the opposition UNO coalition, backed by communists, social democrats and Christian Democrats, of rightful victory in the 1972 poll, and crushed the ensuing revolt by constitutionally-minded young officers. By 1972, the two main Salvadorean guerrilla groups were in operation: the Popular Liberation Forces (FPL) formed by communists exasperated at the party's continued faith in electoral methods, and the People's Revolutionary Army (ERP), centred on a cadre of disaffected young Christian Democrats. Nationwide working-class activism gave rise by 1974 to the first of El Salvador's mass popular organizations, the Unified Popular Action Front (FAPU).

While the Salvadorean military and its official party, the PCN, met their crisis by more narrowly circumscribing the space for political activity, the Hondurans reacted otherwise. Here, the challenge was different and less radical — sweeping demands from the peasantry for agrarian reform, which ushered in a three-year interlude, from 1972 to 1975, of reformist liberal rule. An uneasy tripartite alliance between military, labour and business kept Honduras clear of violent social upheavals.

For the Guatemalan generals, 1973 brought the first serious revival of urban mass militancy since the defeat of 1954. Teachers led the way, with their 1973 strike. In no time, their example was emulated by electricity, railway and communications workers. The military high command was united in its belief that "the Army is the only force capable, morally and materially, of governing Guatemala."[14]

By election time, the military was sure that the bloodbath of the Arana years had done its job. The economy was booming; the Army had not only ascended to state power, but had become the dominant economic fraction of the ruling class. The military puppet-masters could again afford the illusion of electoral pluralism, knowing that they pulled the strings of centrist and reformist participation. Laugerud's campaign could even indulge itself with the promise of a slight *apertura*. However, the rules of the election were clear: a civilian candidate would not be permitted to win.

Acquiescently, two parties dropped their original civilian nominees in favour of military officers. Against Laugerud's civilian-military coalition, the Revolutionary Party fielded Colonel Ernesto Paíz Novales. Unlike 1966, when it had offered Julio César Méndez Montenegro as its candidate, there was no pretence this time of the PR pushing a reformist alternative. That role fell to a coalition not dissimilar to that which had fielded Colonel Ernesto Claramount in neighbouring El Salvador in 1972, with disastrous consequences. The sacrificial lamb in Guatemala was former Army Chief of Staff, General Efraín Ríos Montt, standing on a joint slate of Christian Democrats and social democrats.

To Arana's horror, Ríos Montt took 45% of the vote, clearly unthinkable. By the time the Army had sealed off the ballot boxes, a recount showed Laugerud with a healthy 5.5% winning margin. Ríos Montt, though raging at "a regime of absolute illegality", was outgunned and outmanned. As a military man, he understood military realities. After a closed-doors meeting with the incoming president — during which money allegedly changed hands — he accepted diplomatic exile as military attaché in Madrid.[15] Never again would significant numbers of Guatemalan voters place their faith in peaceful reform through the ballot box, and Ríos Montt would have to wait eight years before claiming the presidency.[16]

Secure in its fraudulent victory, the Army shored up its political defences. Since 1970, Mario Sandoval Alarcón's MLN had been its main electoral ally. As president of Congress under Arana, Sandoval Alarcón had fortified his power base, channelling state funds into financing his paramilitary supporters.[17] But the Army felt increasingly uneasy with the marriage. Economically, the rural oligarchy had been eclipsed by the modern agro-exporters, industrialists and financiers; politically, the MLN's warrior-monk image was a liability. By 1974, Laugerud had broken much of the MLN's freelance terror machine, and within the military he was busy chiselling away at MLN backing in the officer corps.

Nonetheless, the fascists' organised power base was an undeniable asset, and Laugerud felt obliged to select Sandoval Alarcón as his vice-presidential running mate. The alliance was not destined to be an easy one. Within no time, the pugnacious MLN chief was denouncing his president as a communist because of a modest programme of rural co-operative development designed to win over peasant support. Anti-communist bonds notwithstanding, the Army decided that new political alliances would be more expedient. The military's Democratic Institutional Party (PID) made overtures to the moribund PR and the right wing of the badly divided Christian Democrats. Though it has continued to be Guatemala's best organized party, the MLN never fully recovered. Its marginalization from affairs of state finally provoked a split within the MLN in 1975, and the exodus of many of the party's young Turks.

One further element was crucial to Laugerud's rightist military-civilian alliance. This was the Organized Aranista Central (CAO). First conceived as an electoral machine in 1970, the CAO had taken on a life of its own as a personal vehicle for ex-president Arana's ambitions of long-term political power on the model of his crony Somoza. Throughout, Arana remained the real power behind Laugerud's throne. His influence was scarcely concealed: his CAO cohort Luís Alfonso López was corruptly "elected" president of Congress in 1976 amid a bribery scandal, and according to one Army officer, Arana "was in the *Casa Presidencial* almost every day".[18] During the Laugerud administration, Arana used his influence to extend his financial tentacles further into a veritable empire of meat packing, fisheries, timber, construction, vehicle importing, cement works, publishing, broadcasting and breweries.[19]

The Gathering Rural Storm

The vast cotton plantations of Guatemala's south coast stink of toxic chemicals; small crop-duster planes wheel constantly over the hot flatlands, spraying even as the migrant Indian cotton-pickers are bent to their task. Set back from the fields are communal dormitory shacks, described by the International Labour Office as "totally unacceptable with regard to hygiene, health, education and morality". Malaria is rampant; babies are poisoned by the insecticide residues in their mothers' milk. Herded to the fields like cattle, 70 people crammed to a flatbed truck, 600,000 Indian peasant families migrate to the coast each year for three months to earn a meagre wage which their highland subsistence plots can no longer give them.[20]

The brutal reversal of agrarian reform after 1954 set in motion pressures which, by the Laugerud and Lucas regimes, threatened explosion. Both were caught between the unremitting demand of the poor for land and greater purchasing power, and the clamour for expansion by latifundistas in an economy still geared to agro-exports (see Table 1).

From 1960 to 1974, the agro-exporting sector of the Guatemalan economy outperformed that of all but two other Latin American nations. But behind the accumulating wealth lurked another story of mounting rural misery and impoverishment, as export plantations engulfed arable land which had been producing for domestic consumption. From 1961 to 1973, annual increases in staple food production averaged a mere 1.6% (corn), 2.3% (wheat) and 4.8% (beans). Peasant farms lost 26% of their acreage over the 1970s; the area devoted to export crops swelled by 45%. The tendency for each generation to divide farms into smaller units for its children was aggravated by the brutal uprooting of peasants by the Army and landowners' paramilitary thugs.[21]

Since 1954, no Guatemalan regime has contemplated a confiscatory agrarian reform. Only two options have been explored for redressing the inequalities in land tenure, which are more severe than in either El Salvador

Table 1
Export Earnings from Agriculture and Industry, 1970-1978 ($ million)

Agriculture	1970	1971	1972	1973	1974	1975	1976	1977	1978
Coffee	100.6	96.3	105.3	145.6	173.0	164.2	243.0	526.5	455.0
Cotton	27.2	26.0	40.9	47.9	71.0	75.9	87.8	152.1	161.6
Bananas	13.6	14.4	25.7	24.7	31.4	35.1	45.7	45.6	49.9
Sugar	9.2	9.9	16.1	21.9	49.6	115.6	106.7	81.8	28.6
Beef	12.7	17.4	18.1	25.1	21.5	17.0	14.5	27.9	27.5
Other	22.1	17.7	18.4	23.4	34.3	22.0	57.6	69.9	80.0
Agriculture total	*185.2*	*181.6*	*224.5*	*288.6*	*380.8*	*429.7*	*555.2*	*903.7*	*802.6*
As % of all exports	62.3	63.3	66.8	65.5	65.4	67.0	70.8	76.7	69.2

Industry	1970	1971	1972	1973	1974	1975	1976	1977	1978
Manufactured goods	107.5	101.8	107.4	146.4	193.1	203.1	221.7	267.8	341.5
Mineral products	4.5	3.4	3.9	6.6	8.4	8.2	7.5	7.3	16.3
Industry total	*112.0*	*105.2*	*111.3*	*153.0*	*201.5*	*211.3*	*229.2*	*275.1*	*357.8*
As % of all exports	37.7	36.7	33.2	34.5	34.6	33.0	29.2	23.3	30.8
Exports total	*297.2*	*286.8*	*335.8*	*441.6*	*582.3*	*640.9*	*784.4*	*1178.8*	*1160.4*

Source: World bank, 1980

or pre-revolutionary Nicaragua. One is colonization of virgin national lands; the other, rarely applied and of marginal importance, is provision under the 1962 Agrarian Reform Law, Decree no. 1551, for the confiscation of land left idle on certain categories of large farms.

Colonization has centred on the underpopulated northern department of the Petén, which borders on Mexico and Belize, and the *Franja Transversal del Norte.* If the *Franja* has been a carnival for the wealthy, it has been a house of horrors for Guatemala's poor. According to the 1973 census, the area was already the traditional home of 120,000 Guatemalans, most of them monolingual Indians —the Kekchí, Quiché, Mam, Ixil and Pocomchí. Community farming rights have been no barrier to the generals and their cohorts. If the Indians have land titles, and many do, they can expect no legal redress through the courts. There is little choice for them but anger, flight and — increasingly — self-defence. They have a long tradition of revolt, ever since the Kekchí rose up in rebellion against the rapacious German, British and Guatemalan coffee planters who streamed into fertile Alta Verapaz, now the heartland of the *Franja,* in the middle of the 19th Century.

On the other hand, the *Franja* was seen as a convenient place to shunt the hordes of peasants driven off their own land further south. Colonizing the frontier as a substitute for agrarian reform had been a dream of Guatemalan presidents since Castillo Armas. The problem, argued the generals, was not land distribution but land shortage.

The first step was to open up the jungles of the Petén in 1966. But the Petén is wretched cropland, of porous karst rock with a thin top soil, soon exhausted. Its pasturage is better suited to cattle-raising. Of course, the few peasant colonizers who did come — seduced by the frontier myth of official propaganda and nostalgia for their own lost smallholdings — had neither capital nor sufficient land to set up as cattle farmers. Those who did were the already prosperous ranchers of the south coast. As both moved northwards, the latifundio-minifundio disparities of the rest of the country were quickly replicated in the Petén.

The Petén was also too remote, its infrastructure too poorly developed, to attract many settlers: a more sophisticated programme was required. After 1970, colonization of what was to become the *Franja* grew to be an obsession with Arana, and new guidelines formed part of the 1971-5 National Development Plan. The expanded *Franja* project was officially unveiled in 1976 under Laugerud. Under a smokescreen of "agrarian frontier" rhetoric, the military hoped to lure a new work-force into the region as cheap captive labour for the transnationals and the generals' own ranches.

Provisional land titles and small, poor-quality subsistence plots left new peasant settlers easy prey to eviction. Soil quality in the northern parts of Huehuetenango, El Quiché, Alta Verapaz and Izabal turned out to be little better than the Petén. Official studies estimated that only 7% of the land area was viable for regular crop production, and 35% for cattle-raising. 58% was unsuited to any kind of cultivation. Agronomists assessed the rocky plots of under 19 acres granted to each family under the pilot colonization scheme to be insufficient to support more than five years of subsistence farming.

The initial pilot area — the remote Ixcán, in Guatemala's north-west corner — was to be organized into co-operatives. Traditionally, the very word co-operatives had been a political heresy to landowners, but now US AID provided a $5.6 million soft loan in 1976 to settle 5,000 families in co-operative settlements.

But the project was stillborn, and four years later World Bank economists would complain that the planned co-operativization had never spread beyond the initial pilot area. For one thing, the regime had little serious interest in promoting co-operatives, which were regarded by many officers as tantamount to communism. For another, most peasants refused the lure. Those who migrated faced land and labour abuses at the hands of the National Electrification Institute (INDE), which was in charge of developing the new hydroelectric schemes, or from the petroleum and nickel companies investing in the region. Early proposals to settle 70,000 families in the Ixcán over a 20 year period were soon scrapped. Eventually, the Army resorted to settlement by coercion: in 1978, troops attempted to relocate 12,000 *campesinos* in the Ixcán.

President Laugerud's timid decision to seek greater social stability by promoting rural credit and service co-operatives in the highland areas made sound capitalist logic. But it antagonized the agro-exporters, who feared that any greater economic self-sufficiency in the *altiplano* communities would dry up their dependable supply of cheap migrant labour.[22] Highland gang-bosses and usurers, in charge of providing and financing this labour pool, began to find themselves short of work. "When we organized the co-operative," reminisced one peasant of the Laugerud period, "these people lost their source of easy money and started denouncing us to the government as communists." Many peasants and their supporters in local Christian communities found themselves targeted for harassment and death by the far Right. The debate over co-operatives began to produce fissures within the military itself. Its more far-sighted members, especially those who ran the National Reconstruction Committee — set up after the February 1976 earthquake — saw the value of co-operatives in winning over political support for the regime. But they saw the very co-operative leaders chosen by the Army at a local level picked off as "communists" on the orders of the more reactionary members of the high command.

Many co-operative members found themselves worse off financially than when they had migrated. An élite minority of suppliers — not only ladino traders, but members of an expanding Indian bourgeoisie — monopolized the distribution of fertilizers, seeds and credits, granaries, mills and storage facilities, and passed the burden of rising world market prices and local inflation on to the minifundistas.

If they continued to migrate, the peasants faced increased unemployment by the end of the decade, as the big plantations sank their capital into mechanization. At Pantaleón, for example, the country's largest sugar-refining complex, the labour force was cut back by one-third between 1975 and 1981.[23]

The tourist brochures like to speak of tranquil Indian communities "untouched by time". But like most tourists, Guatemala's military rulers failed to grasp the explosive change in rural class structures under the impact of accelerated capitalist development. Though migrant labour has existed since the inception of cash-crops, traditional rural relationships crumbled fast as the expansion of cotton and sugar lands and peasant dispossession swelled the ranks of the migrant rural semi-proletariat to 49% of the total rural labour force by the end of the 1970s.[24] Ties to community and culture find it hard to resist a brutal experience of modern wage labour. Furthermore, the growth of a bourgeoisie of indigenous origins —especially in western Guatemala, around the second city of Quezaltenango — gave the Indian population a taste of class exploitation within their own ethnic community.

On the plantations, ladino and indigenous workers shared the same conditions, the same injustices. Initially suspicious of each other, their common predicament eroded many prejudices, laying the basis for a new kind of joint political action, which by the accession of the Lucas regime would shake the military's rule to its very foundations.

Open the Door an Inch . . .

Laugerud's attempts to stabilize military rule embraced a series of tactics. First, consolidate the PID-PR-CAO power axis, squeezing out the MLN. Then separate off the right wings of the Christian Democrats and social democrats, exposing what the generals insisted was a handful of "communists directed, financed and incited by the Cuban government".[25] Opening up some space for democratic activity, settling troublesome urban strikes by negotiation and lowering the tenor of the repression might win over key leadership elements of the urban labour movement and isolate the radical Left.[26] Sustained economic growth, boosted by the boom in the construction industry in the wake of the 1976 earthquake, gave the generals confidence to proceed with their plans.

Their confidence was ill-founded; their reforms too slight, too late. Inflation, a new phenomenon since 1973, was eroding workers' already meagre living standards. The 1974 electoral fraud told large sectors of the mass movement that even basic democratic freedoms could not be reclaimed within the framework laid down by the armed force. It taught them too that the traditional leadership of reformist parties, which failed to offer alternative strategies in the face of the fraud, was bankrupt. Urban tensions erupted on a scale which the armed forces had never expected.

Table 2
Evolution of Domestic Consumer Price Index 1961-1981

(avg.) 61-65	(avg.) 66-70	1971	1972	1973	1974	1975	1976	1977	1978	1979	1980	1981
Inflation: 0.1%	1.5%	-0.5%	0.5%	10.0%	16.0%	13.1%	10.7%	12.6%	7.9%	11.5%	12.0%	12.4%

Sources: United Nations Economic Survey of Latin America, 1979; Inter-American Development Bank Annual Report, 1981; *Boletin Estadistico del Banco de Guatemala*; This Week in Central America and Panama.

Union leaders, too, were taken aback by the sheer scale of an angry movement which, thought moribund, now burst on to the streets. The funeral of a murdered union activist could trigger a teeming protest by thousands, chanting "We don't want elections, we want revolution." Striking mineworkers from the remote highland town of Ixtahuacán found their 300 Kilometre march to the capital in November 1977 joined by 100,000 united peasant and worker sympathizers. A powerful National Committee of Trade Union Unity (CNUS) crystallized around a 1976 strike at the local Coca Cola franchise, EGSA, and the same year's devastating earthquake, whose main impact fell on urban slum-dwellers and highland peasants.[27]

None of this should suggest of course that the entire mass movement became instant revolutionaries. True, the Christian Democrats and their fellow reformist parties* lost credibility by reaffirming electoral methods

---

* Two parties vied for recognition by the Socialist International. They were the United Front of the Revolution (FUR) and the Democratic Socialist Party (PSD).

after 1974. But they and many of their working-class followers believed that the Laugerud *apertura*, though limited, could be pushed. If not in time for the 1978 elections, a restoration of democracy could surely come, they believed, by 1982.

Laugerud's reforms were too lukewarm to neutralize the Left, but were enough to allow it some space in which to reorganize. As the mass movement swelled in size and confidence, its positions grew more radical. The National Workers' Federation (CNT), largest member organization within CNUS, severed its ties to the Christian Democratic Latin America Workers' Federation (CLAT). The militant new Committee of Peasant Unity (CUC) began to register sweeping successes in organizing south coast plantation workers and highland migrants. After the earthquake, church groups working in the Indian highlands and foreign-aid financed urban slum projects became an explosive new force in opposition to the regime. Even the most modest community demands — a new stand-pipe in the *barrio*, a drainage system, electric lighting in the streets — took on threatening political dimensions. And a revived guerrilla movement began to inflict stinging blows on the Army.

. . . Slam it Shut Again

Under pressure from his right flank, Laugerud backtracked. Far from stabilizing his regime, his tactics had only succeeded in undermining it further. Real reforms were unacceptable to the agro-exporting class, MLN supporters and Army loyalists alike, and token reforms only opened a Pandora's box. Locked in the classic agrarian mentality of those whose products are shipped straight overseas with little regard for the demands of a local market, the bunker vision of the Right only hardened in response to the US State Department's 1977 designation of Guatemala as a "gross and consistent violator of human rights".

By the time of Lucas García's inauguration in 1978, after the by now customary electoral fraud, the armed forces and the rest of the bourgeoisie faced starkly drawn options: thoroughgoing reforms or the full weight of state terrorism against all opponents. Unable to countenance the political repercussions of reform, the regime took the only recourse it knew. After all, terror had always worked before.

Notes

1. No comprehensive analysis yet exists of Guatemala in the 1970s. The best available short studies are Aguilera, *Estado militar*; Piero Gleijeses, "Guatemala: Crisis and Response", unpublished MS (July 1982); Concerned Guatemala Scholars, *Dare to Struggle, Dare to Win* (New York, 1981). Jonas and Tobis' *Guatemala* is the most complete analysis of the political economy of Guatemala, but only covers the period up to 1974, when military control of the state was not yet complete.
2. Poitevin, *El proceso de industrialización*, p.190.
3. Aguilera, *Estado militar*.

4. "Guatemala contra Exmibal", (Guatemala, Universidad de San Carlos, Facultad de Ciencias, 1970).
5. Jonas and Tobis, *Guatemala,* p.97.
6. Ibid., pp.109-11.
7. *Miami Herald,* 8 December, 1974.
8. *El Nuevo Diario* (Guatemala City), 10 October, 1978 and 18 February, 1980; *La Hora* (Guatemala City), 7 November, 1978; *El Gráfico* (Guatemala City), 20 November, 1978; *Prensa Libre* (Guatemala City), 2 September, 1977.
9. *Latin America Economic Report,* 14 November, 1975.
10. US Embassy, *Subsidiaries and Affiliates of American Firms in Guatemala,* March 1980. The most up-to-date listing of US corporations operating in the country appears in Tom Barry, Beth Wood and Deb Preusch, *Dollars and Dictators: A Guide to Central America* (Albuquerque, New Mexico, The Resource Center, 1982), pp.131-8.
11. *New York Times,* 9 July, 1980.
12. See Debray, *The Revolution on Trial,* pp.344-5.
13. *Latin America,* 2 November, 1973.
14. *Inforpress,* no.22.
15. Gleijeses, *Crisis and Response.*
16. On the 1974 elections, see *Christian Science Monitor,* 23 January, 1974; *Washington Post,* 1 March, 1974; *New York Times,* 2 March, 1974; *Miami Herald,* 8 and 15 March, 1974.
17. *El Día* (Mexico City), 6 March, 1982.
18. *Latin America,* 25 June, 1976; *Miami Herald,* 29 March, 1978.
19. *Latin America,* 24 January, 1975.
20. Edelberto Torres-Rivas, "La proletarización del campesinado en Guatemala", *Estudios Sociales Centroamericanos,* no.2, (May-August 1972), pp.83-99. Graphic descriptions of plantation life appear in articles by Alan Riding in the *New York Times,* 13 September, 1975 and 9 November, 1977.
21. World Bank, *Guatemala;* Concerned Guatemala Scholars, *Dare to Struggle.*
22. *New York Times,* 13 September, 1975.
23. *Mother Jones* (San Francisco, California), November 1981.
24. Edelberto Torres-Rivas, "Guatemala: Crisis and Political Violence", *NACLA Report on the Americas,* Vol.XIV, no.1 (January-February 1980). See also Leonel Luna, "El racismo y la revolución guatemalteca", *Polémica,* no.3, 1982, pp.47-57.
25. *El Imparcial* (Guatemala City), 18 May, 1976.
26. Piero Gleijeses, "Perspectives of a Regime's Transformation in Guatemala", paper prepared for the Second Expert Discussion on Central American Perspectives after the Sandinista Revolution in Nicaragua, sponsored by the Friedrich Ebert Foundation, Bonn, West Germany, March 1981.
27. The Coca Cola saga would rivet international eyes on the Guatemalan labour movement for the next five years. For details, see International Union of Food and Allied Workers Associations, *The Coca Cola Guatemala Campaign, 1979-1981* (Geneva, Switzerland, 1981); CIDAMO, "The Workers' Movement in Guatemala", *NACLA Report on the Americas,* Vol.XIV, no.1 (January-February 1980); Miguel Angel Albízurez, "Struggles and Experiences of the Guatemalan Trade Union Movement, 1976-June 1978", *Latin American Perspectives,* Nos.25-26, (Spring and Summer, 1980).

3. Lucas García —
the Descent into Chaos

"It's everyone for himself."
Lucas' Interior Minister, Donaldo Alvarez Ruíz, 1979.

Until Carter, Washington had endorsed the intransigence of every regime since 1954 at critical turning points. It favoured military over civilian options not only in 1963 — when guerrillas were on the upsurge — but again in 1968 and 1970 — when they had been beaten down.

Though successive US administrations may have had widely divergent agendas for Latin America, each found the political centre in Guatemala too fragile to sustain a challenge to military rule. Guatemala's intrinsic economic importance, though certainly a factor in American calculations, was less important than the political legacy of the 1954 counter-revolution, to which Washington had acted as midwife. Maintaining the Guatemalan "example" and the skewed political model that it bred became a near obsession, outweighing the qualms of Washington doves.

But the model was becoming indefensible. To perplexed observers, it seemed as if the Lucas regime — domestically isolated and an international pariah —suffered from an acute death-wish. Yet its behaviour was a logical extension of the process that US administrations had rubber-stamped since 1954. As Lucas confronted powerful mass resistance, more mature than the guerrilla movements of the 1960s, the Guatemalan ruling class asked: why not respond again with terror?

But this time was different. All-out terror did not destroy the popular movement, but only forced it to find new means of organization and survival. State violence rebounded against the regime, each new wave of killings providing an ever more militant opposition with more recruits. At the same time, the first tremors of recession shook the private sector out of its dream world. The military bourgeoisie, monopolistic, scandalously corrupt, and having a stranglehold on state power, had isolated itself from all its civilian counterparts. As cash crop prices plummeted and the brutal global recession reverberated through Guatemala's open economy in 1980-1, the old policies abruptly proved unable to satisfy coffee growers, cotton exporters and industrialists at the same time.

Teenage cadets at the Adolfo Hall military academy

Jean-Marie Simon

The military's first instincts told it to use this period of high inflation to branch out into ever more aggressive forms of speculative accumulation. And it used state power to protect its own monopolies, denying competitors the preferential treatment they demanded in order to ride out the recession. Control of credit flows allowed the armed forces to shape this unequal competition, even if in doing so the clique around Lucas García was in fact sounding its own death knell.

The military's refusal to climb down from its money-making roller-coaster fuelled right-wing schisms. Disputes, previously limited to the rift between the MLN and the more dynamic sectors, now affected all groups. All-out class war rocked the economy, and many capitalists began to desert the fast-sinking ship of state.

The death agony of Somoza in Nicaragua reminded the ruling class of its mortality. In October 1978, Lucas triggered a 60% effective general strike and rioting throughout the capital city and the north-western highlands, when he doubled urban bus fares. Demonstrators, emulating the Sandinista insurrection they had seen on television the previous month, wore face-masks, threw together barricades and confronted the military openly.

Within nine months, Somoza had fled to Miami, and the Sandinista-led junta was in power. Hundreds of Somoza's closest aides and high-ranking members of his National Guard made their exile in Guatemala City. Here, they found ready sympathizers in the Guatemalan armed forces, which cursed Carter (or "Jimmy Castro", as Lucas liked to call him) for betraying a loyal ally and vowed not to repeat Somoza's traumatic military collapse. Even before Somoza's downfall, while US State Department mediators were casting around for a moderate centrist option to head off a military victory by the FSLN, the Guatemalan military set about killing off any remaining local centrists who might prove attractive to Washington.

Between 1978 and 1981, 20 leaders of the social democratic United Front of the Revolution (FUR) were assassinated, including party leader Manuel Colom Argueta; 16 politicians of the Democratic Socialist Party (PSD) met the same fate, and again their party chief — Alberto Fuentes Mohr — was among the dead. Christian Democrat secretary-general Vinicio Cerezo was luckier, surviving three assassination attempts by pure luck. But 70 of his party's activists and local mayors fell to the death squads.[1] The butchery of the centre, as well as a clear tactic for forcing Washington doubters behind the *ancien régime,* was a symptom of the military's impotence. All attempts to mediate social divisions foundered: where there had been "limited democracy", there was now only limitless state terrorism.

There is an old anecdote that Nicaraguans tell about elections under the Somoza regime: a Conservative opponent of Somoza's, the story goes, has just lost another presidential election. Next morning, he storms into the dictator's office. "Look here, you son of a bitch," he shouts, "I've come to hear you tell me the truth — that I won the elections." With a smile, Somoza replies, "Yes, it's true. You won the elections, but I won the count. And you would do well to remember that the guy who loses is a bigger son of a bitch than the guy who wins."

> "The people do not care about elections because of
> their experiences in the past. We cannot talk about an
> electoral method of change."
> Vice president Villagrán Kramer, 1979.

As in Nicaragua, so in Guatemala. In 1974, 1978 and again in 1982 (by which time the electoral model would have forever outlived its usefulness to the military), elections were manifestly fraudulent. In each case, the officially endorsed military candidate won a preordained victory over a limited range of officially endorsed candidates. As the statistics show (see Table 3) "limited democracy" became steadily discredited among the electorate.[2]

Table 3
Guatemalan Election Results 1958-1978

Year Winner	Abstention	Adult population voting for winner
1958 Gen. Miguel Ydígoras Fuentes	33.2%	12.7%
1963 elections cancelled		
1966 Julio César Méndez Montenegro	43.7%	10.0%
1970 Gen. Carlos Arana Osorio	46.2%	10.5%
1974 Gen. Kjell Laugerud García	58.0%	8.4%
1978 Gen. Romeo Lucas García	63.5%	8.3%

Lucas, then, came to power on a record low voter turnout. Within a year, even his vice-president, Francisco Villagrán Kramer, would declare that "the people do not care about elections because of their experiences in the past. We cannot talk about an electoral method of change."

The MLN — again the legitimate winners of another flagrantly fraudulent election — protested, but Arana's goon squads and the military high command intervened to press home Lucas' election.[3] As Laugerud had been before him, Lucas was the protégé of former president Arana Osorio — reputedly because Arana saw him as the least independent-minded, least intelligent and most pliable of the high command.

In the early part of his campaign, Lucas displayed some base of support among the urban middle classes, but in any organizational sense that support was extremely shallow. With elections such a charade, the Army's Democratic Institutional Party (PID) and the Revolutionary Party (PR), which formed the core of Lucas' electoral alliance, had no need to be effective political instruments. Instead, they served merely as platforms for patronage and personal enrichment.

The consensus behind the Army was increasingly unstable. The earlier temporary alliances of convenience with other rightist forces — whether MLN, PR or CAO — seemed exhausted under Lucas. The stage seemed set for the military to carry out a threat which Arana had made in 1973 — to remove the parties altogether from the political arena, and abandon any pretence at cloaking the class dictatorship in the trappings of constitutional legality.

The centrist opposition parties were badly split. Opportunistic leaders wanted to gain a stake in the political process; other activists wanted to use every inch of legal space, believing that their middle-class supporters might still be brought back in out of the cold. Lucas shrewdly capitalized on their confusion. The military dangled the carrot of legal registration, which obliged by tacitly endorsing Lucas' victory and keeping aloof initially from the new, broad-based opposition Democratic Front Against Repression (FDCR), which emerged early in 1979. But the price of registration for the social democratic FUR was the head of their leader, Colom Argueta.

Christian Democrats, now divided into feuding left and right wings — led by Vinicio Cerezo and René de León Schlotter respectively — had spent the 1970s flirting with the idea of building a "centrist alliance" with the PID.[4] Rebuffed in 1974, they none the less again fielded a military candidate, General Ricardo Peralta Méndez, in 1978.[5] Even to describe the Cerezo faction as "left" is misleading, for as in El Salvador, the genuinely radical currents within the Christian Democratic party had been driven to leave the party after the 1974 election fraud, many of them to join the guerrilla movement.

Whatever strength the reformist parties now had was concentrated in Guatemala City, the second city of Quezaltenango and one or two other urban centres. The FUR, which had held the mayor's job in the capital through Colom Argueta from 1970 to 1974, still retained some of its old influence there. The PSD similarly had never made inroads into the rural population. And the Christian Democrats, influential through the rural co-operative movement under Laugerud, now saw their national structure dismembered by repression.

Lucas also managed to cut some ground away from his reformist enemies by fielding an experienced centrist politician, Dr Francisco Villagrán Kramer, as his vice-presidential running mate. During the 1960s, Villagrán Kramer had been involved with embryonic social democratic parties, but by now he had severed all institutional links to the FUR and PSD, and stood very much as an individual. Villagrán Kramer's clean reputation offered the Lucas regime a last veneer of respectability with the electorate and a last bridge to Washington, even though it was soon clear that he wielded no real power inside Guatemala, and was quite unable to stem the abuses of the armed forces. By now, the United States Congress had suspended military aid to Guatemala on human rights grounds.

Villagrán Kramer's own aim, he told a US reporter, was "to avoid a Custer's Last Stand in Guatemala".[6] For his pains, he was predictably labelled a Marxist by the MLN, and accused of being "an agent of both the

United States and the Soviet Union" by Colonel Oscar Mendoza Azurdia, who would eventually succeed Villagrán Kramer as vice-president when the latter finally resigned in despair.[7]

Though it had been cheated of victory in the elections, the MLN remained the single largest party in congress, with 20 out of 61 deputies' seats. But its estrangement from the military power-centre was by now complete. It would spend the four years of the Lucas regime in disgruntled opposition, trying vainly to recover some influence within the officer corps, which would be essential for any renewed assault on power. But its decline in this area was already made manifest by its choice of presidential candidate in 1978. No serving Army officer would accept the albatross of an MLN nomination round his neck, and the party was left with no option but to field retired Colonel Enrique Peralta Azurdia, leader of the 1963 coup.[8]

The Death Squads Run Wild

> "Of course, the death squads were organised under the patronage and approval of the government and the Army. They have lists of people that are suspected of being communists, and they kill them. It's a war, you see, a war between the communists and the anti-communists. They have the sympathy of most of the Guatemalan people."
> Raúl García Granados.

Any notion that Lucas would start his rule with a semblance of democratic opening, as Laugerud had done four years earlier, was soon dispelled. In July 1978, Lucas took office; within three months, he faced the direct challenge of a near-insurrection in Guatemala City over the proposed bus fare increases. How would he respond? Initially, there seemed to be some hesitation about whether to crush or accommodate the strike movement — hesitation that exasperated the fiercely right-wing police chief, Colonel Germán Chupina. The colonel, given to hiring out his Mobile Military Police (PMA) as vigilantes to private businessmen, assigned police provocateurs to inflame the throngs and thus justify blanket repression.[9] Rumour had it that some members of the high command still entertained doubts about a policy of unrestrained terror, but those vestiges were removed in June 1979 when the Left took responsibility for assassinating Army Chief of Staff, Major-General David Cancinos, organizer of the death squads and a figure mentioned as likely presidential candidate in 1982. The military was united in its hard-line response.

The new Secret Anti-Communist Army, a death squad repeatedly linked to Chupina's office, issued a death-list of 40 prominent opposition figures, and set about the task of exterminating them. Terror escalated to unheard-of levels. Corpses appeared at the rate of ten a day, hideously disfigured by torture, strewn along the roadsides, in storm drains, under viaducts. By 1981, the body count during Lucas' term of office had reached 6,000.[10] "Of course," noted Raúl García Granados, a close business associate of Lucas',

> the death squads were organized under the patronage and approval of the government and the Army. They have lists of people that are suspected of being communists, and they kill them. It's a war, you see, a war between the communists and the anti-communists. They have the support of most of the Guatemalan people.

Hombres desconocidos — unknown men — every Guatemalan knows the words; thousands have experienced what they mean. Those who knock on the door at dead of night and speed off in unmarked Cherokee Chief station wagons, dragging away the "communists" whose mutilated bodies will later be left on public display. Pinned to them as often as not will be crude hand-lettered notes warning others that "this is how traitors end up".

The first death squad, the National Anti-Communist Organization, took up operations in 1960. And during the peak years of counterinsurgency, from 1966-8, the squads bloomed like poisonous flowers, 17 new ones in 1967 and 1968 alone.[11] They took to giving themselves flamboyant names — *Ojo por Ojo* (An Eye for an Eye), *Rosa Púrpura* (Purple Rose), *El Buitre Justiciero* (The Hawk of Justice). They mutilated their victims' faces and genitals and boasted of their exploits in apocalyptically worded communiqués. The New Anti-Communist Organization (NOA) announced publicly that it would cut off the tongue and left hand of its convicted enemies. The open publication of death lists and victims' photographs helped contribute to a national psychosis of terror.

In the countryside, the security forces of the Mobile Military Police and the Hacienda (Treasury) Police, private landowners and freelance thugs connected to the fascist MLN used terror in ways that made one group indistinguishable from the others. Since military commissioners, pillars of the local repressive apparatus, were authorized to bear arms such as machine-guns (normally restricted to the Army), many farmers and businessmen simply took out credentials as commissioners as a convenient way of setting up their own officially sanctioned hit-squads.[12] In other cases, officers within the security forces would use the death squads as enforcers for their own private rackets and fiefdoms.[13]

Fifteen years of this behaviour had provided the right climate for private enterprise to reap the harvest of economic growth. The use of official and semi-official violence was rarely concealed, especially in the years when the MLN held a share in power. The earliest mass disappearances of the 1960s indicated quite clearly the links between the death squads, the military and the security forces. The kidnapping and subsequent execution of 28 leaders of the outlawed Guatemalan communist party (PGT) in 1966 was later tied by the testimony of an Army deserter to the Retalhuleu military base, the central Army barracks of Matamoros and units of police intelligence, the widely feared *judiciales.* The most active of the death squads of the 1960s, MANO (The Hand) had its headquarters at the Matamoros base, and NOA operated out of the air force base at La Aurora.

Despite these overt connections, the military continued to depict the death squads as a spontaneous "civic response" to the Antichrist of communism, a conscious stratagem to offer seemingly independent corroboration of its own harsh rule.[14] By the late 1970s, any distinction between institutional terror — exercised by the state on behalf of the ruling class — and freelance terror from extra-legal groups of the bourgeoisie had blurred so far as to become meaningless. So had the pretence that death squad killings were the result of fictitious encounters between "extreme Left" and "extreme Right". while the armed forces valiantly held the line in the centre. The war against communism, Arana Osorio had argued — prefiguring a line that Argentinian generals would later echo — was a dirty business. Innocent people would inevitably get hurt. A 1981 Amnesty International report, entitled "Guatemala: A Government Programme of Political Murder", laid to rest any remaining idea that the death squads operated independently of the top echelons of the Army and security forces by tracing its headquarters to the *Guardia Presidencial,* just a block from the rear of the National Palace, and its chain of command all the way to Lucas García's office.

The Psychosis of Terror

The major death squad of the Lucas period, the Secret Anti-Communist Army (ESA) faced a new kind of target — an organized mass movement which had made an unprecedented recovery from the defeats of the post-1954 period. The response of the ESA was awesome in scale as it sought to decapitate opposition. Manuel Colom Argueta, secretary-general of the United Front of the Revolution (FUR) described the tactics of the death squads: "Every single murder is of a key person — people in each sector or movement who have the ability to organise the population around a cause."[15] It was to be his last interview: only days later, he was gunned down in the street in broad daylight. Within weeks, Democratic Socialist Party leader Alberto Fuentes Mohr was also dead, his murder agreed upon at a March 1979 meeting between senior Army officers and high-ranking representatives of the private sector.[16]

Colom Argueta's remarks were absolutely true at the time of his death. But after the killing had targeted key union, peasant and political leaders, it moved on to figures of intermediate importance, and finally degenerated into random carnage against anyone suspected of "dangerous" opinions: 311 peasant activists were killed during 1980 alone, and 400 students and faculty members of the University of San Carlos butchered over a period of four months.[17] By that time — entering the latter half of Lucas' term — the killing was becoming positively unproductive, and driving whole sections of the urban middle class against the regime.

A decade earlier, Régis Debray had written of the effects of the terror: "Administered in large enough doses over a long period, it has an anaesthetic effect . . . the obscene becomes commonplace, the abnormal normal."[18] By 1980, the obscenity was still commonplace, but the anaesthetic was beginning to wear off. A mass movement which had learned to modify its psychological reactions and improve its clandestine structures managed to survive the rampant terror. The exhaustion of state terrorism as an effective means of domination knocked another pin away from under the fast-crumbling Lucas regime. For the private sector, the Army's recourse to systematic terror, elevating the last resort of capitalist rule to a first principle, was decidedly *not* the problem. What *was* a problem was only its failure to go on producing results.

Worst, and most surprising, rifts began to develop within the armed forces, and most acutely between Arana Osorio — founding father of the militarized state — and Lucas García, its current exponent. Lucas' wild blood-letting frightened the middle class; his monopoly of state power exposed even Arana to the chill winds of unequal economic competition: and his irrational behaviour, wholly unresponsive to US leverage, antagonized the American administration. Arana meanwhile, a favourite son of Washington since the successful counterinsurgency operations of the late 1960s, still enjoyed the support of influential backers in the CIA, Pentagon and Republican Party, who discreetly began to back his return to the political stage at the head of a "cleaner" and "more scientific" form of repression.

Taking Care of Business

They arrive at meetings in chauffeur-driven bulletproof Mercedes with smoked-glass windows. Bodyguards stand watch over the boardroom while behind the doors military uniforms, with the insignia of generals and colonels, mingle with the sober, Miami-tailored business suits. The speeches revolve around a single theme: how to eradicate communism and return to the status quo of the mid-1970s.

Those in business suits are not political party leaders, as they might have been a decade earlier. The parties have been rendered superfluous by the irrelevance of the electoral process as a serious forum for political competition. Instead, the Guatemalan élite has supplanted democratic forms with elements of corporatism, holding itself accountable only to a narrow, and ever-diminishing, spectrum of powerful private interests. It is not classic Mussolini-style corporatism: the regime has never tried seriously to work with the trade union movement, while terror has alienated the middle-class professional associations and the predominantly conservative Catholic hierarchy. Only the armed forces and the business community — U.S. and local — remained in the equation by the latter half of the 1970s.[19]

Into the breach left by the political parties, as in El Salvador and *Somocista* Nicaragua where democratic traditions have been equally weak, have come the private business federations. Guatemala's business groups are the largest and most influential in Central America.[20] The most important umbrella organization is CACIF, the Comité Coordinador de Asociaciones Agrícolas, Comerciales, Industriales y Financieras, founded in 1957. From the military's assumption of power in the 1963 coup, CACIF gave unswerving support for military rule and customarily provided each successive regime with its minister of economy.[21] The National Confederation of Trade Union Unity (CNUS) has frequently accused CACIF and its sister organization AGA — the Guatemalan Association of Agriculturalists — of operating the rural death squads. Who better than an employer, reasons CNUS, could compile such hit-lists of troublesome trade unionists and peasant labour organizers?[22] Yet CACIF, for all its militant defence of the existing order, is far from monolithic, and has often done a poor job of mitigating the feuds that arise between the powerful individual chambers of industry, commerce and agriculture. In an era of moderate-to-high inflation, restricted credit flows and intense sectoral competition — such as the late 1970s — the autonomous political role of the CACIF's member groups has often outstripped that of the umbrella body itself.

Side by side with these ostensibly "apolitical" federations stand the rabid private enterprise lobbies, which devoted considerable money and energies to wooing US Republican politicians even before the Reagan Administration took office in January 1981.[23] After his forced resignation from the vice-presidency, Francisco Villagrán Kramer characterized their ideological stance sardonically to a visiting American journalist. "*Amigos del País*," he declared — referring to the longest established professional body in Guatemala, which traces its founding charter back to 1974 and the heyday of Spanish colonial rule, "is equivalent to the John Birch Society, and the Guatemalan Freedom Foundation is even more to the Right."[24]

It is scarcely surprising that *Amigos del País* and the Guatemalan Freedom Foundation should have close political ties to the military government of a violently right-wing society. What is more noteworthy are the close economic and political connections that have developed between these lobbies and the resident US business community. Linked to the Guatemalan system as much by their political history as by their dollar assets (many US investors made Guatemala their home after taking part in the 1954 invasion as CIA pilots and planners), American businessmen consider themselves an integral part of the local ruling class.[25]

Over the years, their most characteristic and voluble spokesman has been Fred Sherwood. A pilot with the invading Castillo Armas forces in 1954, Sherwood subsequently became president of the American Chamber of Commerce in Guatemala (AMCHAM) and has extensive industrial and agribusiness interests. His attitude to doing business is blunt, and based on a close understanding between foreign investors and the military: "[The government is] very, very cooperative. There's just no restrictions at all. So that makes it nice."[26] Another interviewer asked Sherwood whether State

"[The government is] very, very cooperative. There's just no restrictions at all. So that makes it nice."
CIA aviator, businessman and former AMCHAM president Fred Sherwood.

Department pressure during the Carter Administration for the Guatemalan government to halt death squad activity was justified. "Hell no," he replied,

Why should we do anything about the death squads? They're bumping off the commies, our enemies. I'd give them more power. Hell, I'd give them more cartridges if I could, and everyone else would too. They're bumping off our enemies, which are also the enemies of the United States. Why should we criticise them?"[27]

Banking on Guatemala

No other foreign corporation has gone as far in building institutional ties to the Guatemalan regime than the Bank of America (BoA). A subsidiary of Bank America Corporation, the largest bank-holding company in the United States with 1981 end-of-year assets of $121 billion, BoA opened branches in Guatemala City in 1957, 1959 and 1968.[28] As a principal founder of the Latin American Agribusiness Development Corporation (LAAD), it became the main agricultural lending agency in Guatemala, second only to government as a source of agro-export capital. By 1970, 40% of all its Guatemala loans were being channeled into agribusiness development.[29]

As the only private bank authorized by the Guatemalan government to make loans in excess of $5 million, BoA has become the primary source of financing for large-scale infrastructural projects. In 1975, BoA led a private bank syndicate loan of $15 million, representing participation in the $105 million Inter-American Development Bank credit to the Chixoy hydro-electric plant.[30]

"When you've got a situation like you have here, you need the strongest government you can get. If you use human rights in a country with guerrillas, you're not going to get anywhere . . . "
BoA manager Keith Parker.

All this has brought the bank favoured status in Guatemala; it was the only foreign firm granted corporate membership in *Amigos del Pais*, which it allegedly retained until at least 1980. Individual executives of BoA continue to figure on the exclusive 211-strong membership roster of *Amigos del Pais*.[31]

BoA's local manager, Keith Parker, has acquired a Sherwood-like reputation as an outspoken defender of harsh military rule:

> When you've got a situation like you have here, you need the strongest government you can get. If you use human rights in a country with guerrillas, you're not going to get anywhere . . . What they should do is declare martial law. There you catch somebody; they go to a military court. Three colonels are sitting there; you're guilty, you're shot. It works very well.

This corporate pressure in favour of the Guatemalan status quo proved more resilient than even the support of the local business community, especially as human rights arm-twisting from the Carter Administration began to force the military regime into a corner. AMCHAM became an especially strident defender of the Lucas government. Painting Guatemala as a "beleaguered citadel", and decrying the "doctrinaire adherence to slogans" of the Carter period, its lobbyists buttonholed Washington decision-makers and testified to congressional committees in praise of Lucas García's vigorous defence of Free World values.

AMCHAM, then, remained faithful to Lucas' barbaric regime even as CACIF saw the writing on the wall and began to distance itself from the military. Irritated at its repeated exclusion from a cabinet full of military officers and party hacks of the PID and PR, the private sector seethed with frustration at Lucas' inept economic management, the rampant corruption of his government and its failure to crush a rising threat from the Left. By 1981, there was a clear rupture in the crucial alliance between CACIF and the Army, even if businessmen were poorly placed to bring about any real change in the structures of power. Their investment confidence slumped and their capital began to flood out of the country towards Miami. Even as AMCHAM kept up its fierce anti-communist diatribe on Capitol Hill, more realistic leaders of CACIF were closeted in session with the United States Embassy to find ways out of the impasse into which the Lucas García regime had led the country.[32]

The Garrison State
The private sector's main complaint was the changing nature of the military's role over the decade of the 1970s. As ideological controls, the politics of mediation, military-business dialogue and naked state terrorism each successively failed to perform their purpose, the military had centralized and consolidated its powers. In doing so, the armed forces had overstepped their "normal limits", and invaded spheres of activity customarily reserved for civil society or the civilian state apparatus. The increasing overlap between the purely coercive role of the military and its ownership — as an autonomous economic group — of many of the key means of production severely distorted the profile and function of the state.

The military caste enjoys special privileges. Officers have access to special stores where luxury consumer imports, from stereo equipment to

Scotch whisky, are sold to them at knock-down prices. Military entrepreneurs have moved aggressively into hotel and real estate speculation on the shores of beautiful Lake Atitlán, Guatemala's prime tourist attraction.

But more worrying for the civilian bourgeoisie than this new wealth is the sophisticated machinery that the military have put in place for its acquisition and protection. In a decade, they have created an array of institutions and institutional controls designed to fuse the armed forces with the state. Military men, by the time of the Lucas regime, ran 46 semi-autonomous state institutions; and military-controlled agencies included a pension and investment fund — the Institute for Military Social Security (IPM) — and the *Banco del Ejército* (Army Bank).

The IPM put up a portion of the capital for the inauguration of the Bank of America, Army Bank by President Carlos Arana Osorio in 1972, but even more was siphoned out of public funds. An appropriation of $5 million launched the bank, whose charter called for it to open credit lines for cattle-raising, industry and real estate development. Since those early days, the Army Bank has become — in Guatemalan terms — a financial monster, with active capital of $119.2 million in 1981.[33] In 1981, Lucas García's Congress approved a further injection of $20 million of state funds.[34]

In collaboration with the bank of America, the Army bank co-financed the luxury 800-unit Santa Rosita housing project for military personnel. IPM funds, this time in consort with the South African-registered Trade and Project Management Service, put up funds for the military to open its own cement company, *Cementos Guastatoya,* thereby infringing a long-agreed civilian monopoly over the lucrative cement industry.[35] IPM money is also behind the Army's purchase of a profitable multi-storey parking building in downtown Guatemala City.

The profits from these enterprises find their way into the pockets of senior military officers and into consolidating the armed forces as an institution.[36] This growing domination of the economy by those who wield state power is by no stretch of the imagination state capitalism. Indeed, under successive military rulers, the consistent overall trend has been towards the privatization of the economy. Rather, the military (both as an institution and in the figures of individual cliques of colonels and generals), has chosen to take possession of what it identifies as key areas of economic activity. Its criteria are economic self-interest, its particular conception of the national security state, and its loosening grip on other — purely political — forms of domination. Here, of course, the logic of Army rule, and its decomposition over the 1970s, is laid bare: in the wake of economic voracity came a weakening of political legitimacy, which in turn dictated further incursions into direct economic control under the guise of "national security".

This military expansionism has affected not only the country's economic base. As it forfeits its ideological hold, so the military has also moved into direct control of culture and education. Army grants pay for young officers to study the "subjects of the future" — electronics and computer technology, mining and petroleum engineering. Since 1978, there has been ambitious talk of a military university. In 1979, the armed forces established their own Department of Radio and Television, and they also own Channel 5 of Guatemalan television.[37] Parallel legislation has tightened control of the press and placed new restrictions on the dissemination of information.

Fiddling While Guatemala Burns

The uncontrolled violence with which the military has responded to any flickering of popular resistance suggests that the main conflict in Guatemala is between the state and the mass of the populace. While true, this is only part of the story. Equally serious has been the state's failure to do its job as the effective manager of a capitalist economy.

If at least part of the state's task is to mediate class conflict, the Guatemalan military state has proved too voracious even to bother with mediating *intra*-class disputes. The military, as an increasingly independent economic power, used the political and economic levers at its disposal only for self-enrichment, and not to manoeuvre a stable bourgeois consensus into place behind its rule. If coffee exporters, for example, asked for a tax break, they were entirely likely to be given a tax *increase,* designed to fatten state revenues for the military's own pet projects. This conflict produced a decisive break between the coffee growers of AGA and ANACAFE and the Lucas García regime in the summer of 1981.

When the effectiveness of terror and the sustained growth of the economy both began to evaporate under Lucas, previously masked tensions within the ranks of the private sector exploded. With recession sharpening capitalist competition for shrinking profit margins, the individual private sector chambers clamoured for special treatment. But instead they found that the military only insisted on being cut in on all the most profitable enterprises.

Businessmen excluded from the corridors of power began to mutter that Guatemala was becoming "Somozanised". A principal target of their wrath was the armed forces' monopoly of wealth in the *Franja Transversal del Norte* development zone. The mid-1970s bonanza of wealth in the *Franja* proved a useful way for the Army high command to secure its inner circle of loyalists. Presidents Arana, Laugerud and Lucas all handed out *Franja* properties to high and middle-ranking officers. With the help of FYDEP, the government agency in charge of developing the northern department of El Petén, favoured cohorts acquired finance and land titles, broadening their scope of economic activity from cattle ranching into rubber and *chicle* production for export. By 1975, Laugerud's ministers of agriculture and industry, and a number of congressional deputies from the official PID party counted among the main beneficiaries.

Thanks to the presence of large-scale capital investment projects, land values skyrocketed. Preferential access to governmental and private bank finance would increasingly allow landowners to introduce modern agrarian technology. Economic competitors were expressly excluded, and the far-right MLN was the earliest to smart at the Army monopoly, railing that ostensibly public land had passed massively into the hands of private individuals, "thanks to the special influence of interested parties".

Though Laugerud's generals got rich, when it came to exploiting the *Franja* no one could touch General Romeo Lucas García. A native of Alta Verapaz and a fluent speaker of Kekchí, the local Indian language, Lucas had been in charge of development programmes in the area before assuming the presidential sash in 1978. With his home base in Cobán, he amassed a fortune valued at more than $10 million in land alone. Precise estimates of the extent of Lucas' properties are hard to come by, but they range from 81,000 to 135,000 acres. Sizeable chunks were part of a 125,000 acre section of the *Franja* destined for peasant families by the National Institute of Agrarian Transformation (INTA), but bought up by military officers.

In 1979, INTA moved its headquarters from Guatemala City to Raxruja, a small settlement in the department of Alta Verapaz, lying between Lucas' principal landholdings in Sebol and the Rubelsanto oilfields. The Army evicted 120 families settled by INTA in Raxruja on the pretext that the area was destined to become a military reserve; in fact, the land was promptly handed over to Lucas. In partnership with his nephew, Raúl García Granados, scion of one of Guatemala's richest families, Lucas would eventually own 14 large farms in the *Franja*. He stood at the apex of an interlocking alliance of generals which included ex-president Arana, Defence Minister Otto Spiegler and Hans Laugerud, brother of the former president. Spiegler himself controlled a further 7,900 acres as director of the military consortium known as *Promoción 45*.

The plum of Lucas García's holdings was the Yalpemech farm. The Army's Engineering Corps, jointly with INTA and the Shenandoah Oil Corporation, built a new transversal highway as far as the Ixcán, on Guatemala's north-western border with Mexico. At its intersection with another new highway, leading north from the departmental capital of Cobán into the flatlands of El Petén, lay the 25,000 prime acres of Yalpemech. Lucas and García Granados, knowing in advance of the new road plan, had purchased the land in 1975 from the Dieseldorf family, the richest coffee barons in all of Alta Verapaz, for only $175,000. Within a year, they had established the *Agropecuaria Yalpemech S.A.,* revaluing the land upwards to $300,000. And within months, they mortgaged it to obtain a $750,000 loan from the Bank of America National Trust and Savings Association.[38]

This kind of behaviour was beyond the pale as far as civilian competitors were concerned. The government bureaucracy, packed with self-seeking military officers and technocrats, showed neither inclination nor capacity for pulling the economy out of its nosedive. Plunder took the place of planning. By 1981, the military and its immediate right-wing allies were isolated and fast losing control. Former president Arana, usurped by his own protégés, was by now evolving his own political and economic alternative in the form of a highly personalized political party, the CAN. Through this increasingly vocal grouping, he proposed the unrestrained machinery of the free market as a path to economic recovery. His harsh Chilean-style monetarism, blaming state intervention for the country's economic ills, began to sound like a coherent long-term alternative to many disenchanted businessmen.

For a long time, the unity of the armed forces provided a bulwark against discontent among civilian opponents. After all, deprived of access to the armed forces in a highly militarized society, the businessmen and parties were largely impotent to force change. But ultimately, the military élite even allowed the legendary cohesion within their own ranks to crumble. Once decomposition took hold, it was hard to contain. The monopoly of power, accompanied by corruption on a monstrous scale, gave potential for cracks even within the officer class, as generals and colonels controlled what captains and lieutenants could not yet aspire to. In the most celebrated case of Mafia-style activity — an arms-buying racket controlled by eight generals — runaway sums were involved. Young officers reported that between 1975 and 1981 the Guatemalan military registered $175 million worth of arms purchases from Israel, Italy, Belgium and Yugoslavia. The generals reported the value of the sales as $425 million, salting away the difference in private bank accounts in the tax haven of the Cayman Islands.[39]

Disgust at corruption under Lucas was compounded by the demoralization of young officers in the field, fighting and dying in a bitter —perhaps unwinnable — war against an ever more popular revolutionary movement, resenting their flabby, desk-bound superiors. Recruitment of rank-and-file soldiers as cannon-fodder, press-ganged in swoops on Indian markets and village assemblies, to be indoctrinated with hatred of their race and their communities, began to prove more difficult than ever. Young peasant conscripts found that they had an alternative to turn to by 1980 — in the form of a rebel army which grew in a rhythm that responded precisely to the mounting levels of state violence.[40]

In such an atmosphere, command structures break down; professionalism disintegrates; normal promotion procedures are set aside, leapfrogged by personal favourites of the high command. More and more officers come to realize that the Army has no long-range vision for maintaining its own survival, let alone a political programme that can keep civilian adversaries at bay. As the final guarantee of its power, the Guatemalan Army has been able to rely for two decades on its own monolithic internal cohesion. Under Lucas, that too fell apart — a further Achilles' heel of the military state.

Notes

1. *Washington Post,* 14 May, 1981; *ALAI,* 4 December, 1981.
2. On election figures, see Instituto de Investigaciones Polfticas y Sociales, "Los partidos polfticos y el estado guatemalteco desde 1944 hasta nuestros dfas", Universidad Centroamericana (UCA), San Salvador, 1980; Gabriel Aguilera, *Estado Militar;* and *Between the Lines* (Los Angeles, California), Vol. 1, no.4, November-December 1981.
3. *Latin America Political Report,* 17 March, 1978.
4. *Latin America Political Report,* 17 September, 1976.

5. On Christian Democracy, elections and the military, see *Inforpress,* 4 March, 1982.
6. *Washington Post,* 4 September, 1980.
7. Ibid.
8. José Fajardo, *Centroamérica, todos los rostros del conflicto* (Bogotá, Editorial Oveja Negra, 1980) p.164.
9. *Latin America Political Report,* 13 October and 17 November, 1978.
10. See Daniel L. Premo, "Political Assassination in Guatemala: A Case of Institutionalised Terror", *Journal of Inter-American Studies and World Affairs,* Vol. 23, no.4, (November 1981) p.448. Also, Council on Hemispheric Affairs (COHA), *Washington Report on the Hemisphere,* 7 April, 1981; Washington Office on Latin America (WOLA), *Update Latin America,* March-April 1981.
11. George Black, "Central America: Crisis in the Backyard", *New Left Review,* no.135 (September-October 1982) pp.20-2; Aguilera, *Estado Militar.*
12. Aguilera (ibid.) documents a total of 32 active death-squads operating between 1960 and 1980. New ones are apparently still in formation, the most recent being the August 1981 League for the Extermination of the Indian Race. See *Unomásuno* (Mexico City), 10 February, 1982.
13. *Latin America Political Report,* 28 January, 1977.
14. *Mother Jones* (San Francisco, California), November 1981.
15. *Latin America Political Report,* 30 March, 1979.
16. *Latin America Political Report,* 13 April, 1979.
17. *Siete Días en la USAC* (Guatemala City), 7 May, 1979.
18. Debray, *The Revolution on Trial,* p.360.
19. See Mario Solórzano, "Quién cree en las elecciones?" *ALAI,* 3 April, 1981.
20. The business federations are listed in full in José Rodolfo Maldonado Ruiz, *Poder político en Guatemala de algunos grupos sociales organizados en asociaciones no políticas* (Guatemala City, Universidad Rafael Landivar, 1980).
21. Poitevin, *El proceso de industrialización,* p.190.
22. Premo, *Political Assassination,* p.499; Roger Plant, *Guatemala: Unnatural Disaster* (London, Latin America Bureau, 1978) p.52.
23. See Allan Nairn, "Controversial Reagan Campaign Links with Guatemalan Government and Private Sector Leaders", *COHA Research memorandum,* 30 October, 1980.
24. *Washington Post,* 8 September, 1980.
25. See, for example, the testimony by US businessman Fred Sherwood, CBS News Special, "Central America in Revolt", 20 March, 1982.
26. Ibid.
27. Allan Nairn, "To Defend our Way of Life: An Interview with a U.S. Businessman", in Jonathan L. Fried et al. (eds.), *Guatemala in Rebellion: Unfinished History* (New York, Grove Press, 1983) p.90.
28. *New York Times,* 12 March, 1982; *NACLA Newsletter,* Vol.IV, no.5 (September 1970) p.9.
29. Ibid., p.5.
30. Bank of America, Annual Report, 1976.
31. Nairn, "Subsidization of Terror".
32. Yvon Le Bot and Louise Morin, "Le rôle du patronat et des militaires dans le coup d'état au Guatémala", *Le Monde Diplomatique* (May 1982).
33. Banco del Ejército, *Balance General Condensado,* 1972; *Inforpress,* 20 August, 1981.
34. *Diario Impacto* (Guatemala City), 14 October, 1981.
35. Aguilera, *Estado militar.*
36. Ibid.
37. *Inforpress,* 7 June, 1979.
38. Analysis of the *Franja Transversal del Norte* is drawn, *inter alia,* from the following sources: Thomas J. Maloney, "El Impacto Social del Esquema de Desarrollo de la Franja Transversal del Norte sobre los Maya-Kekchí en Guatemala", *Estudios Sociales Centroamérica,* No.29 (May-August 1981), pp.91-104; Nancy Peckenham, "Land Settlement in the Peten", *Latin American Perspectives,* Nos.25-6 (Spring and Summer 1980), pp.169-77; Salvador Sánchez, "La Franja Transversal de Guatemala", *Le Monde Diplomatique en Español,* October 1979; Gabriel Aguilera, "The Massacre at Panzós and Capitalist Development in Guatemala", *Monthly Review,* Vol. 31, no.7 (December 1979), pp.13-23; *Guatemala!* (Berkeley, California) Vol. 1, no.3 (1978); *Central America Report,* Vol. V, no.23 (12 June, 1978); *Latin America Economic Report,* 26 January, 1979; various editions of *La Tarde* and *El Diario de Centroamérica* (both Guatemala City).

39. Cynthia Arnson and Flora Montealegre, *IPS Resource Update* (Washington DC), June 1982.
40. Shelton H. Davis and Julie Hodson, *Witnesses to Political Violence in Guatemala: The Suppression of a Rural Develop,ment Movement* (Boston, Oxfam America, 1982) p.33; also *Washington,Post,* 28 March, 1980.

PART TWO

The Thirty Years War

George Black

in collaboration with
Milton Jamail and
Norma Stoltz Chinchilla

4. 1954 – 1972:
the Road to Ixcán

"Todas las puertas cerradas,
*Sólo un camino nos dejan."**
Quiché Indian song

Guerrilla warfare; armed struggle. To some, the words conjure up tiny self-seeking cliques, power-hungry bandits committed to violence for its own sake. To others, perhaps more sympathetic, the image is one of raw heroism, military adventure stripped of political substance. On both sets of myths, the cliché and rhetoric of the Right thrives: Reagan's "Soviet-Cuban inspired terrorism", or the "violent minorities" in the nightmares of former Assistant Secretary of State for Inter-American affairs Thomas O. Enders.[1]

The truth is at once more inspirational and more prosaic. The recourse to armed struggle is a rational decision made in extraordinary circumstances by ordinary — sometimes exceptional —men and women, with a vision — at times lucid, at others confused — of a new social order. It is rational only if they perceive all other avenues of change as having been exhausted, for otherwise they will not be joined. If they apply dogma blindly, they will fail. If they grasp the peculiarities of their country — economic and social, political and cultural — and apply that understanding creatively, they may achieve victory. In doing so, they will grope for models to guide them: Cuba, as the only example of a successful Latin American revolution, during the 1960s; Vietnam, for lessons on confronting US troop involvement, in the years that followed; Nicaragua, for hints of the threats facing a society in transition in Central America, after 1979. And they will face, and try and resolve, a series of polarities: between urban and rural work, political and

---

* "All the doors are closed.
They leave us only one way."

Guatemala's Mayan Indian population has become the main protagonist of the war

Anne Nelson

Jean-Marie Simon

military action, leadership conceptions and mass involvement. In Guatemala, they will seek above all ways of uniting the Ladino population and the Indian majority.

The course of Guatemalan history — a frustrated democratic interlude and its traumatic aftermath, followed by the sustained monopoly of power by the military — led many to conclude in the early 1960s that only thoroughgoing social transformation could guarantee an improvement in their lives, and only armed struggle could bring about social transformation. In the intervening two decades of repressive government, tens of thousands have chosen to follow suit. As repression and counter-insurgency escalated into a war of extermination, their participation was dictated as often as not by the sheer logic of survival.

Yet in a political system such as Guatemala's, the radical methods of armed warfare do not necessarily presage a radical social programme immediately the revolutionary movement takes state power. After Nicaragua, where the victorious *Frente Sandinista de Liberación Nacional* (FSLN) enjoyed an unusually favourable international balance of forces, an all-out military victory of revolutionary forces in Central America is unlikely to be repeated. El Salvador has shown the steadily diminishing influence within the Left of intransigent opposition to negotiated settlements. Both countries indicate the appalling economic constraints that will face a victorious revolution. Electoral channels have been barred to Left and Centre alike in Guatemala; there are centrist politicians and churchpeople who have opted rationally for armed struggle. As Guatemalan scholar Edelberto Torres-Rivas argues, it is not only socialism that can issue from the barrel of a gun in contemporary Central America.[2]

In building strong ties with the mass of the population, those who initiate a revolutionary war must offer a channel for organizing and clearly expressing popular aspirations. But beyond this, they must offer protection. Victory does not come overnight. If conditions are not judged right for an insurrection in the short term, then a protracted popular war is harsher, more bitter, more full of risks. Any such war carries a heavy toll in human lives; mistakes over timetable and strategy will make that human cost higher.

The mortal risks involved in confronting a murderous system produce acts of extraordinary heroism and wisdom. But the path of armed struggle, carried out against an enemy mobilized for survival, with vastly superior resources and options, is booby-trapped with blind alleys, errors of judgment and unresolved strategy disputes which fester in the enforced separation of clandestinity. No liberation war is immune to mistakes, setbacks and failures. The question is whether it can overcome them.

Learning From Experience

Clandestine armed activity aimed at the overthrow of the Guatemalan government has a 23-year history. Arising from an aborted military coup in

November 1960, the first guerrilla organization emerged in 1962, with a group of disillusioned ex-Army officers at their head. By 1966, though operating mainly in the arid and underpopulated eastern mountains of Guatemala, they had come to pose a serious threat to the survival of the regime. But by 1968, their ranks had been decimated, victims of tactical and strategic errors and a massive counterinsurgency campaign sponsored by the United States.[3]

By the early 1980s, however, their successors had grown explosively. US State Department estimates put their strength as high as 6,000 armed combatants, not to mention the many thousands more organized into paramilitary and civilian support groups. The guerrillas of the 1960s, at their zenith, had no more than 500 active fighters. More important, they had become much more thoroughly integrated into the cultural, political and social reality of Guatemala. By early 1982, when Lucas García went to the polls, the new politico-military organizations of the Left, in collaboration with civilian opposition groups, seemed set to mount a serious challenge for power.

Why did the movement of the 1960s fall such easy victim to the Guatemalan military and its US advisers? How did the groups decimated 15 years ago manage to rebound so successfully? And what lessons did they learn from those early experiences?

Under The Spotlight

In the period following the victory of the guerrillas led by Fidel Castro in Cuba in 1959, the press could not get enough of Latin American guerrillas in their mountain *focos*. Colombia, Venezuela and — above all — Guatemala became a media show. As soon as clandestine organizations had begun operations in Guatemala in 1962,

> every American provincial newspaper felt obliged to send its correspondent to be photographed with a group of armed guerrillas . . . the Guatemalan guerrilla movement became the great tourist attraction of the moment.[4]

But this fascination with publicity was not one-sided; the guerrillas enjoyed their new-found notoriety. Their willingness to talk and be photographed with a bare minimum of security precautions was a symptom of the overconfidence that would later help bring about their defeat. "They were too much talked about, and far too ready to be photographed; nor did they always conceal the identity of their peasant collaborators" noted Régis Debray. He went on to note sardonically that

> many of them thought their goal had already been achieved. By the time they had given enough interviews, they came to believe the things they had heard on the best authority: their own.[5]

Today, the lesson has been learned. Cautious in their dealings with the press, Guatemala's contemporary guerrilla leaders prefer to write about themselves; only a handful of sympathetic journalists, for the most part

Latin American, have been permitted to visit their camps and interview top commanders.[6] The silent, unknown quality of their struggle has left many observers perplexed, but it is the result of stern self-criticism by the Left of the movement's impetuous early years. "During the 1960s," explained Rolando Morán, commander-in-chief of the *Ejército Guerrillero de los Pobres* (Guerrilla Army of the Poor: EGP), in a rare interview with the Mexican journalist Mario Menéndez Rodríguez, "we used to broadcast things which in reality contained not one iota of truth."[7]

The Origins: 1954 and 1960

The downfall of the Arbenz government and its abandonment by the armed forces is the pivotal moment of modern Guatemalan history. Some would go even further than this: British writer Richard Gott, in his compendious study of rural guerrillas, asserts that "the history of guerrilla movements in Latin America, indeed the contemporary history of Latin America itself, cannot be understood without reference to this cardinal event."[8] Carlos Fonseca Amador, founder of Nicaragua's FSLN in 1961, recalled that his first memories of an incipient revolutionary awareness were those of the Arbenz government. And a yet more celebrated revolutionary, a young Argentinian doctor named Ché Guevara, was an impassioned actor and observer during the final days of the revolutionary experiment.

Every attempt by Latin Americans since 1954 to break free of United States domination has taken the Guatemalan experience deeply to heart. As Debray explains,

> The fall of Arbenz's national democratic regime in 1954 was decisive for the Latin American revolutionary movements of our time — in a negative sense since it was their matrix. Its terrible warning haunted the Cuban leaders and taught them the most basic lesson of revolutionary Marxism as updated and demonstrated on American soil: the only way to secure the revolution is to destroy the bourgeois state apparatus, mobilize and arm the people, and disarm the enemy.[9]

The likelihood of direct United States intervention was a parallel warning. 1954 had seen intervention on the economic, diplomatic, propagandistic and paramilitary levels. The Bay of Pigs invasion in 1961, the deployment of 23,000 US troops in the Dominican Republic crisis of 1965 and the further use of Green Berets in Guatemala and Bolivia in the mid and late 1960s all taught the Left that from now on any popular movement would have to develop the capacity to defend itself against US troops as well as the local military.[10]

Ultimately, of course, it is the Guatemalans themselves who have best learned the lessons of their past. Today's revolutionary movement explicitly traces its heritage back to 1944. For them, the 1944-54 interlude of democratic reform is "a real and living example of what a revolution is".[11] "Real and living" not just in theoretical terms but as a collective memory which has been deeply internalized. For the peasantry, the reversal of political and economic gains — above all the renewed loss of their land — was an equally tangible example of the nature of counter-revolution. Memories of the Arbenz period were a powerful basis for the support which the first guerrillas would receive. "In all the peasant areas we have visited," commented César Montes, a principal leader of the *Fuerzas Armadas Rebeldes* (Rebel Armed Forces: FAR), "we easily explain ourselves by saying that [our] struggle is merely the prolongation by other means of the 1944 revolution."[12]

The catalyst that set the struggle in motion was an abortive military coup against the regime of President Miguel Ydígoras Fuentes in 1960, the first outburst of armed resistance to the government since 1954. Upset by low pay, endemic governmental corruption and the presence of Cuban rightist exiles in training for the Bay of Pigs invasion, a group of junior Army officers decided to act. On the night of 13 November, they launched a military uprising at the barracks of Fort Matamoros on the outskirts of Guatemala City. The leader of the coup attempt was Colonel Rafael Sessen Pereira, his closest associates the 19-year-old Second Lieutenant Luís Turcios Lima and the 22-year-old Lieutenant Marco Antonio Yon Sosa. By 17 November, the short-lived coup attempt had sputtered and failed after rebel-held areas were bombed by the freshly trained Cuban exile pilots. United States naval vessels were swiftly dispatched to the Guatemalan coast as a back-up should the revolt have continued.

With that code of gentlemanliness peculiar to thugs, the Guatemalan Army was reluctant to punish members of its own officer corps. This worked in favour of the conspirators: none of them was brought to trial. Instead, Yon Sosa, Turcios Lima and their fellow plotter Alejandro de León went into a short, self-imposed exile. They would soon return to carry on the fight by other means. But there was no hasty rush to the mountains; instead, the young officers spent the next year in painstaking dialogue with reformist politicians and parties of every stripe, including the *Unión Revolucionaria Democrática* (URD) of future vice-president Francisco Villagrán Kramer. The contacts were fruitless; the young officers concluded that no viable political opening existed.

Disillusioned by these overtures, they turned instead to the Guatemalan communist party, known as the *Partido Guatemalteco del Trabajo* (Guatemalan Labour Party: PGT), with whom they would later enter into alliance. Theoretical Marxism was not uppermost in the officers' minds. One visiting American journalist concluded from a discussion with Turcios Lima that

> If he has an *alter ego,* it would not be Lenin or Mao or even Castro, whose works he has read and admires, but Augusto Sandino, the Nicaraguan general who fought the U.S. Marines sent to Nicaragua during the Coolidge and Hoover administrations.[13]

What impressed them about the PGT was the sense that it could combine a strong personal commitment to the poor with a convincing analysis. Indeed, of all the political parties, only the PGT's analysis of the national situation seemed to the young officers to contain any germ of rational sense.[14]

On 6 February, 1962, Yon Sosa and Turcios Lima formed the first guerrilla front, "the conscious beginning of guerrilla war in Guatemala".[15] In honour of their comrade, killed by police the previous year, they named it the Alejandro de León November 13 Revolutionary Movement (MR–13).

The First Guerrillas

Beset by poor thinking, the MR-13 operation quickly fizzled out. Yon Sosa later admitted that his men were unfamiliar with the population of their chosen theatre of operations, the torrid eastern department of Izabal, where they captured national headlines by the audacious seizure of the military posts of Mariscos and Morales. César Montes, too, ascribed failure to a poor reading of potential local support, a lack of definite direction, clear strategic orientation and adequate organizational structures.[16]

Though the *guerrilla* failed, the Ydígoras Fuentes regime was shaken by a wave of anti-government strikes, riots and student demonstrations in Guatemala City in March 1962. The student leadership called for a general strike to oust Ydígoras, while three political parties — the *Movimiento de Liberación Nacional* (MLN), the *Partido Revolucionario* (PR) and the Christian Democrats, buried their differences and issued a joint statement demanding Ydígoras Fuentes' resignation.

The demands aroused some working-class sympathy, and a number of Guatemala city slums rose up in near-insurrection. But the defeats of 1954 had left deep scars. They had dealt a crushing blow to working-class self-confidence and organizational capabilities; mere sympathy was insufficient.[17] Such working-class struggles as took place in the 1960s were economic and defensive in character; political leadership came overwhelmingly from middle-class professionals and students.

The urban proletariat, for one thing, was still tiny, despite the recent advances of industrialization under the impact of the Central American Common Market. The 1946 census had shown an urban proletariat of 21,661; by 1974, that figure had climbed to only 65,731 — still a mere 3% of the economically active population.[18] Moreoever, any systematic communication was difficult and hazardous between urban factory workers, rural labourers on the coastal plantations, workers in highland mining enclaves and the banana fields of the Caribbean lowlands. The uneven development of militant class consciousness was further battered by the widespread repression which followed on the heels of the audacious actions of the still isolated guerrilla bands.[19] Ydígoras Fuentes was short of political capital and knew it; his response to the riots was brutal and effective. Army reserves fanned out through the city in open confrontation with demonstrators. At least 20 students died, and for the moment the revolutionary opposition collapsed.

At the height of this urban agitation in March 1962, the PGT opened up a tiny new guerrilla front — numbering no more than 30 men — in the Concuá mountains of Baja Verapaz. Again, an ex-military officer, Lieutenant-Colonel Carlos Paz Tejada (an old Arbenz loyalist) was given command. But the front had no coherent plan, and was swiftly annihilated by the Army. In December of the same year, a new unified group was unveiled under the name of the *Fuerzas Armadas Rebeldes* (FAR). It was composed of the tattered remnants of MR-13, the PGT *guerrilla*'s survivors and the student-based *Movimiento 12 de Abril,* which had been organized during the riots.

Although politically clearer than its predecessors, the FAR embraced several more or less autonomous groups, with no single centralized leadership or strategy. It split its forces into three separate guerrilla fronts, inspired by the *foco* model. The theory of *foquismo,* successful in Cuba and most clearly articulated by Régis Debray in his earlier writings, called for small armed groups to be established in specific rural areas, whose example would then "detonate" mass consciousness and involvement. On one front, the MR-13 fought under Yon Sosa's direction; Turcios Lima and Ricardo Ramírez led the *Frente Guerrillero Edgar Ibarra* (FGEI); and a third was made up of former PGT guerrilla cadre.

From the outset, they were dogged by a fatal inability to mesh their military and political work. The guerrilla leadership was, after all, composed of radicalized army officers, expert in the techniques of rural warfare but politically unsophisticated. Both Yon Sosa — trained at Fort Gulick in the Panama Canal Zone — and Turcios Lima — trained at Fort Benning, Georgia — turned their US-acquired counterinsurgency skills against the Guatemalan Army.[20] But they would only concern themselves with military aspects of the struggle. Under their agreement with the communists, they would do the fighting, while the PGT would do the thinking, being conceived of as "*the* political organization, the 'brains' for the Left".[21]

Political Pipe-Dreams

The PGT laboured under the illusion that it could recreate an Arbenz-style reformist government by forging alliances with a virtually non-existent national bourgeoisie. This, they supposed, would modernize the economy, revive bourgeois democracy and create an industrial working class as the necessary preconditions for revolution in Guatemala. The communists, after their 1962 congress, claimed to endorse the notion of armed struggle, but failed to make any corresponding change in their party structures which would have allowed them to embrace military work. From this date onwards, the PGT was effectively destined to play a similar role to its Salvadorean counterpart — a permanent cradle or crucible for leftist activists, but condemned to remain on the sidelines as the guerrilla struggle — and later the mass movement — gathered impetus.

Activists under Yon Sosa challenged the PGT's right to be considered the sole brains of the movement. Working mainly in the department of Izabal, MR-13 called explicitly for insurrection and the prompt installation of a socialist government. Again, the political naïvety of its leadership cost it dearly. The demands of MR-13 were the handiwork of a small number of cadres of the Trotskyist Fourth International, to whom the trusting Yon Sosa assigned more and more responsibility. For the most telling example of their "socialism tomorrow" utopianism, one need look no further than a glowing two-part series of articles by Adolfo Gilly, in the American socialist magazine *Monthly Review*.[22] Eventually Yon Sosa would expel the Trotskyist group from MR-13 in 1966, but not before their stance had brought a split within the FAR alliance.

Many observers criticized the way in which MR-13 exposed its peasant supporters. Armed self-defence groups were poorly equipped to defend "liberated" territory. With no organized popular army to hold military repression at bay, peasants became easy targets for government troops. Debray argued that the MR-13 tactics "can aquire the character of real provocations, causing defeats that oblige the people to retreat politically as the only way of protecting themselves against repression".[23] He was right: the Army's 1966-8 wave of terror slaughtered rural sympathizers by their hundreds.

Turcios Lima's Edgar Ibarra Front (FGEI), meanwhile, fighting in the arid hills of the Sierra de las Minas, developed into one of the strongest guerrilla forces in the continent. Under a fresh unitary agreement in 1965, the FGEI would furnish the combatants and the PGT the organizational structures. From this alliance, the second version of the FAR was born. While the FAR began to register major military successes, it still lacked the necessary machinery to protect its civilian supporters, and again the peasantry bore the brunt of Army terror.

By 1967, FAR leaders saw the wisdom of some fundamental new ideas which were beginning to emerge from the experiences of the Edgar Ibarra Front. They grasped the weakness of *foco* theory, seeing that their actions had palpably *not* succeeded in igniting a mass uprising. A new term began to creep into their discussions — prolonged popular war, or popular revolutionary war. This would be a long, patient process of blending together economic, political and military modes of struggle into a single, multifaceted war. Such a war would necessarily be "a long-term one, which will last ten, perhaps twenty years. Our first objective is to last out, to survive."[24]

Civilian Government, Military Terror

Events the previous year had helped convince the FAR of the need for a revaluation of its political strategy. In March 1966, Julio César Méndez Montenegro, reformist candidate of the *Partido Revolucionario,* was elected president of the republic. During his campaign, Méndez Montenegro had offered negotiations with the armed Left — a heresy to the Army high command. His candidacy on a reform platform seemed to offer an unexpected political opening in the midst of the sharpening war, and it undercut the FAR's conviction that armed struggle was the only way forward. The FAR floundered its way through the months of Méndez Montenegro's campaign. It encouraged its supporters to vote for the PR ticket, and in doing so forfeited the initiative. Despite their internal weaknesses, the guerrillas' actions had achieved wide resonance; by pre-election time they were immensely popular and had kept the regime off balance for three years. Under Peralta Azurdia's rule, with a president disdainful of allowing too much US military assistance, the barracks-bound and ponderous Army had simply been no match for the guerrillas in the field.

But the pivotal decisions taken around election time changed all that. Peasant supporters were disoriented by the FAR's call to vote, and urban middle-class sympathizers, with more intrinsic faith in the ballot-box, were demobilized by the election.[25] Neither group had much suspicion that the call to vote for Méndez Montenegro was the result of another serious rift within the guerrilla movement — an effective upstaging of Turcios Lima's "no vote" position by the more conciliatory arguments of the PGT.

The illusion of democratic elections was only one means of taking the steam out of the left. The Pentagon, which by now was deeply alarmed by events in Guatemala, and the Army, also insisted on other, harsher medicine. The FAR had no means of suspecting the deal that had been struck as a precondition for the elections going ahead: in order to take office, Méndez Montenegro would have to hand over conduct of the war to the armed forces and a new influx of US military advisers.

In July, immediately after his inauguration, Méndez Montenegro offered the guerrillas an unexpected amnesty. When the FAR turned down the proposal flatly, the president gave the Army the green light. The outcome was a mass slaughter in the east of the country, military containment of the political crisis at the cost of indiscriminate state violence. Many guerrillas figured in the list of 8,000 dead, but the vast majority were non-combatants.

In the aftermath of their defeat, the armed actions of the Left opted for spectacle rather than organization. The desperate kidnapping and execution of US Ambassador John Gordon Mein and West German Ambassador Karl von Spretti brought the movement international notoriety, but spectacle was no substitute for internal coherence and a considered plan of action. By 1969, the remnants of the FAR were in disarray.[26]

The Post-Mortem

The conscious decision to carry out a top-to-bottom analysis of their mistakes, during an enforced withdrawal from military action, marks out the Guatemalan Left from all other contemporary Latin American experiences; never before has a revolutionary movement been near-annihilated at the zenith of its power and influence and then staged an effective comeback which would again present it as a possible contender for state power.

By the early months of 1967 — or arguably as early as October 1966 — the guerrillas had forfeited their initiative. Sporadic activity did continue — fresh attempts to create new fronts, a heightened emphasis on urban organizing — but an armed movement considered one of the most powerful on the continent had reached its lowest ebb. The overpowering strength of the Guatemalan armed forces seems the immediate cause of defeat. But the roots of failure lie much deeper, in a gamut of political and ideological dilemmas ranging from personal antagonisms to profound theoretical schisms. Looking back on their early experiences, most of today's revolutionaries would reach consensus on the causes of their decline in the 1960s.

The guerrillas "lacked a coherent organization that could have effectively put a strategy into practice, or even adequately reflected the aspirations of the people".[27] This held true from the days of the original MR-13, through the first FAR — a loose amalgam of several distinct political tendencies.— to the conflicts which would later bedevil the FAR–PGT alliance. There was never the degree of unification necessary to co-ordinate the struggle effectively.

An overall strategy was absent, in many ways a function of the movement's lack of a precise ideology beyond the vague anger at social injustice which drove them to take up arms in 1962. The leaders groped for outside models to guide them, above all the Cuban experience, in the absence of indigenous models. They talked to Left, Right and Centre alike about finding a solution.[28] One segment of the movement, the MR-13, turned briefly to Trotskyist advice, while the communist PGT provided some ideological framework for the FAR, though at the price of separating political and military considerations. The PGT, furthermore, viewed the guerrillas as an auxiliary pressure group, designed to hasten change within the institutional framework of bourgeois democracy.[29]

The early guerrillas failed to build any organic relationship with the mass of their supporters. As such, they "never really constituted a vanguard of the dominated classes but rather functioned at their margin".[30] Outsiders in their chosen terrain of eastern Guatemala, they failed to build any solid ties to the predominantly Ladino population of small and medium-scale peasant proprietors. When working in Indian areas — which was a rarity — they employed organizing techniques that failed to take into account the particularities of indigenous culture.[31]

Critically, the guerrilla movement failed to recognize and embrace the revolutionary potential of the Mayan Indian communities which make up more than half the Guatemalan population. Indeed, the PGT explicitly denied that the Indians — not only peasants, but culturally "backward" to boot — had any such potential. Although some Kekchí Indians from the departments of Alta Verapaz and Baja Verapaz fought in the guerrilla rank and file in the Sierra de las Minas, there was little or no Indian involvement in leadership. Today's Guatemalan Left would come to share the central concerns posed in Régis Debray's analysis; he argued that:

> The prime problem for the Guatemalan revolution is to integrate the Indians into the planning, the execution and above all the leadership of the revolutionary war. It is also the most difficult problem to solve: How is this war to become their war?[32]

Early leaders such as Turcios Lima and César Montes *did* touch briefly on the ethnic and national questions, and on the interplay of class and ethnicity, in their writings. César Montes, something of a visionary in this sphere, would state that

> We know that it is the Indians, half the population, who will determine the outcome of the revolution in this country ... but there are four centuries of justified Indian distrust of *ladinos*.[33]

But it would not be until the mid-1970s that the guerrillas — and above all the Indians themselves — would overcome that historic distrust and begin to address the unanswered questions of the previous decade.[34]

> "We know that it is the Indians, half the population, who will determine the outcome of the revolution in this country ... but there are four centuries of justified Indian distrust of *ladinos*."
> FAR leader César Montes, 1967.

Under the regimes of Colonel Enrique Peralta Azurdia and Julio César Méndez Montenegro, democratic opponents working through civilian parties still enjoyed some small leeway for legal activity. Their decision to go on seeking space within the electoral system further isolated the guerrilla movement. A high price was paid later for this illusion, as one of the contemporary politico-military organizations would reflect:

> With the temporary defeat of the armed movement, the Army was left in charge. It worked systematically and brutally to eliminate all demands, and finally all possibility of participation within institutional channels.[35]

During the 1966 elections, the guerrillas misread the political conjuncture. Overconfident and romantic in their assessment, they let down their guard, calling a temporary halt to armed activity and appearing to endorse the electoral process. They allowed the rhythm and laws of the election to dictate their tactics instead of preserving an independent political analysis.

Security measures, for a clandestine organization, were abysmal, in large measure a reflection of the over-emphasis on military skills and poor training in political consciousness. People came and went freely to and from the mountain camps of the Sierra de las Minas, and on more than one occasion ex-combatants either went over to the military or were forced after their capture to lead troops to guerrilla hideouts, which were then dismantled with ease. One visiting foreign journalist was aghast at the laxity of even elementary security. Reporting in the *Toronto Daily Star,* Norman Gall wrote that

It was impressive to see how many peasants came in and out apparently without restriction. Delegations from the village committees and peasant women carrying gifts of fruit and vegetables arrived.[36]

Though the Guatemalan Army made a hash of its anti-guerrilla campaign under Peralta Azurdia, the introduction of US Green Berets, Vietnam-style counterinsurgency tactics, advanced new technology such as remote sensing and night-vision scopes, plus the overall professionalization of the armed forces under President Méndez Montenegro, tipped the scales fatally in favour of the regime. "It seems improbable," commented Gott, "that the Guatemalan Army could have dealt with the guerrillas so speedily had it not been for this outside assistance."[37] With massive aerial bombings, ground search-and-destroy missions and the horrors of napalm in the eastern mountains came the first of the death squads, nominally independent of the military. All these tactics served to cut down the guerrilla movement's supporters, real or imagined.

Nor was the counterinsurgency limited to massive firepower; with it came a sophisticated civic action programme of bridge-building, food distribution and selected medical care for targeted villages.[38] Though devastating, the military offensive acted primarily to precipitate a *political* disintegration latent within the Left's own shortcomings.

Rebirth

In the wake of defeat came silence. Believing that Guatemala was pacified, presidents Arana Osorio and Laugerud García became complacent. But ducking the repression, sidestepping, the surviving members of the guerrillas of the 1960s dispersed.

They realized that the reasons for their defeat were essentially political, and that superficial adjustments in military or operational tactics would not avert catastrophe. A new military approach was certainly called for to counter the Army's new sophistication in recruiting counterintelligence informants, and in technical areas such as aerial mapping and photo-intelligence. But more important than this, the Left required a thorough political overhaul of its conception and strategy of the armed struggle. Each group understood this basic lesson, and each recognized — though from different perspectives — that the revolution could not be made unless the mass of the population made it.

And that of course is the key: rethinking by leadership, no matter how profound, does not make a revolution; nor does it take place in a vacuum. What shaped the resurgence of the 1970s was the changing reality of Guatemala, growing impoverishment in the midst of an economic boom, mounting levels of state violence against dissent and the progressive closure of legal channels for political activity. Above all, the rhythm of resistance in the 1970s would be conditioned by the dramatic irruption of a mass movement, both urban and rural, in the years from 1976 to 1980.

Armed struggle remained at the core of the Left's strategy, though approaches to the question continued to diverge. The defeats of the 1960s, the EGP would later argue in a statement which came to represent a majority position within the second generation of the armed Left,

> did not demonstrate the impossibility of armed struggle, but rather the need to link more closely armed struggle and the entire spectrum of popular and democratic struggles around economic, social and political demands. Or rather, the need to incorporate the entire population in a process of Popular Revolutionary War, with armed struggle as the centre of the process . . .
>
> By different routes, with ideas that put the accent on mobilising this or that sector of the population, with different degrees of success, the scattered remains of the revolutionary movement of the first decade reinitiated their activities under new premises.[39]

These were years of patient and anonymous work, of slow and laborious advances, of painful and hesitant convergence between different organizations and political beliefs. Patience was the keynote; the movement would try at all costs to avoid a relapse into the facile triumphalism of 1966.

Keeping track of the movement's shifts, alliances and realignments in the years from 1969 to 1972 is no easy matter. Some withdrew altogether from the country for political and military training; others returned to grassroots rural work and collaboration with church conscientization groups which were springing up in the countryside in the years following the 1968 Conference of Latin American Bishops at Medellín in Colombia; others still devoted their energies to urban labour organizing. The nucleus of the old MR-13 fought on alone for several years, though politically isolated and weakened by Yon Sosa's murder in exile by Mexican troops in 1970, until it finally fell apart.

Between 1968 and 1971, those who opted to stay behind in Guatemala had a requently tense relationship. The old FAR painfully marshalled its forces for new, short-lived guerrilla *focos*. One ephemeral camp took shape at Las Tortugas, on the border of northern Quiché and the department of Alta Verapaz, in 1968-9. Later, the FAR would make renewed attempts to set up a front in the jungles of the southern Petén.

The communist PGT remained wary of armed warfare, though their Fourth Party Congress of December 1969 paid lip-service to the notion of a prolonged and multifaceted revolutionary war that would embrace all forms of action from the economic to the military. On paper at least, the PGT agreed with the theoretical currents emerging from the old Edgar Ibarra Guerrilla Front that such a war "will take time, because the people have not yet got their own army, and if they are to take power and keep it, they must create one".[40] But in practice, the PGT failed to make any corresponding adjustments in its work, and became progressively more marginal to the course of the revolution.

After its sixth military reverse in the wilds of the Petén in 1971, the FAR shifted its base of operations to the capital city and the south coast sugar and cotton export plantations, opening the way for a more effective collaboration with the PGT. This at least applied in terms of the audience that the two organizations addressed. At times separately, and at other times in concert, the two groups worked hard in the still feeble labour unions, their goal a mass-based party of the working class.[41] Under the harsh early years of the Arana government, the tactic was fraught with danger. The PGT, still insisting on keeping a semi-open and highly visible presence, was hit hard by the security forces, who wiped out the majority of the party's Central Committee in 1972.

The FAR's new tactics of switching to urban work, meanwhile, provoked a sharp reaction from many of the organization's membership, above all those who had been devoting their energies to winning Indian support in the heavily populated western departments of Quezaltenango and San Marcos. This segment of the FAR, known commonly as the *regional de occidente*, was deeply critical of the FAR's failure to give adequate weight to the ethnic question and its apparent endorsement of a PGT stance which, to many, bordered on racism.

From the dispute, a new guerrilla nucleus emerged; 95% of its original members, by its own assessment, were Indian. After a few months of work on the south coast and the *bocacosta* or piedmont — the hilly agricultural belt that separates the plantation flatlands from the highlands — the new group withdrew into the Indian mountains of the Sierra Madre in September 1971. From this base, its members argued, they could make contact with both the indigenous subsistence farmers of the *altiplano* and the labourers of the *bocacosta*. They held out little hope of operating effectively with the urban working class, in the belief that the savagery of Arana Osorio's first two years as president had neutralized their potential for involvement in the struggle.

Here in the mountains of the Sierra Madre they remained for eight silent years, slowly expanding their strength and increasing their political proselytizing without firing a single shot. In doing so, they gave the lie to widely held beliefs about the imperative need for guerrilla organizations to engage the enemy in combat if it is to survive. When they finally publicly unveiled the existence of the organization in September 1979, they called themselves the *Organización del Pueblo en Armas* (Organization of the People in Arms: ORPA).[42]

Ixcán

On 19 January, 1972, as ORPA's founders were in the early stages of building their support network in the west, a group of 16 men — most of them survivors from the Edgar Ibarra Guerrilla Front (FGEI) — crossed the desolate border from Mexico into north-western Guatemala. The zone in which they found themselves, carefully selected after long debate, is called the Ixcán. Here, the towering peaks of the chain of mountains called the Cuchumatanes falls away abruptly towards the jungles of the north. The

16 men reasoned that the Ixcán was a perfect location — both socially and for security reasons — on which to establish a guerrilla front. To them, it was "the geographical, political and social region of Guatemala where the state apparatus and imperialist penetration were at their weakest".[43] At the same time, this backward area, almost entirely lacking in infrastructural development, harboured a microcosm of Guatemala's rural contradictions. The new *guerrilleros* judged that the local peasantry — both Indian and Ladino — had explosive potential to become the protagonists of a revolutionary war.

Settlers in the Ixcán in the early 1970s were wretchedly poor and isolated groups of migrant *campesinos,* with fresh and bitter experience of being evicted from their lands. In the Ixcán, they hoped to eke out a precarious subsistence from the inhospitable lands of the rain forest. Later, their numbers would be swelled by settlers attracted by a pilot colonization scheme launched by USAID and the Guatemalan government in the middle of the decade. At the same time, the volatile region would receive a further progressive stimulus from the presence of American Maryknoll missionaries who sponsored a co-operativization programme in the Ixcán.

The nearest population centres of any size were the three towns of Nebaj, Chajul and San Juan Cotzal, collectively known as the "Ixil Triangle". The three villages form a distinct ethnic and linguistic unity: 92% of the triangle's 60,000 population are Ixil Indians. More than any other of Guatemala's 22 Maya-descended ethnic groups, the Ixiles know the humiliation of annual migration to the coastal plantations. The triangle is dominated economically by a handful of immense coffee plantations owned by the Arenas and Brol families. A minority of Ladinos, often politically connected to the far-right MLN, function as gang-bosses — or *contratistas* — for south coast farmers. In collaboration with local units of the *Policia Nacional* and the regime's military commissioners, the *contratistas* have quasi-legal powers to arrest and imprison peasants in privately run debtors' jails. Within three years of the initial approaches of the new embryonic guerrilla organization to this socially explosive region, the Ixiles would form a solid heartland of support, as militants and sympathizers of the *Ejército Guerrillero de los Pobres* (Guerrilla Army of the Poor: EGP).

For tedious months of agonizingly slow progress, the harsh reality of the Ixcán seemed far removed from the dream of a mass-based revolutionary organization.[44] But years later, when the EGP had grown to be the numerically strongest of four contemporary politico-military organizations, its leaders would reflect on the rich lessons of the Ixcán. In many ways, those lessons synthesize what the early stages of guerrilla warfare are all about.

> It was just as important to preserve our rifles against rust as it was to bolster the spirits of combatants who felt discouraged; just as important to possess a compass and maps, in order not to get lost, as to enrich every day the political and

ideological views which guided us; just as important to work out in advance our rations of salt, maize and deer-meat as to enrich our consciousness with nightly political discussions; just as important to learn how to hunt wild mountain animals as to learn how to conduct political work with the people of the hamlets in order to win them over to our cause; just as important to learn how to follow tracks, wade through rivers and build rafts, as to identify and fight the mistaken ideas which survive in all of us and lead us into muddled errors; and just as important to love the yellow flower of the *tamborillo* in February, as to learn how to love and truly respect our *compañeros.*[45]

In almost three years, this original nucleus of the EGP fired only a single shot at the armed forces, concentrating instead on building support painstakingly among the poor subsistence farmers of the region, both Indian and Ladino. An assembly in the jungle in 1975 faced a crucial decision: whether or not to go public. Though the EGP had a mere 50

Table 4
Categories for Comparing the Guatemalan Guerrillas
of the 1960s and 1980s

	1960s	*1980s*
Size	300-500, with up to six thousand active supporters	4,000-6,000 combatants with a mass support base
Leadership	ex-military officers and PGT cadre	survivors of the 1960s, leaders from the indigenous and Christian communities
Role of Indians	marginal; some involvement in FGEI	crucial to EGP and ORPA; main reason for growth and scope of movement
Role of PGT	crucial; overall political direction of FAR	marginal; internally divided; weakest of four groups (though many ex-members are now guerrilla leaders)
Strategic Conception	*foco*	popular revolutionary war
Social Base	narrow and unconsolidated	mass based; tightly organised especially in Indian highland areas
Region	eastern areas, departments of Zacapa and Izabal	primarily western highlands but activity in 14 out of 22 departments
Urban/rural Relationship	movement run from Guatemala City	movement directed from the countryside in conjunction with urban members

combatants under arms, hundreds of peasants clamoured for guns to fight the Army. The existence of the armed Left in the region was "an open secret shared by thousands".[46] The time was ripe, the new organization decided, for its first armed action, and with it the public acknowledgement of the EGP's existence. Their target, in an operation planned for 7 June, 1975, was Luís Arenas Barrera, a landowner whose rapacity made him an object of fear throughout the north-west. Peasants called him "The Tiger of Ixcán".

News of Arenas' assassination spread through the mountains like wildfire; by early the next morning, the sky was alive with the drone of helicopter and aeroplane engines. Lumbering C-47 transports disgorged hundreds of paratroopers over the Ixcan, occupying all key points in the region. The war for El Quiché was on.

Notes

1. US Department of State, Bureau of Public Affairs, *Strategic Situation in Central America and the Caribbean*, statement by Thomas O. Enders, Assistant Secretary of State for Inter-American Affairs, before the Subcommittee on Western Hemisphere Affairs of the Senate Foreign Relations Committee, 14 December, 1981.
2. Edelberto Torres-Rivas, "Ocho claves para comprender la crisis centroamericana", *Polémica*, No.1 (1981).
3. Aguilera, *Terror and Violence*.
4. Debray, *The Revolution on Trial*, p.299. See for example Norman Gall, "Impoverished Peasants Make Good Fighters for Red Insurgents", *Philadelphia Evening Bulletin*, 14 November, 1966; and "Guatemalan Guerrillas Slaughtered; Church Objects to Bloodbath", *National Catholic Reporter*, 7 June, 1967; Georgie Anne Geyer, "The Blood of Guatemala", *The Nation*, 8 July, 1968; Henry Gininger, "Guatemala is a Battleground", *New York Times Magazine*, 16 June, 1968; Alan Howard, "With the Guerrillas in Guatemala", *New York Times Magazine*, 26 June, 1966.
5. Debray, *The Revolution on Trial*, p.299.
6. The most important interviews have been those granted to the Mexican journalist Mario Menéndez Rodríguez, printed in *Por Esto!* (Mexico City, July-August 1981) and the Chilean writer Marta Harnecker, which have appeared in various issues of the Mexican magazines *Punto Final* and *Proceso*, as well as the Ecuadorean review *Nueva*.
7. Menéndez, *Por Esto!* August 1981.
8. Richard Gott, *Guerrilla Movements in Latin America* (Harmondsworth, Penguin Books, 1971) p.39.
9. Debray, *The Revolution on Trial*, pp.270-2.
10. Richard H. Immerman, "Guatemala as Cold War History", *Political Science Quarterly*, Vol. 95, no.4 (Winter 1980-1), pp.652-3.
11. Eduardo Galeano, *Guatemala: Occupied Country* (New York, Monthly Review Press, 1970) p.15.
12. Ibid.
13. Gott, *Guerrilla Movements*, p.75.
14. Gott, *Guerrilla Movements*, pp.50, 62; Debray, *The Revolution on Trial*, pp.321-2.
15. Galeano, *Occupied Country*, p.138.
16. Gott, *Guerrilla Movements*, p.55.
17. Mario López Larrave, *Breve historia del movimiento sindical en Guatemala*, (Guatemala City, Editorial Universitaria, 1979) p.51.
18. Carlos Sarti, "*El desarrollo capitalista, base objetiva de la movilización obrera*", *Anuario de Estudios Centroamericanos*, No.5 (San José, Costa Rica, 1980) p.7.

19. Miguel Angel Albízures, interview in *El Día* (Mexico), 31 March, 1982.
20. Gott, *Guerrilla Movements*, pp.49-50.
21. Concerned Guatemala Scholars, *Dare to Struggle*, p.21.
22. Adolfo Gilly, "The Guerrilla Movement in Guatemala", *Monthly Review*, Vol. 17, nos.1 and 2 (May and June 1965).
23. Debray, *The Revolution on Trial*, p.39.
24. Gott, *Guerrilla Movements*, p.43.
25. Debray, *The Revolution on Trial*, p.296.
26. Concerned Guatemala Scholars, *Dare to Struggle*, p.21.
27. Ibid.
28. A.P. Short, "Conversations with the Guatemalan Delegates in Cuba", *Monthly Review*, Vol. 18, no.9 (February 1967), p.36.
29. Jonas and Tobis, *Guatemala*, p.180.
30. Aguilera, *Terror and Violence*, p.97.
31. *Por Esto!* (August 1981), p.15.
32. Debray, *The Revolution on Trial*, p.307.
33. Eduardo Galeano, *Voces de Nuestro Tiempo*, (Bogotá, Editorial Oveja Negra, 1981) p.135.
34. Indian incorporation into the revolutionary war is dealt with more extensively in chapter 5. Of today's revolutionary organizations, the Guerrilla Army of the Poor (EGP) and the Organization of the People in Arms (ORPA) have dealt with the ethnic and national questions most extensively, albeit from different perspectives. The fullest EGP analysis is contained in *Compañero*, No. 5 (1982). ORPA statements are *Acerca del Racismo*, Nos.1 and 2. FAR and PGT analyses, of some interest though of less substance, are included in the magazine of the Democratic Front Against Repression (FDCR), *Polémica*, (Costa Rica), No.3 (1982).
35. EGP, *Compañero*, No.4 (1982).
36. Norman Gall, "Death is Casual in the Land of the Campesinos", *Toronto Daily Star*, 6 November, 1966.
37. Gott, *Guerrilla Movements*, p.104.
38. Jonas and Tobis, *Guatemala*, p.118.
39. EGP, *Compañero*, No.4.
40. *El camino de la revolución guatemalteca*, (Mexico City, Ediciones Cultura Popular, 1972).
41. Debray, *The Revolution on Trial*, pp.361-2.
42. *Historia de ORPA* (Mexico City, mimeo, 1982).
43. *Por Esto!* (August 1981), p.14.
44. This experience is vividly recounted in Mario Payeras, *Los días de la selva* (Mexico City, Editorial Nuestro Tiempo, 1981). The English version appeared as *Days of the Jungle: The Testimony of a Guatemalan Guerrillero 1972-1976*, with an introduction by George Black, (New York, Monthly Review Press, 1983).
45. Marta Harnecker interview with Mario Payeras, (mimeo, 1981).
46. Payeras, *Días de la selva*, p.83.

5. 1972–1982:
the Road from Ixcán

Popular Revolutionary War

In response to the guerrilla presence in the Quiché came state violence with a modicum of civic "pacification" programmes aimed at the Ixcán and the Ixil Triangle villages. By February 1976, the town of Chajul was under military occupation. That same year, the government launched its pilot Ixcán co-operative scheme, which in good Vietnam fashion called for 64 "model hamlets", each with a service complex consisting of a school, drinking water, a church, a market, a communal meeting hall and access roads. The demands of landowners and foreign corporate investors in the *Franja Transversal del Norte* now meshed. The Army placed a permanent detachment of 400 troops at Playa Grande in the Ixcán, western roadhead of a new highway through the *Franja*. In Huehuetenango, also on the Mexican border, the military would launch a concerted offensive against the militant local labour unions, especially those involved in the 1977 march of striking mineworkers from San Ildefonso Ixtahuacán. Cobán, home town of General Romeo Lucas García, would become the military nerve-centre of the *Franja,* and additional new Army bases would be put in place to protect oil installations close to the Ixcán.

The Army was responding to a new kind of threat; it was soon clear that the EGP, and the simultaneous appearance of ORPA, together with new forms of work from the FAR and PGT, signalled the birth of a new breed of revolutionary organizations. They were the direct descendants of the guerrillas of the 1960s, but had taken the errors and defeats of that decade deeply to heart. The *foquista* efforts of the 1960s had withered on the vine, failing for want of a clear strategy for mass involvement in the war. Military action had not ignited mass insurrection, and, in the end, the guerrilla groups had been destroyed by the Army. Now, the survivors were back, organizing in the countryside and — by the mid-1970s — working in the heart of the urban mass movement as well. From now on, the time scale and the strategic conception behind the revolution would be different. The survivors argued for a prolonged popular war, based on the general mobilization of the populace and the creation of a self-sufficient infrastructure. It would seek to organize the population at every level — as

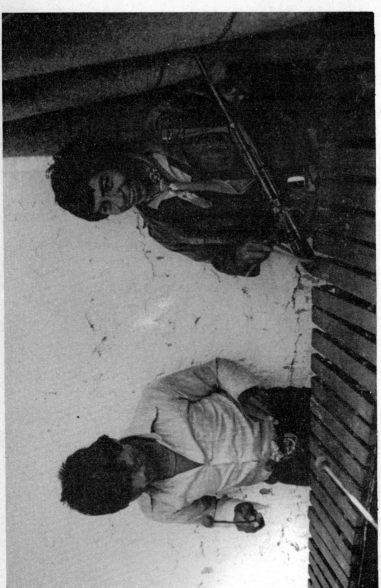

Jean-Marie Simon

Guerrillas with Marimba and gun

fighters in the regular guerrilla units, as paramilitary groups for the defence of local communities, and in a plethora of economic and social tasks ranging from food provision and shelter to intelligence and communications.

> "It was just as important for us to love the yellow flower of the tamborillo in February, as to learn how to love and truly respect our compañeros."
> Mario Payeras.

The prolonged war strategy would move through a series of phases: first would come "implantation", the creation of a solid guerrilla base and its political infrastructure, spreading the word to more and more communities through "armed propaganda". Next, the war would become "generalized" in the countryside, with the Left accumulating strength and extending its social, political and military influence. These stages would precede the moment when the movement felt equipped to take on the armed forces — and perhaps invading US troops — in frontal combat. Only at this point would there be talk of establishing "liberated zones". The culminating stage would be mass insurrection, which many of Guatemala's revolutionary leaders believe is likely to follow levels of military combat not yet witnessed in the region.[1]

The Guatemalan revolution must be fought on three geographical fronts, each with its own special characteristics and problems. There are the rugged Indian highlands, ideal terrain for guerrilla warfare and with weak central government authority. Then there is the rich coastal agricultural belt, with a stronger Army presence pitted against a hostile and (from the late 1970s) organized work-force; and finally the cities, bastion of the regime and hardest to organize.

In a radically new approach, which to many traditional doctrinaire leftists bordered on heresy, the EGP proposed to build its initial bastions of support in the western highlands. It was an abrupt shift from the attitude of the communist PGT and many urban labour organizers, who had seen the peasantry in general — and Indian peasants in particular — as poor raw material for a revolution. The EGP argued that the war must be that of the Indian majority, and only through a social revolution could their centuries of cultural oppression be overcome.[2] Besides, they added, the dismissal of Indians as potential revolutionaries was out of touch with the realities of Guatemala's economic modernization. Any notion of an "intact" and romanticized Mayan social order was absurd; many facets of the Indian communities were the imposition of Spanish colonizers bent on maintaining a captive labour force and weakening indigenous opposition to colonial rule. And since the 1950s the Indians knew only too well — from the despoiling of their lands and the annual forced migration to plantation wage labour — what modern exploitation and class oppression were all about.

Guatemala's Indians

From a single Maya–Quiché root, 22 quite distinct ethnic and linguistic groups have flowered. In the rural marketplaces of the *altiplano,* the different colours and designs of woven and embroidered costumes, or *traje,* may well denote Indian groups who cannot communicate with one another except in Spanish, though they trade with each other and though their home villages may only be a few miles apart.

Three million of Guatemala's people — 40% of the total population — belong to the four largest groups, Quiché, Mam, Cakchiquel and Kekchí. Achí, Aguacateco, Chuj, Ixil, Jacalteco, K'anjobal, Pocomam (eastern and central), Pocomchí, Tzutuhil and Uspanteco ... these lesser groups account for some 700,000 more, one-tenth of the population.

The Spanish *conquistadores* who arrived in what is now Guatemala in 1524 brought with them the requirements of a powerful feudal — not yet capitalist — economy. For Pedro de Alvarado and his cohorts, the only viable option in Central America for the extraction of wealth was to maintain a large labour force, first for export-oriented agriculture (their main concern) and then for mining (a distant second). Their attempts to press the Indian population into the service of the Crown would have to contend with the social structures which they found already in place: those of an incipiently multinational society where the Mam, Quiché, Cakchiquel and Tzutuhil Indians were in the process of consolidating autonomous nation-states. It would take the Spaniards five years to subdue the rebellious Cakchiquel nation, and in the years from 1524 to 1527, historians would record eight major massacres of up to 3,000 Indians at a time.[3]

Throughout the world, imperial conquest of indigenous populations took three forms: extermination, the reservation system and the rationalization of the labour force. The Spanish conquest did not set about the physical elimination of the Indians as did the settlers of the United States. It needed them too much. And requiring a large captive labour pool, the feudal empire did not herd them into racist enclaves, as the British did to the blacks in Southern Africa. Instead, it turned existing social structures and their divisions to its own advantage, tightly demarcating village and ethnic communities and introducing to each easy means of identification and control such as distinctive dress — the *traje* which survives to this day. The prevailing hierarchies of indigenous class structures also became a useful weapon, with local caciques enlisted to do the work of the Crown. Extensive intermarriage between Spaniard and Indian gave birth to the Ladino, and with the explosive mix of colonizer and colonized, expanding empire and aspirant nation-state, a socio-ethnic pyramid of great complexity took shape.

The conquest further fragmented the unity of indigenous communities. First came the expropriation of ancestral Indian lands and the virtual enslavement of their inhabitants; next, Indian servitude within the colonial land-holding system of *repartimientos, encomiendas* and *mandamientos.* In the wake of economic dislocation came ideological assault; the Catholic

Church at its most brutal brought spiritual enslavement, fostering the ideology of European racial supremacy and the code of absolute submission to colonial and religious authority.

But pre-conquest forms of land tenure and community organization survived this onslaught, and not by accident. The material base of Mayan society — communally oriented subsistence farming — was overtaken in importance by the more advanced Spanish colonial plantation system; but the price that the colonizers paid for keeping a subjugated work-force on tap in tightly demarcated local areas was its defiant *cultural* resistance. For four centuries, Guatemala's Indians kept oppression at bay. Their weapon was that collection of beliefs and practices they call *costumbres,* or customs — from hermetic social rituals and village costumes to a religious syncretism which has meshed Roman Catholicism with earlier animistic Mayan ritual.

Passive resistance drew itself tighter through the theft of more Indian lands for coffee production during the 19th Century Liberal presidency of Justo Rufino Barrios, and the seizure of still more to make way for cotton and sugar expansion in the mid-20th Century. It deepened as the generals of the 1970s moved in with spectacular land-grabs in the northern portion of El Quiché, Huehuetenango and Alta Verapaz, and as the Army press-ganged Indian youth into a force which would "kill their noble sentiments, those which characterize our people, and change them into killers".[4] On occasion, it would burst forth into armed revolt, as it did more than a dozen times in the course of the 19th century, and again in 1905, 1906 and 1944.[5] The fatalistic Indian of popular myth is roundly belied by history. Instead, the tenacious hold on a collective Indian identity — of language, birth place, customs, the all-important relationship to the land — "cannot be quantified. It is all over, it crops up everywhere, it is Guatemala itself."[6]

Class differentiation among the ethnic Mayans is quite as complex as the fine racial distinctions which separate Indian and Ladino. The continued coexistence of antiquated and modern modes of production guarantees as much. The subsistence *minifundio* persists: it is the source for cheap migrant plantation labourers, and it is the enduring spiritual heart of Mayan civilization. Purely precapitalist subsistence farmers are tied into the modern agrarian economy only marginally, through their necessary contact with the market. But these days they are in the minority. The norm for today's rural Indian is more likely to be nine months as a peasant and three as a migrant plantation worker. Such an arrangement applies, for instance, to three-quarters of all adult males in an area such as the Ixil Triangle. In the cotton and sugar fields, migrant semi-proletarians will outnumber year-round rural wage labourers.

The transition to capitalism, nonetheless, and the cycle of proletarianization, remains incomplete. The economic system as presently structured can neither absorb the existing work-force nor create a meaningful domestic consumer market. Its failure to generate adequate levels of employment sends droves of hopeful migrants to the cities for work in industry, domestic or other services, or to the pitiful twilight existence of the underemployed *marginado,* selling chewing gum, newspapers and cigarettes on street corners or living by petty crime.

Partial modernization has created a finely tuned range of social classes between peasant and proletarian. Urbanization has dispossessed marginal peasants on city outskirts; state credits, although uneven, have created a stratum of more prosperous peasant farmers; in some areas, Indian middlemen monopolize the local distribution of fertilizers, seeds and other agricultural inputs. New rural access roads and communications have opened up increased possibilities for integrating markets, while others — tied to the spreading tentacles of petroleum companies and local industrialists, have brought only displacement for small farmers in their wake. Tourism and internal migration uproot entire Indian communities and thrust them into small-scale service industries and artisanal activities — handicrafts, for example, or family-run restaurants.[7]

Of all these groups, it is the semi-proletarianized Indians who have played the most innovative political role. The powerful new farmworkers' union that sprang up in the late 1970s — the *Comité de Unidad Compesina* (Peasant Unity Committee: CUC) — paid particular attention to the theoretical and practical dilemmas of their participation in the war. The seasonal migrants were, so the CUC believed, dramatically integrated into modern class society while still retaining a heavy dose of the "old ways". Culturally oppressed and economically exploited, they were open to unified political action (because of their real class experience) with Ladino rural workers, despite the gulf of racism which had historically kept the two groups separate. For the most politically active segments of Indian society, there seemed to be a practical convergence between cultural and class demands, all synthesized in a vision of the ancient Mayan civilization. As the famous declaration of Indian peoples at Iximché in 1980 expressed it, their demand was

> for a society of equality and respect, so that our Indian peoples can develop their culture, now broken by the criminal invaders; for a just economy where no one exploits others . . . for the just distribution and use of our wealth as in the times when the life and culture of our ancestors flourished.[8]

Actors and Stages

In a society such as Guatemala's, in which an ethnic majority is deprived of political power, any failure to arrive at a clear definition of the ethnic question will inevitably pose an obstacle to the unity of the Left. Yet the Indian population alone will not win the war. Though both ORPA and the EGP considered Indians to be the principal force behind the revolution, with their "double suffering" of national and class oppression, the programme to bring about national liberation and revolutionary change is of necessity much broader. It demands alliances with other classes whose requirements the revolutionary organizations — by their very nature —

would be incapable of addressing.

Over the course of the 1970s, many groups came to understand that the existing political order offered them no hope. Whether subsistence farmers, rural migrant labourers or sharecroppers; urban factory workers, the unemployed or marginal slum-dwellers; radicalized students and young middle-class professionals, or even business people cut out of the economic schema of the generals — all became to one degree or another active opponents of the regime.

Coming from such different backgrounds each group has found out in its own way, each fighting its own work-place battles, that the military regime offers no space for dissent or for legal participation through institutional channels. For some, the struggle to win recognition of their trade union has brought disillusionment about the old peaceable tactics; for others, faith in gradual change through the electoral system was travestied by the repeated evidence of fraud — in 1974 and again in 1978 — and by the daily manifestations of corruption in public affairs; for others still, the fight for land was from the outset a battle for survival.

Effective opposition also means finding a synthesis from among widely differing ideologies. In the common fight, traditional communists and disillusioned social democrats rub shoulders with Roman Catholics inspired by the theology of liberation and progressive Protestants; the historic grievances of 22 ethnic groups find common cause with the rebellious anger of the long-term unemployed. At one extreme lies the peril of unregenerated "workerism", which holds that only the urban factories can lead the fight; at the other lurks the risk of exaggerated *indigenismo* whose adherents press for ethnic demands to the exclusion of all others.

It is from this mosaic of class, race and ideology that the arduous path of unity must be forged and the broadest possible social spectrum involved. Radicalization, and with it the acceptance of armed struggle as the only feasible way forward, does not come to all these sectors at the same rhythm. But between 1976 and 1980, one sector after another learned from bitter experience that peaceful change was a chimera, and that the politico-military organizations of the Left might represent a viable means of interweaving the myriad forms of struggle. In those four years, a rush of momentous events marked key moments in the growth and interlocking of the mass movement:

* 1976: a strike at Guatemala's Coca Cola franchise brings a pivotal defence of the right to labour union organization.
* May 1978: more than 100 Kekchí Indians, protesting over land abuses, are killed by the Army at Panzós, a decisive moment for the progressive Catholic clergy.
* October 1978: Guatemala City erupts in riots against proposed bus fare increases, and urban slum-dwellers emerge as a potent force.
* January 1980: government security forces storm the Spanish Embassy in the capital; 39 people — mainly peasants occupying the Embassy to draw attention to Army repression in El Quiché — die in the blazing building.

* March 1980: a sugar-workers' strike led by the clandestine CUC paralyses the South Coast plantations. For the first time, Indian and Ladino workers unite in joint political action.

Throughout this period, at each key moment, the doors of legal protest were slammed shut by the regime. One social sector after another learned its own organizational potential and tne military brutality which awaited dissent. The mildest defensive protest meant military confrontation, perhaps death, and the movement had to learn to respond accordingly. After each fresh strike, each new massacre, there could be no turning back.

Schoolteachers Show the Way

As the rural guerrilla movements began to put down fresh roots, the lingering urban guerrilla fronts of the early 1970s were finally caving in. The regime appeared suffocatingly in control of the cities. To survivors of the blanket anti-communism of the post-1954 period, combined with the counterinsurgency terror of the late 1960s, the rebirth of grassroots popular organizations must have seemed a remote fantasy.

Yet quite abruptly a new mass movement had indeed begun to stir in the spring and summer months of 1973. Economic boom years had brought some new urban employment and a working class ready to flex its muscles, while at the same time rising inflation — it would soar from 0.5% in 1972 to 10% in 1973 and peak at 16% in 1974 — eroded living standards and fuelled discontent. With the eyes of the world on Guatemala's upcoming presidential elections, there seemed to be the promise of some limited space for opposition and protest.

It began with a national teachers' strike. During the previous year, there had been strikes or threatened strikes in several areas of the public sector — electrical and communications workers, university and court employees. Yielding to this pressure in a pre-election year, the Arana Osorio government passed a law in early 1973 stipulating that public employees should receive a salary increase every two years and making severance pay obligatory. Significantly though, the teaching profession — which accounts for nearly half of all public sector employees — was expressly excluded. An earlier law had provided for annual inflation-linked salary increases for teachers, but in practice salaries had remained frozen since 1962. A new teacher could expect starting pay of $89.33 per month; one at the top of the scale, after 25 years of service, would make $176.77 per month.

The protest began in the western towns of Quezaltenango and San Marcos but rapidly spread throughout the country and brought out 20,000 teachers in support of a 50% wage claim. Teachers had always been a militant and mobilized group. They had been prominent in the movement which overthrew the dictator Ubico and were one of the main pillars of support for the "revolutionary" governments of 1944-54. As such, they were targeted for harsh treatment in subsequent years, accused of being riddled with "communist influence".

Organizing a strike, or even a trade union, in Guatemala has always been a risky proposition. When workers on the foreign-owned railways undertook their second national strike in 1924, the government intervened and imprisoned the principal leaders. In the same year, when dockworkers employed by the United Fruit Company demanded wage increases, an eight-hour day and an end to discrimination against black workers, troops moved in to break the strike, leaving a number of workers dead and 22 of the strike leaders under arrest. Under the tyranny of Ubico from 1931-44, all organizing rights were abrogated; the very words "unionism", "strike" and "labour rights" prohibited by law.[9] Anyone daring to use them, according to labour historian Mario López Larrave, was automatically deemed a "communist" or "subversive" and dealt with accordingly.

The brief respite of 1944-54, during which one of the most advanced labour codes in the hemisphere was written into law, was followed by an anti-union savagery so indiscriminate that even the staunchly anti-communist American Institute for Free Labor Development (AIFLD), which had supported the 1954 coup and expected government protection for US-allied unions, felt moved to protest. The fine distinction between a class-conscious union and a co-optable union has never much interested the Guatemalan élite. Reliant on a constantly available, cheap and docile work-force, they have seen any union as a bad union, communist by definition.

The Central American Common Market of the 1960s, bringing a degree of industrial modernization and a flood of foreign investment, did little to improve matters. On the contrary, the government's hard line was a prime incentive for US, Japanese and European businesses to invest in Guatemala. Even those multinationals who were prepared to accommodate labour unions in other Latin American operations became willing or passive partners in the government's campaign to intimidate and eliminate union leaders. In the case of US businessmen, that complicity was more than likely to be enthusiastic. One, interviewed in September 1980, explained the best way of dealing with a troublesome trade unionist: "Shoot him or eliminate him. Assassinate him. Murder him. Whichever word is most applicable."[10] Business methods recalled the ugliest days of *laissez faire* capitalism: factory personnel managers were often military men; Mobile Military Police units would commonly be stationed on the shopfloor in conflictive plants.

The teachers' strike now quickly swelled to include parents, students, public employees, slum-dwellers and industrial workers who took to the streets in sympathy. And as broad support for the strike blossomed, it took on fresh significance. The teachers were not alone in their grievances. A victory for them, winning their wage demand and forcing restitution of strikers who had been sacked, would provide the chance for the labour movement as a whole to drive a wedge into government repression. Then others too — hitherto paralysed by fear — could take hope about expressing their own stifled demands.

On 7 August, 1973, 4,000 people marched through Guatemala City in solidarity with the teachers, defying threats from the government-sanctioned death squads. The Arana regime, startled by this show of strength and aware of the risks of negative pre-election publicity, caved in to the teachers' demands. This was something new; the tiny movement pressed forward. In 1974, railway workers struck. Though the military succeeded in breaking their protest, other unions — such as electricians and tobacco workers — were more successful. The government's own tame Federated Workers Central (CTF) all but collapsed in 1973 as more and more of its members shifted leftwards.[11] Bank employees, university staff and municipal workers all unionised for the first time.

Table 5
Percentage of Economically Active Population Organized in Unions

Year	Total Work-Force	Percentage Organized
1953	967,814	10.33
1975	1,695,520	1.62

Source: Guatemalan Office of Labour

The movement may indeed have been small: by the middle of the decade, only half as many of the industrial labour force were organized as had been under the Arbenz government in 1954. But this new movement had a clear sense of purpose and was determined to set its own autonomous rules. One Guatemalan sociologist reflects upon changes from the 1950s to the 1970s in these terms:

> It is important to recall that the workers' movement that emerged in Guatemala between 1948 and 1954 had a very different character from the movement of the 1970s. It was born and bred in a complacent climate of bourgeois democracy and learned to walk with official support. To be sure, it rapidly gained independence and formulated its own programme. But it was a trade union movement of artisans on the one hand and white collar workers on the other, which remained trapped by its own petty bourgeois base.[12]

The 1970s were quite different, even though it was the teachers — that most petty bourgeois of social groups — that provided the initial spark. A modernizing economy in the context of the absolute absence of political rights helps explain why. By this time, Guatemala had a fairly consolidated "proletarian nucleus" made up of three distinct groups — urban industries geared to the needs of the regional market (foodstuffs, pharmaceuticals, packaging and other light industry); extractive industries (nickel and copper mining and petroleum exploration): and large agribusiness plantations with integrated, mechanized processing facilities (bananas, cotton and sugar). Not only were these new sectors organizing, but they were running up against the heavy-handed response of a regime which had left itself little or no margin for political manoeuvre. The unions of the 1970s threatened to break through the barrier of fear and co-optation, and the traditionally timid union leadership of the previous decade — for the most part Christian Democrat — was alarmed.

New Unity, New Methods

The basic strategy of the nascent union movement was to open up "democratic space", making working-class organization possible. But even this was an uphill fight. Following formal legal procedures to have a union registered with the Ministry of Labour, and then petitioning for the right to strike, were integral parts of the process. But it would not stop there. Compliance with legal norms was unlikely to yield results. The slow and corrupt deliberations of the Conciliation Tribunals, whose judges (rarely versed in labour legislation) were likely to be heavily influenced by employers' pressure, dictated a healthy scepticism. That pressure could be blatant — to suspend Tribunal proceedings altogether, giving management time to identify and sack (if not kill) union leaders; or more subtle — making sure that petitions were thrown out on some trivial loophole, such as the petitioner's mispelling of a single worker's or manager's name.

By mid-decade, virtually no major enterprise, whether public or private, Guatemalan or foreign-owned, had escaped bitter labour conflict over union registration rights. The confrontation hotted up after the February 1976 earthquake, when employers took advantage of the chaos to dismiss workers they deemed unruly. Between February and June of that year, officially or unofficially unionized workers were laid off at the Coca Cola bottling plant, the Aurotex textile factory, the IODESA food factory in Escuintla, the Pantaleón sugar refinery, the Transportes Reyes bus company in Guatemala City ... the list reads like a Guatemalan Chamber of Commerce directory.

As the earthquake struck on 4 February, labour union delegates had been meeting intensively to unify their efforts; momentarily, the earthquake shook them out of their stride. Unity discussions were set aside as all hands turned to aid survivors of the disaster.[13] But the lull was short-lived; one of the springtime sackings above all triggered the outrage of the entire Guatemalan labour movement.

> "In Guatemala, murder is called Coca Cola."
> Israel Márquez, former secretary general of the
> Coca Cola plant union.

The flashpoint came on 24 March, when 152 workers were laid off by *Embotelladora Guatemalteca S.A.* (EGSA), local franchise of the Coca Cola Company, owned and managed by John C. Trotter, a fiercely right-wing lawyer from Houston, Texas. Since the previous August, the work-force had been striving to register a legal union and draw up a collective bargaining agreement. Wages and conditions were inferior to those at the non-unionized Pepsi-Cola franchise, operated by the wealthy Castillo family: in fact, the prevailing gallows humour at the plant was that wages were so low that a bottle of Coke was an unaffordable luxury. Now, on 24 March, patience snapped. Enraged by the sackings, the workers took over the factory. Police responded by storming the building and ejecting the occupiers by force.[14]

What now? Would the Coca Cola workers cave in and allow management to break another union? The answer came from the broad range of unions which weighed in to support the strike. It was a pivotal decision. The country was in the traumatic aftershock of the earthquake; a US-owned company had massively abused labour rights; and the repression of recent months had already driven the young movement a long way down the road to unity and an escalated concept of self-defence. Now, if ever, a stand had to be taken.

On 31 March, delegates of 65 unions met to consider their response. From the talks emerged the *Comité Nacional de Unidad Sindical* (National Committee of Trade Union Unity: CNUS), a broad unitary organization designed to confront the repression and defend labour rights — above all the right to organize freely. Its cutting edge was the eight-year-old *Confederación Nacional del Trabajo* (National Confederation of Labour: CNT), by far the largest member grouping. Formed along Christian Democratic lines in 1968, the CNT had been radicalized away from those origins just as segments of the Guatemalan Christian Democratic Party had shifted leftwards. By April 1978, the CNT would finally break from the Christian Democrats' regional labour federation, CLAT, thereby sealing the political independence of the Guatemalan labour movement.[15]

The formation of CNUS made it possible for the first time for workers in different factories, and even in different industrial sectors, to link up in joint action. From 1976 to 1978, each fresh strike would set off solidarity actions in other plants. Factory occupations would be helped along by other groups of workers supplying the raw materials to keep production moving. CNUS proved innovative and creative in its tactics, teaching its members to duck the repression. The story is told of one Japanese-owned plant, where workers had planned a wildcat strike. No, advised CNUS labour lawyers — they had no chance of winning and would only invite police brutality. When the plant owner brought the police in, ready for a forcible eviction, he found the occupying workers quietly at their posts, with production flowing smoothly. On the wall hung a banner, which until then had borne the single word "strike", now two new words had been added: "*de Hambre*" — Hunger. When stoppages and occupations became too dangerous, many groups of workers opted instead for brief,peaceful occupations of embassies and consulates. In 1978, workers at the Duralita building materials factory — a joint venture between Swiss and Guatemalan capital — would go as far as throwing a birthday party for their good-natured "hostage", the Swiss Ambassador. The action gained them a considerable amount of local sympathy and international press coverage.[16]

And via CNUS, the world would sit up and take notice of the long-running Coca Cola dispute. The International Union of Food and Allied Workers (IUF) weighed in with a boycott of Coca Cola products and a worldwide publicity campaign highlighted the stream of Coca Cola workers cut down by the death squads.[17] As one former secretary of the plant union, Israel Márquez, would tell the world, "In Guatemala, murder is called Coca Cola."

The Mineworkers' March

In November 1977, Minas de Guatemala closed its tungsten-mine in San Ildefonso Ixtahuacán in the remote north-west, laying off 300 workers and stepping up intimidation of their union. Isolated way up in the mountains, the Mam Indian miners settled on a new tactic, a 300 kilometre protest march to Guatemala City to demand reinstatement and fresh discussions on a year-old collective bargaining agreement. Immediately, CNT-organized miners at the Oxec mine and construction crews at the huge Chixoy and Aguacapa hydroelectric plants downed tools in sympathy.

As the workers and their families made the long trek down the Pan American highway, Quiché Indian peasants ran from their homes offering food, clothing, money and moral support. Further on down the road, Cakchiquel Indians and poor Ladinos did the same. By Tecpán, 55 miles short of the capital, the miners learned their demands had been met. Yet they walked on to their destination in support of striking workers from the Pantaleón sugar mill, who in turn brought out sympathizers from the industrial estates around Lake Amatitlán. From both directions, streams of workers poured on to the dusty cloverleaf by the Roosevelt Hospital, merging there with a throng of waiting urban supporters. One hundred thousand people took to the streets. Never before had workers and peasants, Indians and Ladinos, and Indians of different ethnic groups showed such solidarity with each other.

For the generals, the miners' march was proof that things had been allowed to get out of hand. By the end of 1977, the surge of strikes, marches and occupations forced both sides to draw battle lines. As CNUS's critiques became bolder and the class content of their declarations more explicit, union members and labour lawyers became moving targets for the death squads. CNUS lawyer and labour historian Mario López Larrave, Ixtahuacán march organizer Mario Mujía of Huehuetenango and scores of others died.

Insisting still that any remaining legal space had to be exploited, CNUS continued to meet openly But security became a nightmare, and rank-and-file criticism mounted that open work was tantamount to suicide. On 21 June, 1980, amid growing disquiet that the concept of "legal space" was an illusion, 27 union leaders met at the dilapidated CNT headquarters in

97

downtown Guatemala City, just a few blocks from the National Palace. They represented the plant unions of Acricasa, Induplast, Tursa, Kerns, Richardson Merrel, Sistemas Electrónicos, Coca Cola, Cedasa and Prensa Libre. As they talked, police units sealed off the block; plain-clothes gunmen broke in and dragged away all 27. They were never seen again. Increasingly, the movement went underground from this point onwards, its methods progressively converging with those of the guerrillas. The defensive demands of CNUS's founding charter — such as an end to court delays in union registration and the elaboration of a new Labour Code in which CNUS would have a voice — began to sound like distant echoes of another age. Secret factory "nuclei" and workers' commissions came to replace open assemblies and legal deputations to the Labour Ministry. In some factories, they began to meet under armed guard, formed into workers' self-defence units.

From the Classrooms . . .

While CNUS moved from foundation through victories and repression to the bitter lessons of enforced clandestinity, other social sectors flooded on to the stage as active opponents of the regime.

As elsewhere in Latin America, students were an active political force during the 1960s and 1970s, especially in the years when the University of San Carlos campus was still located on a number of downtown sites. Their annual parade and publication *No Nos Tientes* (Don't Tempt Us), like its Salvadorean counterpart the *bufonada,* had always given vent to some pretty scurrilous anti-government satire. Yet the student threat had remained ephemeral, the campus split by internecine political squabbles. Until August 1977, that is, when the death squads turned their sights on high school leaders Robín García and Leonel Caballer. A little more than a year later, on the anniversary of the October 1944 revolution, Oliverio Castañeda de León, president of the University Students' Association (AEU) fell next victim. Leaving a mass demonstration that he had just finished addressing, Castañeda fell in broad daylight in a hail of bullets from a specialized commando unit of ten men in four vehicles. Policemen on duty in the Parque Central, just across from the National Palace, stood idly by and watched the whole thing.

The death squads proceeded to declare open hunting season on the San Carlos campus, which was by now in revolt. Covered in revolutionary wall-paintings, it functioned as a virtual liberated area on the outskirts of the city, and as a meeting place for the clandestine organizations. In a four-month long orgy of violence, 400 students and teachers would die.[18] A large segment of the student movement was also underground by this time. Just as the guerrilla movement drew away from the static electoralist politics of the communist PGT, so many students decided that more radical methods were needed than those on offer from the communist-linked AEU. The radical current broke from the AEU to form the *Frente Estudiantil Revolucionario* (FERG), with both high school and university sections. The FERG was named in honour of slain student leader Robín García.

The student leaders' killings were part of a wave of attacks, designed in the words of one Guatemalan scholar, "to create the impression that the terror gangs could act with impunity against any form of popular mobilization".[19] But they also produced an unexpected and unintended response: the mobilization of new sectors and the overcoming of individual fear through a fusion of funeral cortège and protest march, which followed each assassination of a major figure and grew spectacularly in size. With Castañeda's death, the students found out they were not alone. 20,000 turned out for his funeral, and 45,000 for a protest march days later. With students and workers marched ever greater numbers of the middle classes and professional sectors, outraged by the brazen killing of their own kind. For the first time, a serious questioning of a system capable of such violence began to germinate in the minds of the relatively well-to-do. In the funeral processions, they walked together with the poor, a sea of red carnations held high in the air in protest.

. . . And the Slums . . .

Strangest of all — and not least to the participants — the marches brought the middle classes elbow to elbow with the inhabitants of Guatemala City's sordid slums. The influx of migrants to the capital from rural areas had risen steeply since the 1960s, bringing people displaced by the encroachment of export agriculture and mining, the mechanization of large farms and the lack of reliable year-round employment. The 1976 earthquake further swelled the burgeoning squatter settlements. With the earthquake, absolute levels of poverty in the city worsened; many slum-dwellers had seen their frail cardboard and tin shacks swept away by the tremor into the ravines and gullies which ring the capital. Thousands more had flooded into the *villas miseria* from the devastated countryside.

In these slums, known also as *limonadas,* as in the rural areas, progressive Church workers were deeply involved in community organizing; so too were Christian Democrats. From their combined efforts, the *Movimiento Nacional de Pobladores* (National Slum-dwellers' Movement: MONAP) was born. And as in the countryside, Christian community activists and the poor themselves discovered that the humblest local demand for economic improvements — drinking water, or paved streets — was dealt with by the regime as a mortal threat.

CNUS too was now part of the rising tide of slum organizing. It has long been almost an axiom among revolutionaries that slum-dwellers — with no employer and no work-place ties in most cases — are poor stuff for a revolution, treading the line between *lumpen* and aspiring small entrepreneur. But from its inception, CNUS had taken a different view; after all, failing to do so would mean discounting 60% of the entire urban population. CNUS worked to mobilise both factory workers and the unemployed urban poor, arguing convincingly enough that the dividing line between the two is perilously thin in an economy such as Guatemala's. Nor is there a safety net against unemployment: from one day to the next, one can plummet from being a "relatively privileged" industrial worker in a foreign manufacturing concern to being an unemployed, maybe blacklisted, worker with no access to government benefits or health care. In its first major pronouncement on 1 May, 1976, CNUS made its concerns clear. It urged government to provide adequate land and housing for those affected by the earthquake, as well as the regulation of rent increases, controls on food prices and a ban on profiteering in construction materials. Furthermore, it demanded the right to work and the enforcement of the legal minimum wage.[20]

Nicaragua's September 1978 insurrection provided the practical vindication of CNUS's belief that slum-dwellers could indeed be a potent force in the Central American revolution. And bus fares, an apparently trivial issue, provided the spark for *pobladores* to demonstrate their anger in Guatemala.

Following anarchic routes which reflect the number of competing private lines, ancient buses — many of them retired American school buses — rattle and roar their way through the capital. Silencers seem not to exist; nine out of ten buses pump noxious black smoke into the air, where it hangs in palls, trapped between the buildings that line the narrow grid-pattern streets. The Guatemala City bus service is a headache for anyone. But for most slum-dwellers, travelling on the city's ramshackle buses is an economic nightmare. Even for employed workers, daily travel — changing buses once — can eat up a full 15% of their income.[21]

In late September 1978, CNT-led bus drivers struck for a wage increase. The context was explosive. At one level, the strike came in the middle of a year when the economy was performing well — coffee prices were high, the post-earthquake, foreign-financed construction boom was continuing, and the public sector was expanding steadily. And workers, though they had learned some salutary lessons in the Laugerud years, had also learned a lot of self-confidence. At another level, more immediate, the new Lucas García regime was only weeks old and was floundering from right to centre in its search for political alliances. It met the strike call in a state of confused indecision. Finally, the memory of Nicaragua's insurrection on television was fresh and inspiring.

In response to the drivers' strike, the Lucas regime backed the private bus-owners' demand that urban fares should be doubled from 5¢ to 10¢. At once, a CNUS general assembly of workers, students and shanty-town dwellers agreed on a general strike in the public sector, demanded a single publicly owned bus company to rationalize services, and put up barricades to paralyse traffic in the capital.[22] With the strike, which was about 60% effective, economic activity in Guatemala City slowed to a near-standstill. But even more threatening were the barricades. Following the Nicaraguan example, disaffected urban youth wearing face masks blocked the roads with paving stones and burning tyres and peppered traffic-lanes with thumb-tacks. It was a vast spontaneous uprising which the organized mass movement did *not* control. Street fighting erupted in the capital and in towns in the western highlands, with police firing on unarmed crowds; 31 died.[23]

Eventually, however, the pressure told. To the disgust of Army hardliners, the government withdrew the proposed fare increases and instead paid a 3½¢-per-ride subsidy to the owners. Like all victories of the popular movement, it was a costly one. Hundreds of activists lost their jobs, and the militant unions of state employees (CETE), postmen and telecommunications workers were outlawed. The bodies of slum-dwellers arrested and "disappeared" on the barricades began to turn up later, strewn along the roadsides.

... And the Churches
The 1976 earthquake, said the Cardinal, was a punishment from God. And what should be done about it? "Let us confess our sins and pray for sacramental absolution and penitence." No, no, said the bishops. This was not what the earthquake meant at all. Instead, "[it] laid bare the suffering history of our people: a history of people lacerated by injustice, of men made small by oppression".[24] A third body of opinion, in the slums of the capital and the poor Indian highlands, came from parish priests, lay workers and catechists. For them, actions spoke louder than episcopal pronouncements. The earthquake was a moment for the preferential option for the poor to be put into effect.

The Guatemalan Catholic Church is badly divided. Here, even more than in El Salvador or Nicaragua, the emergence of a "people's church" is remarkable. In the colonial capital of Antigua, dozens of churches and convents ruined in the earthquake of 1773 bear witness to imperious Spanish rule and the central role of the Church in the conquest. Since Guatemalan independence in 1821, the conservative function of the Church has rarely wavered. Its economic power was broken late, by the Liberal reforms separating church and state after 1871, but the ideological importance of conservative doctrine to keep the indigenous population in line did not diminish. The Guatemalan Church remained institutionally more important than its Central American counterparts.

Throughout the 1930s the hierarchy identified openly with Falangism. Not surprisingly, it remained vocally opposed to the reforms of Arévalo and Arbenz and blessed the Castillo Armas counter-revolution. When the dictator was assassinated in 1957, Archbishop Mariano Rossell proclaimed him an "authentic martyr" of the Church. His successor, Monseñor Mario Casariego, who took office in 1964 and stayed there until his death in June 1983, was a man in the same mould. Blessing 54 new police radio-patrol cars in March 1967, he congratulated the police for their efforts towards internal security and told them "it is important that you take good care of these vehicles since they were purchased with the money of the people".[25] Casariego remained a personal confidant of successive military presidents, and confessed towards the end of his life that next to the Church the career of a military officer would have been his ideal.

After 1954, the hierarchy encouraged a flood of foreign missionaries to preach the anti-communist word and restore government control over the countryside. The missionaries were concentrated in Indian peasant areas. By 1966, 434 out of 531 priests were foreigners, as were 705 of the 805 religious sisters and all 96 brothers.[26] But the foreign missionaries broke the mould they had been expected to preserve. The co-operative movement of the 1960s, modest though its goals were, was the first step. With the co-operatives came the social training workshops or *cursillos* which brought a shared discussion of Guatemalan social reality in the rural communities.[27] The repression of the co-operatives by landlords who saw them (correctly enough) as a threat to the cheap migrant labour supply opened the eyes of missionaries who had envisaged them as a moderate alternative to radical reform, in line with the Church's "social doctrine". As the co-operative movement foundered, churchpeople turned to ideas of radical structural change, and became a natural primary conduit for filtering the revolutionary message into the Indian highlands.[28]

Church-sponsored grassroots organizations flourished in the wake of the earthquake, seeking fundamental improvements for their communities. At the same time, the Army established itself more firmly in the countryside; the new community organizers ran up against the military at every step. Through Church efforts in the highlands and the slums, new generations of indigenous leaders emerged, and their fruitless efforts to win community battles peacefully led them to question the very roots of the system.

By May 1978, conflicts between religious communities and the Army, and between grassroots Church activists and the conservative sectors of the hierarchy, came to boiling point. On the 29th, a crowd of Kekchí Indians (variously estimated at between 700 and 1500) marched into the small town of Panzós. There, they had been given to believe, mayor Overdick would settle their long-simmering grievances over land tenure and explain the disappearance of three peasant leaders kidnapped some weeks earlier.

Land disputes had been raging through the new *Franja Transversal del Norte,* and the ancestral farming rights of the Kekchí of Alta Verapaz had been abused more than most. As the Exmibal nickel-mine — close to Panzós on Lake Izabal — began operations, Indians on the banks of the Río Polochic were forcibly relocated to make way for strip mining. Plans for the new transversal highway made matters worse. Landowners such as coffee baron Ricardo Sapper Cordúa, who took over three whole Kekchí villages in a 3,375 acre land-grab in June 1976, simply ignored the counter-claims to the land from the local Indians.

But the Kekchí, instead of finding the answer to their question in Panzós, found only 150 troops from the military garrison at Zacapa, called in by local landowners, cantoned in the town hall. Together with right-wing vigilantes posted on surrounding rooftops, they opened fire on the demonstration. When the dust settled, the body count began: 119 said one report; at least 140, said another; over a hundred, was the consensus. At such times, precise statistics become almost an indecent luxury. What many witnesses agreed on was that the graves had been pre-dug with earth-moving equipment owned by local MLN politician Flavio Monzón.[29]

The regime's version was not slow in coming: Defence minister Otto Spiegeler, with Lucas García the owner of huge tracts of farmland in the *Franja,* blamed *religiosos* for stirring up the peasants. "They used tape recorded messages in Kekchí," Spiegeler would claim,

> to arouse people to demand land. Hence one of their slogans on Monday morning was "The land belongs to God and those who work it." This and other slogans were taught them by guerrillas and religious.

In the aftermath of the massacre, the government expelled a Spanish nun who had worked for years in Alta Verapaz. The Christian base communities and co-operatives wasted no time in reacting. At least ten religious groups published press denunciations of the mass killing, including the 24-member Conference of Guatemalan Religious (CONFREGUA) and the newly formed Justice and Peace Committee, which grouped together Catholic lay intellectuals and religious. Moving rapidly from a stand against repression into active opposition to the existing social order, Justice and Peace swiftly became one of the most broadly based of the popular organizations.[30]

The regime was not prepared to countenance dissent from this quarter. In rural areas, clergy took their place in the Army's shooting gallery; Father Bill Woods of the Maryknoll order, killed in an unexplained plane crash near his co-operative in the Ixcán; Faustino Villanueva, Spanish mission-ary, machine-gunned in his church in El Quiché in July 1980; Stan Rother, conservative priest from Oklahoma, shot to death at his mission in the tourist town of Santiago Atitlán. The list goes on . . . 16 deaths between 1976 and 1981. Eventually even the Bishop of El Quiché, Monseñor Juan Gerardi, would leave the country, declaring that further pastoral work was impossible because of the repression. Two attempts had been made on his own life. Over the summer of 1980, Bishop Gerardi spent three months in Rome and had three audiences with Pope John Paul II. On his return to Guatemala in November, he was refused entry at the airport. Not a single church kept its doors open in the whole mountainous department. Many of the priests who left were Spanish, and they would leave the country to form the core of the Guatemalan Church in Exile.

But Cardinal Casariego was not impressed, and in 1979 seven of his bishops resigned, disheartened by the cardinal's obstruction of episcopal efforts to denounce human rights violations.[31] A fresh group of bishops distanced themselves more and more from the radical stance of their clergy. In response to government charges of Church involvement in "subversion", the hierarchy cut its activist priests adrift:

> If a priest or religious opts to . . . enlist in any political faction or subversive group, he ceases to belong to the pastoral organisms of the Church, and the hierarchy cannot therefore take any responsibility for his subsequent actions.[32]

But growing numbers of the base church refused to be deterred by the repression. A protest march against the Panzós massacre on 8 June, 1978 drew 60,000 demonstrators. Nuns and priests in clerical garb walked shoulder to shoulder with workers and peasants. As one onlooker commented: "This is what Guatemala has been waiting for from the Church — for 400 years."[33]

A New Voice for the Countryside

From the moment of its first public appearance on 1 May, 1978, it was clear that the *Comité de Unidad Campesina* (Peasant Unity Committee: CUC) was no ordinary peasant organization. In that Labour Day parade was the largest Indian turnout ever witnessed in Guatemala. They came in their hundreds — children, grandparents, entire families — with their flags, scarves, hand-painted *petate* banners, their nylon tarpaulins to shield them against the rain, carrying hoes, machetes and torches. They marched in well disciplined rows with their own tight security. For the first time, there were Indian orators. No one had ever seen anything like it.

Guatemala had seen agricultural unions and peasant leagues before, but the CUC was designed as a new kind of political instrument to give the rural movement real coherence for the first time. The CUC arose as a fusion of co-operatives, peasant leagues and — perhaps most important — Christian base groups. It quickly joined CNUS, but unlike its predecessors the CUC did not seek legal recognition from the government or limit its demands to defensive economic improvements. From the outset, the CUC spoke unequivocally: it would "uproot the tree of exploitation".

Laying the groundwork for the CUC's foundation had taken five meticulous years. Each existing political organization was studied during that time to see if it could meet the specific needs of the peasantry and the rural poor, but none fully qualified. Some peasant leaders toyed briefly with the notion of an exclusively Indian body, but as instances of co-operation between Indian and Ladino within CNUS multiplied, the idea waned and was finally discarded. The success of the Ixtahuacán miners' march fully vindicated the proposal to organize across the ethnic divide. The CUC's founders would organize nation-wide — in the communities and on the plantations simultaneously — under a single banner, a single unitary strategy that could bring together not only Indian and Ladino, but also Indian groups hitherto isolated from one another. With the escalation of government violence in the countryside through 1977 and 1978, the new organization could wait no longer. By April 1978, the CUC stood ready to respond.[34]

Its work concentrated on the highland departments of El Quiché and Chimaltenango, but rapidly expanded to the south coast plantations and the north-western areas of San Marcos and Huehuetenango. The genius of the CUC was to work with the same people in two complementary ways. In doing so, it defied traditional scepticism about the feasibility of harnessing the inchoate force of migrant labour — some 600,000 families from different towns and villages, speaking many different languages, often migrating to a different farm each harvest season.[35] In the highlands, the CUC organized them as subsistence farmers, on the south coast as migrant labourers, exposing through this work the overlap between economic exploitation and cultural oppression.[36]

As CNUS began to look vulnerable to the repression, the CUC began to distance itself from the umbrella organization and became more determined in its concern for security precautions. Initially, the CUC provided for the participation of all in its decision-making process, young and old, Indian and Ladino. It kept no membership lists and charged no dues; nor did it have formal leadership structures. Local and regional assemblies were the main forums for the CUC's deliberations, with a six-monthly national assembly whose decisions would be carried out by local organizers. The intensity of government repression led the CUC to meet under armed guard; finally it reduced meetings to get-togethers in twos and threes. The CUC's leaders remained unknown figures until 1980; as members are fond of saying, "our methods of operation are not exactly clandestine, just secretive".

CUC work merged with that of the guerrilla organizations. Their methods included preparation for the war, sabotage and harassment of the Army, mass armed self-defence techniques, political education and mobilization around community demands. The emphasis was on the creative use of available resources and ingenuity in tackling grassroots problems. Plantation workers, for example, faced with a lack of billboards and walls, would paint their slogans on cattle. When landowners began to single out these beasts for slaughter, the workers resorted to stray dogs, and these served as moving rural signboards, reading "¡Viva CUC!" and "GPR" (the acronym for *Guerra Popular Revolucionaria* — Popular Revolutionary War).

In an atmosphere of war, overtly political structures may only invite repression, so the peasants came up with a creative assortment of alternatives. Family parties, religious brotherhoods, even local football tournaments, might provide the best vehicle for education, discussion and organizing.[37] While the CUC's own newspaper *Voz* (Voice) circulated in Indian languages throughout the highlands, other locally produced peasant news sheets and religious study documents complemented the message. Together with indigenous radio stations — the *radiodifusoras populares* — like the *Voz de Atitlán* in Santiago Atitlán, broken up by the Army in 1980, they began to defy the ideological monopoly of the military state.

The philosophy which these new media carried was summed up in the CUC's slogan: *Cabeza clara, corazón solidario, puño combativo* — Clear head, heart of solidarity, combative fist. One leader explains:

> The CUC needs a clear head to analyse our class situation, who are our brothers, sisters and friends, who are our enemies. It needs a heart of solidarity to gather together all rural workers . . . an important step in building the worker-peasant alliance. The CUC adopts a combative fist because we have learned that we conquer our rights with the force of our actions.

From this starting point, the concrete goals of the CUC were those of the revolutionary movement: the right to life, land, jobs and fair wages; equality between Indians and Ladinos; an end to forced military service and an end to the repression. In their formulation, the influence of rural grassroots Christian communities was unmistakeable.

No Turning Back

It was 11 a.m. on 31 January, 1980, when a group of people — mainly Indian peasants from El Quiché — peacefully occupied the Spanish Embassy in Guatemala City. Their request was that ambassador Máximo Cajal should intercede with the Guatemalan government to force an official enquiry into Army atrocities in the highlands. For four years, the Quiché had been under military occupation. Fifty Indians from the town of Uspantán had already visited Congress in August 1979 to protest the disappearance of local villagers; for their pains, they had been beaten and arrested, told that "this is no place for *indios*". On 24 January, Abrahám Rubén Ixcampari, secretary of the social democratic FUR, was assassinated after trying to get a hearing in Congress for the peasants' case. All legal doors seemed closed, so the peasants decided to resort to the Embassy takeover as a last resort.

Inside, Ambassador Cajal was sympathetic; he had been to the Quiché personally and talked to the many priests there who were his compatriots. He knew full well that the peasants' grievances were well-founded. Already, he had spoken on the telephone with Guatemalan government officials and instructed them to keep the security forces well clear of the building since the occupation showed no signs of turning violent. But at 2 o'clock in the afternoon, hundreds of police began massing outside. Even as Cajal yelled to them that they were trampling on international law, advance units were beating down the Embassy doors with axes. A confused din of shots and an explosion ensued; in no time the building was ablaze. Television videos showed the police standing around outside, unconcerned. By the time the fire-engines arrived on the scene, 39 people had been burned alive. Only a single peasant occupier, Gregorio Yuja Xona, survived. Next day, badly burned, he was dragged out of his hospital bed by the customary "unknown assailants", and his mutilated corpse later found dumped at the University of San Carlos. No witnesses.

If Panzós had been a turning point for the Indians, the Spanish Embassy massacre killed off any flickering hope of peaceful protest. In the fire, said the CUC, "Indian and Ladino blood mingled." Class and ethnic protest fused in a single potent symbol.

Paralysing the Plantations

This fusion made its greatest show of force within a month. By February 1980, the CUC had spent two years developing its structures and expanding its membership, knowing that if spark led to fire the organization must be ready to respond. The spark came on the sugar plantations, and the 15-day strike by 75,000 workers in late February and early March brought the countryside to a standstill. Within days, work ground to a halt on 59 plantations, shutting down even Pantaléon, the country's largest refinery, owned by right-wing politician Roberto Herrera Ibarguen. Sugar came first, but cotton and coffee plantations quickly shut down too.

The united show of force by Indians and Ladinos, permanent and seasonal workers, defied the Labour Code's prohibition of work stoppages during harvest time and paralysed the industry at a crucial moment in the production cycle.[38] The spectre of peasants lined up along the Pan American highway, brandishing their machetes in the air, was a nightmare come true for the plantation owners. Labourers blocked all mill entrances, controlled traffic, sabotaged machinery and burned stockpiled crops, defying military and police attempts to dislodge them.[39] Press reports at the time indicated that the occupation of the fortress-like Pantaleón plant had been led by cane-cutters from Nebaj, in the Ixil Triangle.

The strikers' immediate demands were limited to a single issue, for a daily wage rise from $1.12 to $5.00 — still 31¢ short of the amount needed to cover minimal nutritional needs for a family of six. They complained later to visiting journalists of other grievances — that the scales used to calculate piece-work rates were under-weighted, with Indians and Ladinos obliged to weigh in on different scales. But the generals and the agro-exporters alike recognized that the true significance of the strike ran much deeper. For one thing, this kind of unified action across racial barriers, bringing together resident workers (*colonos*), temporary day-labourers (*jornaleros*) and seasonal migrants was utterly unprecedented in Latin America. For another, the cities threatened to join in, with CNUS talking in militant terms of a possible general strike to demand that the urban minimum wage be raised from $2.00 to $7.00 per day.[40]

Over the frenzied objections of the landowners, the government decreed a new rural minimum of $3.20 per day. The turn-around came on day 15 of the strike. With wages frozen since 1973, the increase was not as large as it looked. On the quiet, the military assured the plantation owners that they would not actually be expected to *pay* the increases, but this did little to mollify the growers, who remained incensed by the climbdown.[41] "People of Guatemala," cried the militant cane-growers association, "let us not be persuaded by foreigners and unscrupulous persons to carry out illegal acts that bring only hunger and misery to the country."[42] Agro-exporters lashed out not only at the government's political failure of will but at the real economic consequences of the strike. At one fell swoop, it became apparent how absurd the economic organization of Guatemalan society was: acceptable levels of profit were impossible without super-exploitation. This was particularly true of coffee-planters: while sugar or cotton growers might weather the storm by lay-offs or mechanization, there was no such luxury for coffee exporters. Demand for labour was constant in the coffee fields; the hilly terrain of most plantations and the delicate manual task of berry-picking made mechanization almost impossible.

> "We are witnessing a new scene with actors different from the Indian who removes his hat, places it over his chest and humbly asks his *patrón* for a few *centavos* more, *por la gracia de Dios.*"
> Conservative journalist Roberto Girón Lemus, 1980.

Beyond raging at the government, the most perceptive members of the private sector grasped the full import of the strike, and articulated it as clearly as the Left itself might have done. For conservative journalist Roberto Girón Lemus, director of the daily newspaper *La Nación,*

It represents, principally, an organized demonstration of salaried agricultural workers. And an organized demonstration indicates a state of class consciousness, and class consciousness is arrived at through union education ... This means that we are witnessing a new scene with actors different from the Indian who removes his hat, places it over his chest and humbly asks his *patrón* for a few *centavos* more, *por la gracia de Diós*. This conflict and its results will serve as a yardstick and an example.[43]

Indeed, economic victory was not the strikers' paramount concern; the CUC agreed to the $3.20 a day settlement, withdrawing its initial demand for $5.00 at the behest of other CNUS members.[44] The political lesson of the strike was more important. Again, there was a price to pay in human suffering. One worker died and another two were wounded when security guards opened fire during the occupation of the Pantaleón mill; several strike leaders were hunted down in the countryside and murdered later; and more than 10,000 workers lost their jobs in the aftermath of the strike as employers cut back on their labour force. But the decisive way in which the strike was handled (its exceptional unity never faltered) had stayed the hand of a repressive and cornered military regime from worse excesses of violence.

As at every watershed in the history of the mass movement, tensions arose, and inevitably so. Many urban workers, whose factory organization had been severely mauled by the repression, remained more cowed than the CUC, which — blooded in the reality of a successful confrontation with the state — pressed forward with militant self-confidence. Critique and counter-critique poured forth: some accusing the movement of insufficiently protecting itself against repression; others bemoaning the excessive militarization of some segments of the movement: But there is more to the question of Left unity and disunity than this.

Going Underground

In the year following the Spanish Embassy massacre, events shifted rapidly and radically. The regime militarized class struggle, and the mass movement was faced with the problem of how it was going to respond. Simple empirical observation showed that legal union work was all but extinct, and the few strikes that did take place were quite different in character. In August 1980, for example, Atlantic Coast banana plantation workers went on strike for a wage claim, but central to their tactics — as in other union actions of this period — was the concept of "armed self-defence". Spokesmen for the strikers pointed out that this was the only logical step for them to take, in view of "the experience accumulated at earlier stages in the history of the movement."[45]

The comparisons and similarities with El Salvador, where conflict was at this time moving into overt civil war, are instructive. In Guatemala, the mass movement had several times taken over the streets in 1977-8; events such as Panzós and the Spanish Embassy, plus the constant ravages of the death squads, showed that open public protest was impossible without a heavy death-toll. In El Salvador, over a six-month period from October 1979 to April 1980, from the reformist military coup through a general strike, mass rallies and massacres to the death of an archbishop, the possibilities for open mass work were similarly exhausted.[46] In the months that followed, both governments triumphantly declared that the Left was finished; in both countries, of course, it had devised new methods and gone underground.

Guatemala was quiet for much of 1980, but a hint of new methods came with the traditional 20 October events to mark the anniversary of the 1944 revolution. This year, public protest on traditional lines was out of the question, tantamount to suicide. Instead, the CUC — together with militant segments of the workers, students, Christians and slum-dwellers movement — carried out lightning meetings, erected barricades in slum quarters and painted anti-government graffiti. It hardly brought the regime to its knees, but that was not the point — it was an indicator of the possibility of organizing spontaneous and secretive actions amid the worst of the repression.

In the strikes and the 20 October protests, the conception of "armed popular self-defence" was a key point for debate. In many ways, that debate encapsulates the kind of dilemma that a revolutionary movement faces at this stage of its development, fiercely strained by the pressure of events. The very phrase presupposes a meshing together of military and political activity, of guerrilla organizations and the mass movement, of "revolutionary" with "popular and democratic" sectors. During the 1960s, as we saw earlier, the military-political fusion had not even been seriously present at a theoretical level. During the 1970s, in reaction to earlier failures, it became a strategic axiom — but perhaps the toughest challenge of all is to make the standard *conception* that "armed struggle is the highest expression of the mass political struggle" into an inescapable, concrete reality rather than a mere rhetorical flourish. And that will depend on the course of events. During the ascent of labour organizing in its "open" period from 1976 to 1978, this was not the case. Each of the four politico-military organizations of the Left had seen mass labour movement work as a priority, with the exception of ORPA. But their perspectives were different, and their success patchy. Under the second half of the Laugerud presidency, armed action was not a widely accepted need in the workers' movement, nor did the politico-military organizations have a common approach to the question — that would only come later, with the first steps towards unity in 1979-80.

The mass movement of labour unions, peasants, students, Christians and slum-dwellers must recognize that the nature of political conflict leaves it no option but the recourse to arms. Meanwhile, the guerrilla groups, who present themselves as the vanguard force of that struggle, must be able to settle the question of their own unification around specific criteria — the strategic notion of "popular revolutionary war", or the nature of the worker-peasant alliance. And they must enhance their strength on the ground enough to be seen as a convincing ally and protector of those who choose the risks of armed warfare. That process of unification is fraught with difficulties. Many of them derive not only from the groups' divergent origins and histories, but from their relative size and strength, which will dictate differences in bargaining power as much as differences in vision.

By 1980, the EGP — which by now was the largest of the groups — was arguing that "[the] destruction of other forms of political participation [has] laid the basis for a convergence between the armed revolutionary movement and the popular and democratic sectors".[47] By that year, the politico-military organizations were firmly entrenched on several regional fronts and in more than half of the country's 22 departments, above all in the Indian highlands. In the coastal plantation flatlands and around the capital city, too, the war was advancing rapidly. In departments such as El Quiché and Huehuetenango, this was what the EGP called the "massif-ication" of the war, with armed guerrilla columns operating as the military spearhead of a supple, mass-based political structure. Without one, they believed, the other was futile.

With growing strength in the field, argued one observer and theorist, "the revolutionary movement could at all times be beside and within the mass movement".[48] In this way, each immediate local issue could be related politically to a long-term, strategic vision of the war. In the factories and plantations, this became increasingly true by around 1980; in parts of the highlands, it had been the case for much longer. At the national level, clandestine armed activity began to seem the only viable remaining alternative to those seeking fundamental social change. The guerrilla forces projected themselves as a rational response to an untenable situation, the only ones offering comprehensive solutions, and now backed up by the capacity to give the mass movement the coherent direction it needed.

In the highlands, Marxist analysis, Christian activism and the specific demands of indigenous communities began to coalesce into a single homogenous vision. In these Indian areas, both the EGP and ORPA were spoken of as "our army", and also even as "our new society". Even the United States Embassy was obliged to admit that eight out of ten guerrillas were Indians, and the alarmed Guatemalan Army recognized that "whole peasant families join in as strategic collaborators".[49] The State Department estimated the guerrillas' strength at 3,500 active combatants, plus 10,000 organized in Local Irregular Forces (FIL) and another 30,000-60,000 actively involved supporters.[50]

By 1981, complex and flexible new modes of organizing had taken root in the highland communities. In this war, noted a Mexican visitor to an area of the countryside controlled by ORPA, there were two kinds of people: those who collaborate with the guerrillas, and "those who await death, trapped between terror and starvation".[51] Those who chose the first option engaged in a kaleidoscope of tasks. There was voluntary collective labour on food production for the guerrillas; others organized first aid networks for those wounded by marauding Army patrols, or took charge of the welfare of orphans and widows.[52] Rapid reaction groups learned to evacuate villages under attack from the Army; in other areas, local chapters of the CUC built man-traps, blocked roads and felled trees to impede the military's advance.

Though there was no intention at this stage to designate any part of the highlands a "liberated zone", several did become effective no-go areas for government troops. In parts of El Quiché and Huehuetenango, new democratic village structures sprouted, with village committees handling a range of local affairs from land tenure disputes to the legal business of crime, weddings and funerals.[53] Under the tutelage of guerrilla organizations, new social relations began to develop taking into account and respecting the traditional collective values of the indigenous population.

Ironically, the greatest weakness of groups described by the State Department as "terrorists", and one which would later cost them dearly, was military. Further massive incorporation of the population into the guerrilla forces was impossible because the movement, quite simply, was short of weapons. If the Guatemalan Army feared extinction at the hands of the Left, it was not because a military juggernaut awaited them in the hills. Rather, it was testimony to the breadth and depth of the *political* work which the revolutionaries had carried out among the population.

By early 1982, the revolutionary Left had overcome many of the chief obstacles to its unification. For more than two years they had been inching in that direction. The first step was the *Tripartita,* conceived of as a forum for unity discussions between the EGP, FAR and PGT in 1979 (this was just before ORPA revealed its existence publicly). ORPA joined the unity discussions in October 1980; slowly, joint actions and co-ordinated propaganda work began to take shape, and basic logistical problems were overcome to some extent. It was never easy: for 29 years, scores of guerrilla organizations, labour groups and political parties have tried to complete Guatemala's interrupted history. While leadership grapples with thorny theoretical debates, the mass of more practically minded followers itch with impatience. Middle-level cadre, fiercely loyal to the group they have been fighting with, are the trickiest: worst exposed to the repression, fighting sectarian skirmishes, they must escape the tunnel vision which an underground existence can too easily breed.

A unity agreement came on 25 January, 1982, with the declaration of the four politico-military organizations of the Left to form the Unión Revolucionaria Nacional Guatemalteca (Guatemalan National Revolutionary Unity: URNG). All four endorsed an overall strategy of popular revolutionary war. Their very general five-point statement, less a programme than a platform, stated that:

1. The Revolution will eliminate once and for all the repression against our people and will guarantee to all citizens the supreme rights of life and peace.
2. The Revolution will set down the foundations for resolving the basic needs of the great majority of our people by eliminating the political domination of the repressive rich, both national and foreign, who rule Guatemala.
3. The Revolution will guarantee equality between Indians and Ladinos, and will end cultural oppression and discrimination.
4. The Revolution will guarantee the creation of a New Society, in which all patriotic, popular and democratic sectors will be represented in the government.
5. Based on the principle of self-determination, the Revolution will guarantee a policy of non-alignment and international co-operation which poor countries need in order to develop in the modern world.

As in El Salvador, the local communist party was the smallest and least significant of the member groups. The PGT — or at least the fragment of the party that joined the unity — had to swallow its pride and acknowledge that history had relegated it to play a fringe role in the revolutionary drama. After calling for a complete restructuring of the party on politico-military lines, its leaders admitted that "we know that in the verdict of the Guatemalan people we no longer constitute the vanguard . . . we must be very sincere and very humble."[54]

Guatemala's Politico-Military Organizations

Ejército Guerrillero de los Pobres
(Guerrilla Army of the Poor: EGP)
Formed in 1972 by FGEI survivors and Christians involved in grassroots *concientización* work. Influenced by the Vietnamese experience, they evolved a theory of prolonged popular war tailored to Guatemalan reality. Biggest of the four groups today, with large-scale organized support in the Indian highlands of El Quiché, Alta and Baja Verapaz, Huehuetenango and Chimaltenango. Also operates fronts in the coastal regions of Escuintla and Suchitepéquez, in the capital and the neighbouring department of Sacatepéquez, and (embryonically) in the east. Has given particular emphasis to the ethnic question as its Indian base of support has grown. The EGP has an extensive national structure and works closely with the farmworkers' CUC. Believes in a worker – *campesino* alliance with guerrilla warfare as the dominant form of struggle. Took time to put its commitment to mass organizing into practice, doing so as the mass movement gained impetus after 1976.
Commander-in-Chief: Rolando Morán.

Fuerzas Armadas Rebeldes (Rebel Armed Forces: FAR)
Descendent of the FAR of the 1960s. The FAR's founders returned to Guatemala City after the failure of their guerrilla front in the Petén and decided to concentrate on urban guerrilla warfare. Subsequently opted for intensive mass work in the urban labour movement, with the eventual goal of forming a working-class party. An influx of new members in the mid-1970s brought many disaffected and radical Christian Democrats. The FAR enjoyed considerable influence in the labour movement from 1976 to 1978, first through the CNT and then CNUS. Active in the capital and on the coastal plantations. With the escalation of urban repression, the FAR reinitiated guerrilla activity in 1978, and has now reorganized fronts in Guatemala City, Chimaltenango and three areas of the Petén.
Commander-in-Chief: Pablo Monsanto.

Organización del Pueblo en Armas
(Organization of the People in Arms: ORPA)
Derived from the *Regional de Occidente,* a split from the FAR–PGT alliance in 1971. Launched publicly in September 1979. ORPA developed as an entirely new organization, dedicating its efforts to building an Indian support base for its military actions. ORPA has not believed in conducting mass organizational work in the traditional sense; instead it has worked primarily — and often brilliantly — as a military entity with widespread,

113

loosely organized peasant support. ORPA draws its strength from the predominantly Indian areas of San Marcos, Quezaltenango, Sololá, Totonicapán and Huehuetenango. Also enjoys considerable support from middle-class intellectuals. It regards the elimination of racism as a prime objective, and was heavily influenced by the writings of Franz Fanon. Believes Indians are the country's leading revolutionary force.
Commander-in-Chief: Gaspar Ilom.

Partido Guatemalteco del Trabajo
(Guatemalan Labour Party: PGT)
The *PGT - Núcleo de Dirección Nacional* (National Leadership Nucleus) is a member of the URNG. This segment of the party consists of base militants and some of the old party leadership. It split from the party in 1978 over the question of armed struggle. The main body of the party, known officially as the *Comité Central,* or PGT - CC is criticized by dissidents for failing to carry out the military work agreed upon at the 1969 Party Congress. As well as the National Leadership Nucleus, the PGT Military Commission has also broken from the party rump. All three factions engage in military action, but none is strong. In the labour unions, the PGT - CC has retained considerable influence, and the party has some base among south coast agro-export plantation workers. Many of the leaders of the other revolutionary groups are former PGT cadre, especially from the party's youth wing (JPT).
Secretary General (official PGT): Carlos González.

A fifth politico-military organization, the *Movimiento Revolucionario del Pueblo* (MRP–Ixim), rejects membership of the URNG. Originally formed by ORPA dissidents under the name of *Nuestro Movimiento* (Our Movement), it began military actions as the MRP–Ixim in July 1982. Its mass front is the MUP; espouses an explicitly Marxist-Leninist programme.

Towards a Political Front

As far as the guerrilla organizations were concerned, the question was now to strengthen the unity and resolve remaining differences with the communist party. The broader task was to hasten the formation of a mass political front, based on a worker–peasant alliance, to integrate the political and military aspects of the struggle. The first initiative in this direction had come in February 1979, when CNUS had issued the call for the establishment of the *Frente Democrático Contra la Represión* (Democratic Front Against Repression: FDCR), a loose amalgam of — at least on paper — more than 200 labour unions and grassroots organizations. The FDCR reflected the strong residual rôle of middle-class political leadership: the two social democratic parties, the PSD and FUR, were well represented in its ranks. Essentially, what the FDCR embodied was an alliance between radicalized middle-class intellectuals and the organized working class. It had never formulated a clear common programme, and indeed that had never been its explicit goal. Instead, as the name suggested, the FDCR had seen its function as a defensive response to the regime. It did not seriously come to grips with the double edge of mass organizing in Guatemala — the political and the military.[55]

Hence, many people were startled when the FDCR issued the first call for a "revolutionary, popular and democratic government". Critics said the front had never tried to build structures in line with such a call. Intense debate raged around the question: some claimed that open mass work could continue, others that mass work was impossible because of the repression. The CUC, long disturbed at the lack of security and self-defence among the FDCR's membership, now pulled out of the coalition after the sugar strike. The FDCR's role, it stressed, though useful and necessary for a period, had now been superseded by history. Others agreed — the most militant sectors of factory workers, slum-dwellers, Christians and students.

They posed an alternative — the *Frente Popular 31 de Enero* (31 January Popular Front: FP-31) named in homage to those who had died in the Spanish Embassy. The regional conjuncture in Central America was a tense one: next door in El Salvador, the FMLN was waging its over-hasty January 1981 "General Offensive"; in Washington, Ronald Reagan was assuming the presidency; pressure on Sandinista Nicaragua was mounting. Pushing the war in Guatemala into greater profile on the international stage was one of the concerns of FP-31's founders. But more important was the need they perceived for "much more profound forms of struggle, much more solid and effective".[56] Accordingly, FP-31 would provide "a unitary structure to deepen the support, coordination and solidarity between the mass organizations and as a consequence raise [their] fighting potential".[57] Preparation for a future insurrection would be crucial.

FP-31 claimed extensive membership: after a year, the *Latin America Report* assessed its strength and composition ás follows:[58]
CUC: 6,000 organized members.
Núcleos Obreros Revolucionarios (Revolutionary Workers' Nuclei: NOR): 1,500 members.
Comité de Pobladores (Slum-dwellers' Committee: CDP): 150 members in five suburbs of Guatemala City.
Frente Estudiantil Revolucionario "Robín García" (FERG): 200 members in seven university faculties plus 300 in secondary school chapters.
Cristianos Revolucionarios "Vicente Menchú" (Revolutionary Christians) 4,000 members.

While the FDCR stagnated, its main leadership decimated, the war ever more militarized, FP-31 was prey to accusations of wanting to monopolize the shaping of a future unified mass front. In this atmosphere, there was little progress for a year or more. The next step came hard on the heels of the unity declaration of the armed Left. Within three weeks, in February 1982, 26 noted professionals, labour, peasant and party leaders, Christians and intellectuals formed the *Comité Guatemalteco de Unidad Patriótica* (Guatemala Patriotic Unity Committee: CGUP). Over the succeeding months, the number would swell to over 60. CGUP received the simultaneous endorsement of the FDCR, FP-31 and the guerrilla organizations. Its role was threefold: first, to throw down a political gauntlet to the regime in the run-up to the critical March 1982 elections; second, a limited — though nonetheless important — diplomatic function; and third, as a forum for discussions towards the unified political front long dreamed of by the Left.[59]

The political front was the key missing element. It would not be an exiled group of notables, like CGUP, but an organization rooted in the daily battles inside Guatemala. And that would not come about until each sector currently divided — worker, peasant or student — had overcome its past schisms and achieved its own solid internal unity. The progressive middle class would have a place in its ranks; so, too, might a handful of reform-minded military officers, if any could be found. But its core was intended to be the revolutionary organizations of the workers and *campesinos*.

Notes

1. See interview with Rolando Morán which appeared in *Punto Final* (Mexico).
2. Ibid., and *Compañero* (Mexico), No.5 (1982).
3. *Declaracion de Iximché*, 14 February, 1980.
4. Ibid.
5. Fried et al., *Guatemala in Rebellion*, pp.24-5.
6. *Compañero*, No.5.
7. J. Antonio Bran, "Organización popular y lucha de clases en el campo", in *Cuadernos de Marcha*, (Mexico), No.10 (November-December 1980), pp.15-23.
8. *Declaracion de Iximché*.
9. Miguel Angel Albízurez, "Struggles and Experiences of the Guatemalan Trade Union Movement, 1976-June 1978", *Latin American Perspectives*, Nos.25-6 (Spring and Summer 1980). Edelberto Torres-Rivas, "Guatemala: Crisis and Political Violence", *NACLA Report on the Americas*, Vol. XIV, no.1 (January-February 1980). p.24. On labour unions in the 1960s, see CIDAMO, "The Workers Movement in Guatemala", in *NACLA Report on the Americas*, id., pp.28-33.
10. Nairn, *To Defend our Way of Life*, p.92.
11. CIDAMO, *The Workers Movement*.
12. Torres-Rivas, *Crisis and Political Violence*.
13. Albízurez, *Struggles and Experiences*.
14. For the full history of the Coca Cola dispute and its eventual resolution, see *Food Monitor* (New York, November-December 1980).
15. Albízurez, *Struggles and Experiences;* also Concerned Guatemala Scholars, *Dare to Struggle*, p.27.
16. *Latin America Political Report*, 6 October, 1978.
17. See International Union of Food and Allied Workers' Association (IUF), *The Coca Cola Guatemala Campaign, 1979-1981* (Geneva, 1981).

18. *Siete Días en la USAC,* 7 May, 1979.
19. Aguilera, *Terror and Violence,* p.108.
20. Plant, *Unnatural Disaster,* p.48.
21. *Latin America Political Report,* 13 October, 1978.
22. See Alejandro Bendaña, "Crisis in Nicaragua", *NACLA Report on the Americas,* Vol. XII, no.6 (November-December 1978), p.43.
23. *Latin America Political Report,* 6 and 13 October, 1978.
24. *El Gráfico* (Guatemala City), 20 February, 1976.
25. Melville and Melville, *Another Vietnam,* p.208.
26. Richard Adams, *Crucifixion by Power* (Austin, University of Texas Press, 1970), p.84.
27. Blase Bonpane, "The Church and Revolutionary Struggle in Central America", *Latin American Perspectives,* Nos.25-6 (Spring-Summer 1980), pp.182-6.
28. Iglesia Guatemalteca en el Exilio (IGE), "Algunos apuntes para un análisis sobre los efectos de militarismo sobre los intentos de desarrollo de las comunidades del altiplano de Guatemala", unpublished mimeo (Managua, Nicaragua, 1980).
29. See Aguilera, *The Massacre at Panzós.*
30. Concerned Guatemala Scholars, *Dare to Struggle.*
31. *Latin America Political Report,* 15 June, 1979.
32. *ALAI,* 18 December, 1981.
33. IEPALA, *Guatemala: Un futuro próximo* (Madrid, 1981).
34. Bran, *Organización popular y lucha de clases.*
35. Concerned Guatemala Scholars, *Dare to Struggle,* p.29.
36. Ibid.
37. Bran, *Organización popular y lucha de clases;* Concerned Guatemala Scholars, *Dare to Struggle,* p.35.
38. *Latin America Political Report,* 29 February, 1980, and *Inforpress,* no.382.
39. *Prensa Libre* (Guatemala City), 27 February, 1980, and *Inforpress,* 28 February, 1980.
40. Norma Chinchilla, "Class Struggle in Central America: Background and Overview", *Latin American Perspectives,* Nos.25-6 (Spring and Summer 1980) p.15.
41. See the bulletin from the Asociación de Cañeros, cited in *Inforpress,* 28 February, 1980.
42. Ibid.
43. Ibid.
44. Interview with CNT, in *ALAI,* 12 February, 1982.
45. An interview with the FDCR which appeared in *ALAI,* 27 February, 1981, cites as an example the August 1980 banana workers' strike.
46. See James Dunkerley, *The Long War: Dictatorship and Revolution in El Salvador,* (London, Junction Books, 1982), pp.132-62; a concise and thoughtful analysis of the period is Anne Nelson, "El Salvador's Struggle: The Revolution has a History", *Christianity and Crisis* (New York), Vol. 43, no.10, 13 June, 1983.
47. *Compañero,* No.4 (1981).
48. Bran, *Organización popular y lucha de clases.*
49. *Inforpress,* 3 December, 1981.
50. *New York Times,* 15 March, 1982; see also the testimony of Deputy Assistant Secretary of State Steven W. Bosworth before the House Banking Subcommittee, 5 August, 1982.
51. *Unomásuno* (Mexico City), 25 June, 1982.
52. See descriptions in *Noticias de Guatemala* (San José, Costa Rica), 20 October, 1981.
53. Ibid. Also, author's interviews in Mexico City, June 1982.
54. Interview with the PGT by Marta Harnecker, in *Nueva* (Quito, Ecuador), October-November 1981.
55. Bran, *Organización popular y lucha de clases.*
56. Interview with FP-31, in *ALAI,* 27 March, 1981.
57. Ibid; also founding communiqué of the FP-31, mimeo, 31 January, 1981.
58. *Latin America Regional Report: Mexico and Central America,* 12 February, 1982.
59. NACLA interviews with CGUP leaders in Mexico City, Managua and Washington DC, June-September 1982.

PART THREE

A War of Exterminism

6. The Ríos Montt Experiment

"Do you know why I am a true political leader? Because I am here without your votes."
President Efraín Ríos Montt, broadcast to the nation, 24 May, 1982.

Guatemala City's National Police headquarters is a turreted castle on Sixth Avenue and 14th Street, a Disneyland piece of nostalgia for former colonial grandeur. Three blocks up the avenue lies a microcosm of Guatemala's modern fairy tale: the transnational neon blur of expensive shopping malls, where Donna Summer's voice blasts out of record stores to the milling crowds of chic teenage shoppers wearing designer jeans. Displaced Indians, recent migrants from starvation and terror in the western highlands, shuffle blankly past windows piled high with consumer luxuries.

This day, 9 March, 1982, the streets were empty of shoppers. Storekeepers, fearing trouble, had rolled down their steel shutters. It was two days after the presidential elections, and official figures showed Defence Minister General Aníbal Guevara, hand-picked successor of General Romeo Lucas García, with an implausible 35% of the vote. Informal straw polls on election day had shown him running third out of four, behind the far-right MLN and a centre-right coalition.

A small procession of enraged opposition candidates, flanked by the international press corps, was making its way up Sixth Avenue. Bearing a formal letter of protest, the three victims of yet another electoral fraud were headed for the National Palace. Alejandro Maldonado Aguirre, head of the centre–right coalition, turned to a reporter: "This is not a demonstration; we are simply three citizens walking on the street carrying, peacefully and unarmed, a request for the nullification of the elections."[1] As he spoke, masked plain-clothes secret police and steel-helmeted riot squads in gasmasks fanned out from police headquarters, firing volleys into the air, lobbing smoke bombs and tear-gas grenades at the marchers. A police bus screeched up to the kerb and hauled the three protesting candidates away for interrogation. Their letter was never delivered. In military-ruled Guatemala, tiger eats tiger.

Anne Nelson

*Civil Defence Patrol members, armed with wooden rifles,
at San José Poaquil, Chimaltenango*

Theatre of the Absurd

Though voting was compulsory, and Lucas García raged at voters from their television screens that "to abstain is to collaborate with the enemies of Guatemala", few paid any heed to his warnings. By the Army's own figure less than 46% voted. Independent observers put the turnout as low as 35%.[2]

While voters showed their indifference, even contempt, the campaign did bring into sharp focus the now gaping rifts between political competitors. The Lucas clique of the armed forces fought it out with three opponents, each of whom offered a different prescription for rescuing Guatemala from economic collapse and "communist subversion". All three rejected linkage with the last 12 years of military rule.

Even before election day, Lucas and the Army were floundering in their campaign. Guatemalan electoral law allowed for all manner of last-minute coalition building, and previous military regimes had made alliances of expedience with one or another right-wing party. But this time, the official PID and PR found themselves in embarrassing isolation. The military coalition's declared aim had been to field a single candidate on a joint six-party ticket. It was groping not only for a broader electoral base, but also for a way to cover itself against any disagreeable post-election scrutiny of the abuses and corruption of the Lucas era. But, one after another, each of the opposition parties spurned Lucas' overtures. Only the Christian Democrats continued to flirt with the notion of a broad front until late 1981, but they too eventually fell by the wayside — a victory for the party's more progressive wing. In the end, only the minuscule *Frente de Unidad Nacional* (National Unity Front: FUN) fell into line with the military coalition.

Unification of the other right-wing parties proved equally hopeless. Though National Liberation Movement chief Mario Sandoval Alarcón warned repeatedly of the dangers of splitting the anti-communist vote, there were too many points of friction between his MLN and ex-president Arana's *Central Auténtica Nacionalista* (National Authentic Central: CAN) for the rumoured "Great Anti-Communist Alliance" to take shape.[3] Each would wage its own separate campaign. Any lingering CAN hopes of victory evaporated when Defence Minister Guevara, in a rare moment of political astuteness, recruited former CAN stalwart Ramiro Ponce Monroy as his vice-presidential running-mate. The Christian Democrats, meanwhile, cut adrift from the Army, gravitated into an eleventh hour electoral alliance with the *Partido de Renovación* (National Renovation Party: PNR) (see box on parties).

The sympathies each enjoyed within the dominant classes failed to translate into significant campaign funding. There was little incentive since, without reliable military backing, none was a viable option; since the raging war outside Guatemala City meant that venturing out on to the campaign trail was a hazardous business for all but the official candidate. The Christian Democrats in particular went in fear of their lives in rural areas.

123

The March 1982 Election Line-Up

Frente Democrático Popular
(Popular Democratic Front: FDP)
The official government coalition backed by the armed forces. Its members were the military's own *Partido Institucional Democrático* (Institutional Democratic Party: PID), the *Partido Revolucionario* (Revolutionary Party: PR) and the tiny *Frente de Unidad Nacional* (National Unity Front: FUN). All three offered policies of continuity with the Lucas García period. Their social base was restricted to high-ranking military officers and state functionaries, with the parties operating mainly as vehicles to personal enrichment and government patronage. The FUN, registered as a new party in 1978, espoused an economic programme more nationalist in content than the other two.

Movimiento de Liberación Nacional
(National Liberation Movement: MLN)
Formed directly after the 1954 coup, the MLN is Guatemala's largest political party. Its candidate and leader, Mario Sandoval Alarcón, was viewed as the most likely winner of a clean election. The party traditionally represents large and small coffee planters, as well as some newer cotton and sugar exporting interests. Though it retains some support in the officer corps, it has been marginalized from state power since the 1974-8 Laugerud García administration. Modelled on Franco's Falange and Chile's fascist shock-force *Patria y Libertad* (Fatherland and Freedom), the MLN offers few policies beyond a war of extermination.

Central Auténtica Nacionalista
(Nationalist Authentic Central: CAN)
Founded in 1969 as the personal vehicle of General Carlos Arana Osorio, the CAN's main support derives from sections of urban-based industrial capital, importers and financiers, especially those with ties to foreign capital. Influential within the private sector federation CACIF. Presidential candidate Gustavo Anzueto Vielman, a former minister under Arana, and a member of the right-wing business lobby *Amigos del País,* put forward a radical monetarist programme — "The Path to Peaceful Prosperity" — proposing to abolish 50 out of 56 existing taxes, deregulate consumer prices, remove exchange controls, free interest rates and eliminate all restrictions on foreign capital. This hardline monetarism made Anzueto Vielman a favourite with some sectors of the US Embassy, but the party's power base was too narrow, enmity between it and the current military high command too deep-rooted, for it to have a chance of victory.

Unión Opositora
(Opposition Union: UNO)
This was a coalition of the *Partido Democracia Cristiana Guatemalteca* (Guatemalan Christian Democratic Party PDCG) and the *Partido Nacional Renovador* (National Renovation Party: PNR). Formed after the PDCG abandoned the notion of a broad front with the military. The Christian Democrats, at first closely linked to the agrarian bourgeoisie, had conservative and anti-communist origins in the 1950s, but active involvement in rural peasant leagues and co-operatives during the 1960s led the party to adopt more progressive positions. Severe repression, the dismantling of the co-operative movement and acrimonious debate within the party over its part-icipation in the electoral process left it split and badly weakened. After the 1974 election, many left to join the guerrillas, angry that the party had accepted its fraudulent defeat so tamely. Today, the main strength of the PDCG is among the urban middle classes.

Its coalition partner, the PNR, embraces the more dynamic sectors of urban industrial capital, favouring limited reforms within a capitalist framework. The PNR's populist campaign declared the party "the voice of the silent and silenced majority". Like many top PNR officials, presidential candidate Alejandro Maldonado Aguirre pulled out of the MLN to form this new party in 1977.

The UNO coalition looked the most attractive political option to Washington, the most responsive to the need for some economic reforms, but the military would never let it take power. A coalescence of Army and Christian Democratic interests, as between Napoleón Duarte and the military in El Salvador, was not on the cards.

And anyway, Lucas and the Army were more than likely to overturn any result of which they disapproved.

Faced with this bewildering array of choices, the United States Embassy, too, found itself trapped between the devil and the deep blue sea. For months, it had pressed Lucas to hold clean elections — the best hope for remedying Guatemala's international pariah status and breaking the Congressional resistance to renewed military funding — but he arrogantly ignored the symbols, trusting that like his Salvadorean counterparts he could eventually bend the US Administration to his will. And so it was: the Reagan Administration was obliged to keep its channels open to what was almost certain to be the future government. In short, the March elections — however free from fraud — offered no perspective of real change.

From Boom to Bust

Underlying the ruling-class divisions is Guatemala's economic slump. This is no mere cyclical downturn in the economy, but few had come to terms with the gravity of the problem, least of all the Lucas regime. The parties, too, though angered by the fiasco of economic planning under Lucas, were reacting to a dilemma to which the Guatemalan bourgeoisie — in its naïve faith in perpetual growth — was quite unaccustomed.

They had failed to read the danger signs. Even a report in early 1981 by the Economist Intelligence Unit of London had sounded only a conservative note of caution, certainly no loud alarm bells.[4] The *Economist* survey was tellingly prefaced by a comment on the jubilation with which the private sector had greeted the election of Ronald Reagan in November 1980; in the celebratory firework parties and marimba band concerts was the implicit statement by Guatemalan businessmen that they regarded their plight as essentially *political* in character.

The economic indicators were certainly alarming enough, and familiar from the crisis of other Central American economies. The high growth rates of the 1970s had been on the slide for five years in a row: from 7.8% in 1977, then 5.0% in 1978, 4.5% in 1979, 3.5% in 1980, down to 1.8% in 1981. Sombre official predictions of real GDP growth in 1982 were *minus* 3.5%, but other sources estimated that the negative growth rate could be as bad as −5%.[5] Declining currency reserves were perhaps the gravest symptom of the crisis; from a high of $1.3 billion in 1978, they had plunged to just $450 million by the end of 1980, and the slide showed no signs of abating.[6] Industrial stagnation was accompanied by rising inflation, and rising external debt by increased capital flight.

While everyone acknowledged that there were economic difficulties — and each presidential candidate put forward his own remedies — all thought the problems were short term: the imported effects of global recession, the ravages of the war, the Lucas clique's gangster-like business methods and inept government strategies, all with a consequent loss of business confidence. For them, the answer was to clean up governmental corruption, eliminate the revolutionary movement, tinker with a few economic policies to make the temporary recession more comfortable for the privileged, and rely on the removal of Carter to make the "human rights" climate a little less oppressive. That done, they would wait for things to return to normal.

But Guatemala's problems run much deeper, of course. As in much of Central America, they are rooted in the inherent inflexibility of its cash-crop growth model. When market prices for its limited range of products collapse — as they did during 1981 — there is no alternative economic activity on which to fall back. The disparity between lowered demand for agricultural exports and higher import costs — above all for petroleum — was especially acute. Guatemala's much-vaunted oil boom has come to little; though it exports 30,000 barrels per day of crude, this earns only some

$30 million in income, and with no local refinery facilities, all usable oil has to be imported.

Guatemala, the world's eighth largest coffee producer, suffered a 36% drop in coffee earnings during 1981. The value of cotton exports plummeted by 22%. Another blow, this time wholly unexpected, was the closure of the giant EXMIBAL nickel plant, which had earned the country $59 million in exports the previous year. The parent company, INCO, gave its reason as lowered world nickel prices.[7] With all this, overall export revenues declined from $1.52 billion in 1980 to only $1.23 billion the following year.[8] With the collapse of crop prices and of tourism — Guatemala's exquisite scenery makes this the third largest source of foreign currency earnings — a trade gap of only −$30 million in 1980 had widened to a yawning deficit of more than $200 million in 1981.[9]

Social repercussions from previous ebbs of the international market had customarily been met with repression rather than adjustment. But by 1982, the economic situation was fast moving out of control, and the masses had moved beyond the point of being easily stifled by repression. The political crisis and the economic had become one, and the outlook for Guatemala's dominant classes was grim.

There was no doubt that the revolutionary war, too, had taken a heavy toll in the already sagging economy. Tourism had the biggest casualty. Some 100 companies connected to the tourist trade were driven into liquidation after 1980, and by 1982 the industry was three-quarters paralysed.[10] The US State Department issued a "Travel Advisory" in 1980, urging US citizens not to travel to "high risk" Guatemala, much to the consternation of the local business community.

As in El Salvador, a prime tactic of the revolutionary Left was to hit key infrastructural targets — in Guatemala's case the oil-fields — burn the farms of right-wing landowners and destroy stockpiles of cotton and coffee. Not only aggravating the immediate economic situation, such sabotage also fatally undermines investment confidence. According to a 1981 opinion poll, two-thirds of Guatemalan businessmen interviewed agreed that "the aggravation of the economic crisis is above all due to the political risks run by investments".[11] US Embassy figures showed that private capital investment dropped off by 13% in 1981. The ever lower morale of the business community provoked accelerated capital flight, which in turn worsened conflicts between different sectors of private enterprise. Those who still had the power of accumulation preferred to exercise it abroad, and in dollars, leaving behind and demoralized those with less liquid capital. In this, the Guatemalan bourgeoisie is part of a pronounced regional trend: some economists estimate that there is now more Central American private capital in the United States (most of it in Miami) than remains in the region.

Grappling with the upsurge of the Left and its own internal conflicts, the private sector was pushed to the limits of its tolerance by the serious credit squeeze and the concomitant greed and incompetence of the Lucas government. Original estimates for large government projects, such as the new port facility at San José, the national electricity grid and the new *Anillo Periférico* highway system soared way over budget. While that is hardly uncommon in public planning, in Guatemala it was largely the consequence of monstrous government corruption.

The tight credit restrictions naturally affected small and medium-scale industrialists and growers most seriously, but even the powerful planters felt the lash of Lucas García's chaotic policies. The regime had a particularly vitriolic showdown with the large coffee growers of ANACAFE and the agriculturalists' federation AGA. Already facing a cutback in world coffee export quotas, coffee rust and mounting production costs — which meant that even large-scale growers were losing $40 for each hundredweight produced — AGA and ANACAFE complained bitterly that their members were unable to repay outstanding loans or secure new government credits. When the Lucas government replied by *raising* coffee export taxes, the growers moved into open revolt.[12] Many of them responded by resorting to highly conflictive land rental schemes in lieu of payment for peasant labour. Such attempts to slough their losses on to the 400,000 peasants who depend on the coffee trade for their livelihood only exacerbated class animosity.

Finally, and inevitably, the Lucas government called in the International Monetary Fund. In November 1981, the IMF consented to pump in $110 million to stabilize currency reserves. In exchange, Guatemala would reduce its social expenditures (already the lowest per capita in Central America) and use the savings to revitalize financial flows to the beleaguered private sector. One more log to fuel the fires of revolution.

The economic crisis deepened daily, and Lucas offered no visible way out. With agro-exporters petitioning for tax exemptions on one side, industrialists demanding a rigid package of monetarist measures on the other, and the ranks of the revolutionary movement swelling with thousands who felt they had nothing further to lose, the generals flailed onwards, satisfying nobody.

Losing the War

Out in the field, the fight against the Left was going disastrously. The inept conduct of the armed forces provided a major campaign thrust for the electoral opposition candidates. "The present government," stormed MLN party boss Sandoval Alarcón, "is wholly incapable of putting a brake on the guerrillas."

He was right. West of the capital, in the area code-named "Vietnam", the Left's roots among the population were solid. Large stretches of El Quiché, Huehuetenango and San Marcos turned into virtual no-go areas for the Army, and US diplomats were forbidden to venture any further west than the colonial tourist trap of Antigua, 28 miles from the capital.[13] The Army seemed powerless to halt the advance. Guerrilla columns intercepted traffic on the Pan American and Atlantic Coast highways with relative impunity, cut ditches in provincial roads, ran free in much of the new development area known as the *Franja Transversal del Norte* and controlled long stretches of the Mexican border. Army losses in combat ran unacceptably high, with 57 officers — mainly captains and lieutenants — killed in the course of 1981.[14] In a political and military quagmire, internationally isolated, senior officers began to mutter despondently about inevitable defeat within three years.

Over the summer months of 1981, the security forces launched a major offensive against the armed Left. It began by breaking a series of safe houses in the capital city, from which ORPA suffered worst. In October, the Army — now under the vigorous command of the president's brother, General Benedicto Lucas García — initiated a four-month long pre-election scorched earth campaign. It had a new kind of aggressiveness; in a marked change of strategy, the Army went after the guerrillas' civilian support base; large-scale killings of real or suspected guerrilla sympizers began to characterize military operations. For the first time, field commanders — by taking the war aggressively into areas they had previously neglected — glimpsed the full extent of what they were up against, both socially and militarily. A majority of the officer corps grew convinced from what they witnessed that a radically new solution was necessary at both levels.

The very nature of the revolutionary upsurge by 1981, the profound intermeshing of the armed guerrilla organizations and the mass movement as a whole, dictated that the Army should undertake a corresponding rethink of its strategy. More sophisticated forms of rural counterinsurgency would now have to be blended with traditional modes of political repression; no longer was it sufficient to rely on piecemeal military strikes to deal with guerrilla bands; nor to rely on the death squads to stifle trade unions, political parties and peasant federations by decapitating their leadership. In terms of military logic, this could only mean adopting a scorched earth strategy in the countryside. Not because the military was acting out of some irrational bloodlust, or because individual field commanders "lost control", or because raw recruits committed excesses as a result of poor discipline and training. The savagery is intrinsic to the frontal attack on the peasant population, and it will destroy entire communities where necessary if they are deemed to be "lost" to the Left. Through terror and wholesale violence, the umbilical cord linking the armed Left to the organized communities will be physically ripped away. The guerrillas, duly isolated, can then be destroyed by the Army with more surgical efficency. So, at least, runs the doctrine of counterinsurgency. But as long as Lucas García and his ilk remained in power, it was impossible to advance this new style coherently, in the context of a regime whose political bankruptcy was so absolute.

A Different Kind of Solution

General Angel Aníbal Guevara was declared winner of the 7 March election; but no one knows who won the count. For four days after the opposition party leaders' arrests, Guatemala City seethed with tension. The losers, setting their historic differences to one side for a moment, banded together in an Anti-Fraud Front, but to no avail. On the 13th, riding rough-shod over their protests, Congress hastily ratified Guevara as president.

The farcical election and its sequel proved the last straw. Inevitably, it was the military, and not the civilian political dissidents, who moved to defuse the crisis. As early as January, two months before the election, long simmering resentment of Lucas had matured into the near-unanimous decision of the 900-strong officer class to unseat him.[15] The loudest rumblings of discontent came from the Air Force, which was particularly anxious to break the international isolation blocking delivery of US spare parts for the disabled Huey helicopters so crucial to the aerial counter-insurgency war.

On 23 March, helicopters, troops and armoured vehicles sealed off the presidential palace. All radio stations played martial music, interspersed at 15-minute intervals with announcements appealing for calm. Lucas, caught off guard, offered no resistance, and apart from a brief skirmish with Army old-guard loyalists in the second city of Quezaltenango, the operation was smooth and bloodless. It was the first time in 19 years that the military had been forced to resort to a *coup d'état* to perpetuate its rule.

If some observers had scented the impending coup, few could have predicted the identity of Guatemala's new leader. Dressed in camouflage fatigues, gesticulating wildly to the cameras, a half-remembered Army general treated his audience to a 13 minute diatribe, littered with invocations to God, "my Lord and King". Slowly, some television viewers put a name and a memory to the face. General José Efraín Ríos Montt, defrauded of electoral victory in 1974 at the head of a Christian Democrat-backed coalition, had sunk into obscurity. A 1975 newspaper horoscope had written him off as "a has-been", whose star sign offered no hope of a future in politics; most Guatemalans would have agreed.[16]

Ríos Montt certainly sounded different from his predecessors. The coup, he declared, was designed "to put an end to corruption, guarantee human rights and revitalize our institutions". Most important, he vowed "to change the image of Guatemala . . . especially with the United States".[17] For those who read between the lines, the political drift was clear enough: further attempts to stabilize the ruling class through the two decade-old stratagem of "limited democracy" would be discarded. Instead, the coup would attempt to heal the rancorous intra-class fissures in a way that elections could no longer hope to do. By modernizing its counterinsurgency techniques and abandoning old forms of repression which had outlived their usefulness, it would also look for an escape route from the intolerable existing levels of class conflict.

The Lucas fraction of the Army had certainly proved dysfunctional in every sense. But what would come next? Businessmen were pitted against the military; young officers against the old hierarchy; political parties against the military, the private sector and each other. What new programme could hope to rally and unify the battered forces of the Guatemalan Right?

Something Old, Something New

Just how ambitious and innovative that programme would turn out to be was not as yet apparent. The first clues were dizzying: who was in charge? And what interests did the coup-makers represent?

In fact, two concurrent plots to get rid of Lucas had been underway. On 23 March, they converged, and it was young officers who held the key to events. One group — easily the minority — wanted fresh elections, and spoke of holding them within 60 days; these officers were close to the MLN. The other group, representing the bulk of the intermediate ranks of the officer corps, had no such ideas. Instead, they had a more far-reaching agenda for the restructuring of Guatemalan political life. The confused course of events on the day of the coup were a reflection of the intense horse-trading which went on between these two tendencies.

> "God has raised up a leader of this nation . . .
> a man of destiny, a man of God."
> Jim Durkin, presiding elder of Gospel Outreach.

The call for Ríos Montt to present himself at the National Palace to take charge of the new regime had come in a radio broadcast from Leonel Sisniega Otero, the flamboyant deputy leader of the MLN. Behind him stood a small number of captains and lieutenants including Sisniega's own nephew. At the time of the radio appeal, Ríos Montt was busy counselling at the school parent–teacher association run by the evangelical *Iglesia Cristiana Verbo* — the Christian Church of the Word — where the retired general was an elder.

Journalists waiting for Guatemala's new rulers to arrive at the palace were bewildered. Five ornate chairs had been made ready for the incoming junta, and word had it that the centre seat would be occupied by General Oviedo Morales Paíz, former head of intelligence for the Army General Staff and now military commander of the port town of San José. Later, however, two of the chairs were spirited away. All talk of Morales Paíz evaporated; when it appeared, the junta was down to three men.

In the centre was Ríos Montt; flanking him on his right was general Horacio Maldonado Schaad; on the left, Colonel Fernando Gordillo. Maldonado Schaad, whose name had often been linked to the death squads, had been commander of Lucas García's Guard of Honour Regiment. Now, he enjoyed the backing of the two most right-wing parties, the MLN and the CAN. Gordillo, even closer to the Lucas camp and also to Sisniega Otero, had been an energetic director of counterinsurgency operations in El Quiché and Chimaltenango.[18]

Behind the triumvirate stood a silent trio of young officers. They comprised half of a six-member Advisory Council; as the crest of the young officers' movement, the council held many of the strings of real power. The six were mainly of modest rank; their senior figures were infantry Colonel Mario Enrique Morales and chief of the presidential guard Manuel Argueta Villalta; behind them were Major Angel Arturo Sánchez Guidel, Air Force Captain Mario Augusto Rivas García and infantry Captain Carlos Rodolfo Muñóz Pilona — the latter often considered to be the leading influence within the group. Its youngest member, in his early twenties was the fiery infantry Lieutenant Héctor Mauricio López Bonilla.[19]

For the first few months of the new regime, however, the coalition junta held on. Ríos Montt would have to move cautiously to adjust the balance of power within the ruling class; any abrupt move against opposing sectors of the armed forces or private capital could wreck the experiment. The vested interests left intact by the coup, and Ríos Montt's overriding need for unity in the Army, dictated a fragile compromise with the old guard. Though the coup had united most of the officer corps, Mexican press reports spoke of 200 Lucas loyalists forcing the new junta to accept president–"elect" Guevara as special adviser to the armed forces.[20] And Pentagon sources asserted that a pact had been struck between the outgoing Lucas clique and new Defence Minister General René Mendoza Paloma under which "no Army officer would be arrested or brought to trial as a consequence of the coup".[21]

The promised purge of those involved in the scandalous corruption of the Lucas García years ran aground on these power-broking realities, much to the rage of the MLN, which by this time had been smartly pushed aside by the coup-makers. True, a handful of National Police officers were arraigned, with the full glare of publicity, on charges of rape, homicide and assault. The notorious Detective Corps, run as a virtual private enforcers' unit by former Interior Minister Donaldo Alvarez Ruíz, received a token face-lift. But the real culprits went unmolested. From the civilian bureaucracy, only smaller fish were thrown to the show-trials — railway managers, agricultural marketing officials, port authority contractors. Soldiers raided the house of Alvarez Ruíz, uncovering underground jail cells, 50 stolen vehicles and a $400,000 printing press purchased with state funds to forge election ballot papers. Hidden in a safe-deposit box were scores of gold graduation rings, wrenched from the fingers of police torture victims. But though the crowds outside the house bayed for the head of the ex-minister, "Donaldo" and his associates were already safe in Miami.[22] True to the pact, not a single military officer stood trial.

Palace Coup — a Guatemalan Pinochet?

Ríos Montt's hold on power often appeared tenuous. His first months in power were marked by frequent and barely disguised conflicts with his fellow junta members. Maldonado Schaad in particular exploited his position in order to shield pro-Lucas bureaucrats from prosecution under the vaunted anti-corruption drive. By 9 June, the strains in the triumvirate grew too much for Ríos Montt and his young officer advisers to bear. In a surprise move, the junta leader ousted his two partners in a swift and efficient palace coup, buying off their protests with cheques for $50,000 —an inauspicious if expedient beginning for the new moral order.[23]

The audacious show of authority was a calculated risk, and though it placed absolute executive power in the hands of one man, it could not be described as a clean sweep. There were Lucas supporters left at all ranks, many of them in key barracks. Other Army traditionalists were reluctant hostages to Ríos Montt's unfamiliar moral fervour. Three appointments in particular showed that the old order was still hanging on: Maldonado Schaad's rearguard action against dismissal secured the appointment of Colonel Ricardo Méndez Ruíz — a Lucas loyalist — as Minister of the Interior. Generals Mario López Fuentes (chief of the high command) and Oscar Humberto Mejía Víctores (Defence Minister) were both hard-line rightists. Within the Army and outside it, threats to the new dictator refused to go away: from 9 June until the end of the year, at least four coup attempts were nipped in the bud.[24]

> "Our close examination of the decrees promulgated by President Ríos Montt persuades us that the Guatemalan government has overtly abandoned the rule of law and that it has overtly substituted a system of government that is both despotic and totalitarian."
> Americas Watch Committee

In the wake of the palace coup, Ríos Montt drew a noose tight around all political activity. Human rights monitoring agencies began to use their harshest language to describe his concentration of power. Said the New York-based Americas Watch Committee:

Our close examination of the decrees promulgated by President Ríos Montt persuades us that the Guatemalan government has overtly abandoned the rule of law and that it has overtly substituted a system of government that is both despotic and totalitarian.[25]

Initially, the right-wing and centrist parties had welcomed Ríos Montt. Taking the young officers' apparent commitment to fresh elections on trust, the parties of the Anti-Fraud Front rallied in support, and on the day after the coup an unholy alliance of MLN and Christian Democrats brought 8,000 people on to the square in front of the National Palace to salute the new junta. PNR candidate Maldonado Aguirre was designated as intermediary between the triumvirate and the parties, while Christian Democrat Secretary General Vinicio Cerezo sped off to Washington to lobby support for the new regime.

But the parties' optimism turned sour as Ríos Montt replaced the junta with one-man rule; election talk disappeared from the agenda — instead, there would be informal, token parleys between the party leaders and the general in the National Palace. The armed forces' monopoly of power was to be absolute. In his inaugural speech, Ríos Montt had warned that "we do not want anything to do with political wheeler-dealers (*politiqueros*) and political parties at the moment". With the *autogolpe* in June, his strictures became harsher still: "Political parties in Guatemala are electoral machines and inoperative. For this reason, the Army must now project itself politically."[26]

It projected itself above all to the urban middle class as its long-term power base, many of whom — thrown into panic by Lucas' urban terror — had begun to gravitate leftwards. Cleaning up the cities and removing the counterproductive death squads was a priority for Ríos Montt, to create the reassuring impression that the Army was in control. The rural slaughter, meanwhile, increased — out of sight and out of mind.

Much of the middle class sighed audibly with relief. Enthralled by Ríos Montt's evangelism and his promise of a shining new moral order, they groped for the fantasy of a "third way" between their fear of right-wing terror and their fear of revolution. As overt repression in the capital waned, their selective moral conscience calmed itself. Moods brightened as marimba bands replaced unmarked Cherokee Chief station wagons in the streets of Guatemala City. US government opinion, too, brightened.

The military had still not offered a coherent programme of government, but it did make its political priorities clear early on by publishing a comprehensive Plan of National Security and Development, a more vigorous updating of the recent innovations of General Benedicto Lucas García. Briefly, the plan was posited on the total militarization of political conflict, taking Guatemala further down the road of the full-blown counterinsurgency state.[27] Popular opposition was not just to be overcome, but annihilated (see appendix 1). It would not be a force to reckon with, in the vision of Ríos Montt and the young officers, in any future restructuring of the political order.

Towards a New Political Model

Every Sunday evening, President Ríos Montt would speak to the nation on television. Changing from battle fatigues to a smart lounge suit, he delivered a moral homily from an idyllic tropical garden, filled with the sound of bird-song and canned marimba music. The week after the June palace coup, his Sunday broadcast brought a new message. "Guatemalans," he declared, "are going to stop talking about political divisions, political ideas, political parties."[28]

It was the first warning of a harsh new authoritarianism masquerading as apolitical morality. With the palace coup and the centralization of power came a new legal framework, drastically suppressing political liberties, even those of the conservative and largely subservient news media. The press, in fact, was the first target. Control of the press would allow the Army to cordon off the war from public scrutiny, imposing an image of military self-confidence. Coverage of the war in the countryside was made subject to stringent restrictions, with journalists only permitted to print official Army accounts of firefights and massacres. The word "guerrilla" would no longer be allowed; nor would the names or acronyms of the guerrilla organizations. Instead, the press would speak of "terrorists", "subversives" and "delinquent bands." That, said the Army public relations office proudly, is a trick we picked up from the Americans in Vietnam.

Censorship was accompanied by a harsh and indefinite State of Siege, suspending all major constitutional guarantees. The sweeping powers contained in the decree made it a capital offence — and a quite arbitrarily defined one — "to betray the nation [or to] act against the integrity of the state". Special secret tribunals would be empowered to try a wide variety of crimes.

Ríos Montt at the same time offered an amnesty to both Left and Right, but on terms that the Left could scarcely have been expected to take seriously. The guerrilla organizations swiftly condemned the amnesty as a smokescreen for rehabilitating Army criminals: any solider accused of rape, murder or other atrocities against the civilian population would be granted a free pardon if his actions were committed "while fulfilling duties in anti-subversive actions". As to the Left, Ríos Montt made clear the underlying rationale of the amnesty offer in an address to a convention of the *Asociación de Gerentes de Guatemala* (Guatemalan Managers' Association). Guatemalans were by now getting accustomed to their new president's colourful turn of phrase: "The amnesty gives us the juridical framework for killing," he declared, "anyone who refuses to surrender will be shot."[29]

While limitations on civil liberties in a state of war are hardly unusual, these new measures surpassed all previous controls, and were directed as much against the Right as against the Left. In the same month, the military dashed any hopes of quick elections when it announced that it intended to extend its rule by 30 months, until January 1985. During that period, congress would remain closed and all political party activity outlawed. Rule would be by presidential fiat, the only machinery of consultation a Council of State whose functions would be explicitly apolitical and advisory. It was obvious enough from all this that the restrictions ostensibly imposed to protect national security would also permit the Army, unencumbered, to embark on a sweeping remodelling of Guatemalan political life. Ríos Montt's Basic Statute of Government had decreed that the Army could not participate in politics. For the political parties, this clause of the Statute seemed to presage an Army return to barracks, restoring the military to its "normal" place within a capitalist state.

But the young officers' movement interpreted its "non-political" role as placing it above the sectarian impulses of party politics and in no sense as removing it from the political arena. Ríos Montt shared their Bonapartist view that the Army is the central institution in society, and that this stature imposes upon it certain historic obligations. In discharging those obligations it will show itself less non-political than non-ideological. "Here in Guatemala," said Ríos Montt, "there is no right wing and no left wing. There are only Guatemalans." The contrast between the young officers' Guatemala and "reformist" El Salvador became clear: while in El Salvador the locus of state power would be defined by constant wrangling within a coalition of rightist and centre parties and the military, in Guatemala the armed forces — openly and alone — would dictate the terms of the new political process ushered in by the 23 March coup.

The Young Officers and Ríos Montt

In 1974, when Ríos Montt took his place in the long line of victims of electoral fraud, observers noted his allegiance to reformist military rule on the pattern of the generals who ruled Peru from 1968 to 1975, and after the 1982 coup Washington policy makers moved quickly to refurbish that progressive image. But those tendencies — never prominent — have now been all but expunged from the Guatemalan military. The dapper young officers in neatly pressed fatigues who staff the capital city's public relations offices may have breathed an elusive hint of that Peruvian era; but like Ríos Montt, their authoritarian political agenda was quite different.

The young officers never held a monopoly of power within the armed forces; what counted was that, representing the majority of middle ranks, they managed to build political alliances with key field commanders and to a large extent neutralize the remaining influence of *luquistas* at the highest level. In this sense, a parallel chain of command persisted in the Army, making its policies at times hard to decipher and leaving room for a certain continuity of practice from the old regime.

The *fundamentalistas,* as the young officers were sometimes known, knew that sweeping change could not be wrought overnight. Their problem from the outset was to keep their opponents — both military and civilian — at bay and off balance for long enough for their programme to be enacted, knowing that their monopoly of power over that time (they reckoned three to five years) would only deepen the antagonism of the far Right. Their goal was to create a society which was highly organized and regimented down to the smallest local unit of population, all under the control of the military.

Though profoundly nationalistic, they were prepared to look at foreign political models for lessons; there was a whiff of Peru and rather more of Pinochet's Chile, but above all their eyes turned to Israel, South Korea and Taiwan.[30] Corporatism of one form or another was the common denominator, and Ríos Montt was their man.

In the words of a press release issued to journalists covering the first anniversary of the coup, the Army had decided to hand the reins of power to Ríos Montt "because he was a distinguished, capable and honest soldier, and because his professional and moral background guaranteed that corruption would be stamped out in every sphere of national affairs." While Ríos Montt was partly hostage to the wishes of his officer corps, he was far from being anyone's puppet. His strident born-again evangelism was one unique asset, a useful vehicle for the ideological and moral dimension of the young officers' plan. But most important of all, Ríos Montt was a disciplined career soldier, an authoritarian with dependable anti-communist credentials. He represented a modernized and technologically oriented trend within the Guatemalan Army. Versed in modern counter-insurgency, civic action and psychological warfare, he recognized that hearts and minds matter as much as cadavers.[31] Many of these attitudes derived from his training in the United States, with courses in infantry weaponry at Fort Gulick in the Panama Canal Zone and counter-insurgency techniques at Fort Bragg, North Carolina.[32] The officer corps respected his long rise through the ranks, from private to chief of staff under Arana, commander of the country's most powerful garrison and principal of the military's *Escuela Politécnica* (Polytechnic School).[33]

This apparently model professional career had not left Ríos Montt with clean hands. As Arana's Chief of Staff in 1973, he had commanded the massacre of peasants involved in a land takeover at Sansirisay, in the eastern department of El Progreso. Nor had he kept free of the prevalent guns-to-riches mentality of the armed forces: exiled to Spain as military attaché after the 1974 elections, he left the country a rich man, with extensive estates in Alta Verapaz and El Petén.[34]

For the initial period of his rule, though, it was his counterinsurgency skills which were most in evidence. This emergency period would cleanse the body politic of the "cancer of communism" and eviscerate effective opposition. At the same time, the Army would expand its role — building up its combat strength and being allocated a correspondingly greater slice of the budget, building local level instruments of control and civilian participation (ranging from press-ganged Civil Defence Patrols to community planning committees) and extending its tentacles to more and more of the state apparatus. The concentration of state power in military hands was even more accelerated than under Lucas García. An already impressive list of military controlled institutions now swelled to embrace the Social Security Institute (IGSS), immigration and prison authorities, the Fire Brigade and the National Co-operative Institute (INACOP). The police was placed under the control of the Ministry of Defence, with provision made for the Ministry of the Interior to become the jurisdiction of the military. Article 4 of the June State of Siege provided for the militarization of public transport and education. In July, the first steps were taken in the direction of militarizing local government authorities, as Ríos Montt named all local mayors by decree, with the threat of legal sanctions against any who refused their designated posts.

At the highest level of government, military officers filled six of the 12 cabinet posts; former Army Bank president Leonardo Figueroa Villate received the key finance portfolio. A new legal and constitutional framework also come into play, with the Basic Statute of Government, the 14-point security plan and the indefinite State of Siege as its central instruments. Secret tribunals would allow the military to increase and rationalize its control over the judiciary — as Ríos Montt would say with more than a hint of cynicism, the tribunals and the death penalty would obviate the need for death squad victims to appear strewn along the highways.

Eventually, new electoral laws would be drafted to regulate the future status and conduct of political parties. As we shall see in due course, they proved to be the antithesis of the democratic opening which the parties had clamoured for. Meanwhile, the Council of State would continue its solemn — if largely ornamental — deliberations.

The new, supposedly interim, Council, introduced after the June palace coup, had all the early earmarks of a corporatist venture. In the terminology of some Guatemalan political thinkers of a neo-fascist stripe — believed to have Ríos Montt's ear — such a non-elected Council of State would be a central element in an "equicracy", under which the business of government would be managed by an alliance of the military, private enterprise and non-political professional bodies.[35]

Of the Council of State's 34 members, four represented the various economic sectors (finance, agriculture, commerce and industry); seven the professional sectors (colleges and universities, a judicial association, a municipal organization and the press); and one each the five legally registered parties not expressly excluded for their *luquista* taint. Rounding out the list were ten representatives of the indigenous peoples and one each from rural workers, urban workers, the co-operative movement and the national women's association. A five-member secretariat, hand-picked by Ríos Montt — directed the limited business of the Council.

Under its born-again Christian president, Jorge Serrano Elías, the Council of State made great play of its Indian membership. US State Department officials too, keen to justify a resumption of military sales at this point, eagerly took up the cry that Guatemala's indigenous majority had finally found its voice in affairs of state.[36] But few Indians in the highland war-zone would have recognized the names of their "represent-atives", since they had no hand in choosing them. Most were government employees, designated by the Army-run *Comité Nacional de Reconstrucción* (National Reconstruction Committee) — a key agency in the young officers' scheme — for "security reasons", as one military spokesman said.[37] Much the same applied to the Council's token trade union representation, appointed directly by Ríos Montt after not a single union proved willing to nominate a delegate.

The marginalized political parties had no illusions either about the Council of State. MLN, PDCG, PNR and CAN all refused to have anything to do with it, and when it began its ineffectual labours on 15 September, only the tiny right-wing splinter from the social democratic FUR had taken up its seat. The others boycotted the Council to form their own "Multi-Party Constitutional Front", demanding the "free and clean" elections which the young officers had appeared to promise back in March. "A new alliance is necessary to confront the military and its habits of power," fumed PNR leader Maldonado Aguirre, "so that sovereign rights can be restored to the people."[38]

Packaging the Product — Three Blue Fingers of Virtue

Ríos Montt had a fondness for analogies. In one explanation of his vision of "communitarianism" — a system of social organization that owes nothing to capitalism or socialism, but everything to divine love — he depicted the world as a market-place in which different ideologies were displayed for sale. One political scientist writing from Mexico explored the analogy further:[39] the *product* on offer from Ríos Montt's new, corporatist Guatemala, he argued, was peace and security — the peace of the grave-yards, admittedly, after the chain or rural massacres,but — for the survivors — peace nonetheless. For those who sided with the Army, whether willingly or otherwise, there was also the offer of their basic consumption needs being met. The *market* for this product was, of course, the target population, thoroughly prepared to become its consumers after military terror and material privations. The promise of total physical security is attractive, especially when the alternative is further relentless persecution as a guerrilla sympathizer. Finally, the product will not sell without *packaging*.

> "[Ríos Montt is] a man of great personal integrity, totally committed to restoring democracy." Ronald Reagan, after meeting with Ríos Montt in San Pedro Sula, Honduras, December 1982.

At a meeting with Ronald Reagan in San Pedro, Honduras, in December 1982, Ríos Montt held up three fingers to explain his divine mission. The first finger, he explained to an enraptured US president, signified "I do not steal"; the second, "I do not lie"; and the third, "I do not commit abuses." In the shape of a blue poster, the slogan covered Guatemala during 1983, emblematic of the "new moral order" of the regime. Ríos Montt's folksy Sunday homilies were only part of a sustained public relations drive. Full page government advertisements appeared in the press on a daily basis, and television channels were obliged to carry a daily average of between 20 and 30 minutes of government propaganda.

In the absence of traditional political channels, and even the illusion of pluralism, new forms of legitimation had to be found for the regime. The search led the armed forces into the novel terrain of ideology and morality, and the version offered by Ríos Montt — no matter how colourful or arcane it may have appeared from standard media reports — was the characteristic response of an authoritarian regime in deep crisis.

Class conflict, according to Ríos Montt, had no logical basis for existing. Prevailing economic structures, he added, did not engender class hatred, and therefore had no reason to be altered. Rather, conflict springs from "the rottenness of mankind. The mind hurls out insults like a weapons factory, instead of saying 'I love you.'[40] The rottenness has a name: communism, or the Antichrist, and all means must be used to exterminate it.

"We are neither Russians nor North Americans," Ríos Montt was also fond of saying. "Why can we not simply be Guatemalans?"[41] Side by side with the sweeping appeal of his born-again evangelism went an exhortation to nationalism — without regard to social class — and lip service to the country's Mayan identity. Ríos Montt called it *Guatemalidad.* No mere whim of a quixotic leader, the new nationalism was part of a clearly elaborated strategy of the Army high command. The National Plan of Security and Development called for "building up nationalism as a doctrine opposed to international communism". Military leaders such as the hard-line Defence Minister Mejía Víctores were even more explicit about the doctrine's racist content, declaring that "we must do away with the words 'indigenous' and 'Indian'. Our mission requires the integration of all Guatemalans."[42]

This was getting closer to the true motives behind the new moral and ideological push. More than just the words, counterinsurgency in the guise of nationalism actually does away with the Indian communities themselves, scattering their people and dismembering their cultural traditions. But while physical displacement of entire populations did part of the job of breaking down community cohesion, the Army also drove every possible wedge into existing local conflicts: Indian was pitted against Ladino; Civil Defence Patrol against guerrilla sympathizer; village against village; evangelical against Catholic. And all in the name of nationalism and Christian love.

With God on Our Side

In the ornate National Palace, the coup brought a new look. Piles of cheap, mass-produced Bibles filled bureaucrats' shelves; a hand-lettered sign on the doorman's desk told visitors that "Jesus loves you". Spearheaded by two special presidential advisers, evangelism swept the palace.

Whenever the onerous duties of state permitted, "Brother Efraín" Ríos Montt would drive out to an elegant suburb of Guatemala City for morning worship. In an airy green tent donated to Ríos Montt's Christian Church of the Word by a grateful convert — a Guatemalan circus wrestler named Tarzan the Terrible — the General would join hundreds of fellow believers in hymn singing, hallelujahs and the laying on of hands.

A fierce competition against the Roman Catholics of the post-Medellín "popular church" is underway for community loyalties. The armed forces' romance with evangelism is nothing new. The Lucas regime too had seen its strength as an alternative to liberation theology, and official candidate General Angel Aníbal Guevara had delivered the keynote speech to a pre-1982 election rally of 50,000 evangelical faithful in the national football stadium. Presenting him was Yiye Avila, the Puerto Rican preacher who claims the honour of having evangelized Chilean dictator Augusto Pinochet. The Army too was not slow to grasp the political importance of evangelism in the United States. Support in the US for the Ríos Montt coup was mobilized by stellar evangelical and New Right figures such as Representative Jack Kemp of New York, Pat Robertson of the Christian Broadcasting Network and Lorin Cunningham of Youth With a Mission.

> "We make no distinction between the Catholic Church and the communist subversives." Colonel Roberto Matta, commander of the military region of El Quiché, 1982.

Not that all the sects in Guatemala are conservative, to be sure. Some have identified with the process of social change and have paid the price in death squad killings and harassment. But many, tacitly or overtly, collaborated with the 1982 counterinsurgency drive, organizing joint Protestant–Army rallies against the guerrillas and their Roman Catholic supporters. Posters in their temples equated Catholicism with "communist subversion". In return, they received favours such as free passage through Army road-blocks. Pastors could pass on to their congregations the promise of protection against repression;[43] the other side of that coin was that Protestant pastors could be empowered by the military to report as a possible subversive any villager who did not accept the evangelical Church.

For an Army that had butchered a dozen priests, not to mention countless catechists and grassroots Church organizers of the progressive Catholic Action groups, the opportunity was heaven-sent. Under Ríos Montt, few of their assumptions changed. "We make no distinction," declared Colonel Roberto Matta, in charge of the military region of El Quiché, "between the Catholics and the communist subversives." [44] In mute testimony, only one priest in the department — a timid conservative prelate placed there by the cardinal — kept his church doors open. Elsewhere, the evangelical sects mopped up the debris.

The Guatemalan Catholic Church has for years now been riven between the community-level activism of priests and religious influenced by liberation theology and a largely conservative hierarchy which announced its "moral and spiritual" support for the Ríos Montt dictatorship. But there is more to the rise of the evangelical sects than changes within their Catholic rival and the scars of counterinsurgency. Economic devastation, natural and human violence all provide fertile terrain for talk of the Second Coming. The 1976 earthquake was an important turning point. Evangelicals offered apocalyptic reasons for the disaster and warned that a further year of earthquakes would follow if Catholics did not separate themselves from social action programmes: many did.[45]

Evangelical Protestant sects now reckon that they have brought more than 1.6 million Guatemalans to the Lord — a full 22% of the population. Since 1978, when state violence began to rise rapidly, fundamentalist Church membership has been growing by 23.6% each year. In ten years, their strength quadrupled, and by 1982 there were 6,767 Protestant congregations and temples in Guatemala divided between 110 different sects.[46] Pentecostalists lead the way; dozens of micro-sects like Ríos Montt's Church of the Word, a mission of Gospel Outreach, which is based in Eureka, California, bring up the rear. Rallies in December 1982 to mark the 100th anniversary of evangelism in Guatemala were attended by half a million people.[47] Crowds pack into the national Football stadium for ecstatic prayer meetings — so much that local wits refer to the place as the "First Protestant Church".

As rural violence escalated in the last years of Lucas García and the first of Ríos Montt, the escape into passivity beckoned harder. A massacre in one predominantly Protestant village provoked wild responses about impending apocalypse. Said one observer, "Women cried that what had happened was a prophesy foretold in the Bible".[48]

In the large-scale modernization of the Guatemalan rural economy, too, the sects found rich raw material for making converts. The degradation of plantation wage labour has broken down many traditional ties, overturning long-held moral values and replacing them with alcoholism, wife-beating and acute depression. Protestantism offers the appeal of sobriety, individual self-worth, answers in Christ. As a by-product, it offers landowners enhanced productivity from a newly submissive work-force.

> "He who resists authority is resisting that which has been established by God." Francisco Bache, Assembly of God preacher in Cunén, El Quiché.

The appeal to traditional indigenous values of austerity, hard work and rectitude is not dissimilar to the morality promoted by the revolutionary organizations of the Left. But while the Left has offered organization and participation, the sects instead appeal to individuality and subservience to earthly and heavenly authority. The appeal for the Army hardly needs to be stated, when pastors like Assembly of God preacher Francisco Bache of Cunén in El Quiché can tell villagers that "He who resists authority is resisting that which has been established by God."[49] How much of the response is fear, and how much is conviction? Throughout the new strategic hamlets of the Indian highlands, the temples began to overflow, but there was little guarantee of the depth of conversion. Faced with such a threat, the Indian population is likely to choose to survive, as it has historically, by adopting the protective colouring of the chameleon. Evangelism is a colour the military can never fully trust.

Scientific Counterinsurgency — Just Pins on a Map

Guatemalan field commanders tended to take on a smug look when asked how their "*Plan Victoria 82*" compared to the counterinsurgency efforts underway in neighbouring El Salvador. The problem with the Salvadorean military, the Guatemalan officers claimed, was that they were too dependent on pressures from Washington and too inexperienced in counterinsurgency. After sending 2,000 men out to sweep through Chalatenango or Morazán, they would then pull out and allow the guerrillas to run free. Search-and-destroy missions, the Guatemalans were convinced, were meaningless without a follow-up plan: you had to establish a permanent presence in the target area.[50]

Much of the Ríos Montt military strategy was borrowed from US recommendations of the mid-1970s, formalised in a Programme of Pacification and Eradication of Communism. Planners from the US embassy MilGroup had called for "combining psychological warfare with regular and irregular military tactics . . . to confuse and create the belief that in Guatemala there is a civil war between the peasants and the revolutionary forces."[51] This advice has been fully implemented, even if its US origins have been obscured by the frigid relations between Guatemala and the United States during the Carter Administration. Israeli and Argentine advice, and the Guatemalan Army's own chauvinistic sense of purpose, guided the campaign after increasing frictions with Washington.

Under Lucas, the war in the field had slid badly. Rural slaughter had been indiscriminate, unplanned. The "new" Ríos Montt approach was pre-figured in the dying months of the Lucas regime, when brother Benedicto took over military command. Some even saw him — as he liked to depict himself — as a macho Guatemalan answer to Panama's dynamic populist General Omar Torrijos. "General Benny" might have stopped short of Ríos Montt's *Fusiles y Frijoles* (Guns and Beans) epithet, but he would probably have agreed with his military philosophy that "if you don't take food into people's homes, what you take there is subversion."[52] For neither general was the determination to win over social bases — by persuasion or coercion — incompatible with mass murder. In the weeks before the March 1982 coup, the massacres under "General Benny" escalated — culminating in the slaughter, according to Church and opposition accounts — of more than 500 villagers in Paraxtut in the northern Quiché on the very day of the coup. But it was murder with a scientific purpose and philosophy, not random carnage for its own sake. Benedicto Lucas García had learned his tradecraft at France's famous St. Cyr military academy, and had seen it put to good effect in the counterinsurgency war in Algeria. Ríos Montt had learned his under US instructors, and had been part of the military generation that saw it work in Guatemala in the brutal successes of the late 1960s.

According to the doctrine of the young officers, where the security situation had slipped so badly that the Army could no longer see a distinction between the *guerilleros* and their peasant supporters, then entire Indian villages were to be erased from the map. The methods employed beggar description, but an April 1983 supplement to the *Americas Watch* human rights report gave some idea of them:

> the Army does not waste its bullets on women and children. We were repeatedly told of women being raped before being killed, and of children being picked up by the feet and having their heads smashed against walls, choked to death or killed with machetes and bayonets.[53]

In an opinion piece in the *New York Times*, Wayne Smith — former head of the US interest section in Cuba — went further: "The [Guatemalan] government's atrocities," he said, "make the Sabra and Shatila massacres in Beirut pale by comparison. Guatemala may be the most dangerous powder keg in the region."[54]

"The [Guatemalan] government's atrocities make the Sabra and Shatila massacres in Beirut pale by comparison." Wayne Smith, former head of the US interest section in Cuba, October 1982.

Where the influence of the Left was more ambiguous, terror and threats were used to force guerrilla sympathizers into submission, exposing and isolating the "hard core" revolutionary cadre, who could then be picked off clinically. If the inroads made by the Left were more recent or superficial, then why kill needlessly? Concentrate on the beans here, and less on the guns.

This philosophy translated into the maps which lined the walls of high-command offices in Guatemala and provincial garrisons. Pins of four colours classified the villages of the Indian highlands. Witness to the influence of the guerrillas, many were red — enemy territory — when Ríos Montt took power. By the end of the year, thousands of inhabitants of the red villages were dead — estimates ranged from 3,000 to 10,000 — their huts charred hulls. Hundreds of thousands more escaped from the carnage and ended up who knows where. Some opted to wait out the trauma in neighbouring countries; others died of starvation and disease; many stayed precariously alive on a diet of leaves and grub worms higher in the mountains. Eventually, droves of them were forced down into the towns to "surrender" to the armed forces and be relocated. 5,000 or more delivered themselves up in Choatalúm in Chimaltenango in October 1982; as many again, perhaps, in Chisec in Baja Verapaz. Their story, delivered to visiting reporters under the watchful eye of the military, varied little. "*Fuimos engañados por los subversivos*" — "we were tricked by the subversives"; we have now decided to co-operate with the Army; everything is peaceful now.

Throughout the rebellious *altiplano,* vast stretches were occupied and militarized; anyone in pink and yellow villages was considered suspect. In a year of Ríos Montt's iron rule, the green pins — safe villages — sprouted like trees in a graveyard.

By July 1982, Amnesty International was reporting 2,600 dead in rural massacres. Other human rights groups called the AI figure "conservative and responsible", and at year's end some of them put the total at nearer 10,000.[55] Bishops accused the military of creating a six-mile wide feed-fire zone along the Mexican border; there was sound military and diplomatic logic in the Army doing this — constant pressure on the border and incursions into refugee camps in the Mexican border state of Chiapas might provoke Mexico into militarizing its frontier and so providing a buffer against the Left's formation of a strategic military rearguard outside Guatemala.

The Mexican border sweeps also reflected the Army's concentration in 1982 on cleaning out EGP-held areas before moving on to the rest of the country. The same tactic devastated the interior of El Quiché, Sololá and parts of Chimaltenango, severing guerrilla supply lines and removing the local population. The revolutionary organizations found themselves neither able to free nor to protect the survivors.

Public debate in Guatemala, such as it was outside the country, tended to centre on the body count and the responsibility of the armed forces for the killing. But it is necessary to look beyond moral outrage and beyond explanations about winning back military territory. What was to be built on the ashes of the Indian highlands?

Political Controls and Economic Planning

The heaviest months of military terror — during the summer and autumn of 1982 — were only the first step. This time, the counterinsurgency strategists had the semblance of a long-term plan. The *Comité de Reconstrucción Nacional* (CRN), set up after the 1976 earthquake and run by the military, held some of the answers. The colonels in charge showed off their plans with pride — ambitious architectural scale-models of new rural settlements: strategic hamlets with concrete houses, water supply, a market place, an evangelical church and — central to the design — a military post. The hamlets were no temporary holding operation until the scorched earth phase is over, the 'necessary' number of civilians killed (MLN leader Mario Sandoval Alarcón would estimate half a million) and the displaced thousands decanted back into their home villages. No, once the communities of those who survive had been militarized, there must be long-range resettlement and new development plans for the areas of conflict.[56]

The development of a system of strategic hamlets and controlled towns began around the time of the Choatalúm and Chisec surrenders. The first phase called for the Army to repopulate abandoned towns, starting with the largest, and to destroy any hamlets that were either too remote to control in the long term or were deemed impossible to recover permanently from the Left. In El Quiché and Huehuetenango, towns emptied by military attacks in June and July 1982 were resettled in September and October after the internal refugee population was pressured into going back. Any villagers refusing the order to return risked being treated as subversives; their homes, farmlands and livestock would be confiscated.

In the resettled areas, the Army and security forces consolidated their presence, establishing new barracks and bringing in increased numbers of National and Treasury Police units (*Policía Nacional* and *Policía de Hacienda*). In December 1982, the strength of the security forces was further enlarged with the creation of a new rural *Guardia Civil*. Without the permanent militarization of rural areas, Ríos Montt and his advisers feared that pacification would only be temporary. "Under previous governments," explained one colonel, "the problem was that we pulled out leaving the subversives to take advantage of our absence to win over villages."[57] By May 1983, the high command was opening new command centres all over the country, aiming to consolidate a system of regional military bases in all 22 departments. Chief of Staff General Héctor Mario López Fuentes explained that "we need to continually reinforce not only territorial control, but also control of the people. Where there is military presence throughout the republic, there will be no subversive presence."[58] The Army announced at the same time its intention to open a national munitions factory, using Israeli and Belgian advice, to reduce its reliance on foreign suppliers and the unwelcome criticisms and conditions which they attached to military assistance.

One of the characteristics of fascism and its variants is that it trades the promise of security in exchange for the relinquishing of political freedoms. Even so, many authoritarian and neo-fascist regimes have proved willing to respect the right of the population to non-involvement and neutrality. Not so Ríos Montt's Guatemala. There, counterinsurgency did not stop at killing real or imagined enemies; the corporatist model that followed, in the words of one Mexican analyst, "obliges the peasant to violate the human rights of other [peasants]. The Ríos Montt regime seeks not only victims but accomplices."[59] Its main thrust came in obliging peasants to take part in two emerging structures of local control: one involving a community's most prominent leaders, would supervise local social and economic activities, and would bear the title of *Coordinadoras Institucionales Comunales* (Communal Institutional Coordinating Committees: CIC). The other, charged with mass paramilitary functions, would be known as the *Patrullas de Autodefensa Civil,* or Civil Defence Patrols.

The patrols guard the entrances to the green villages; nervous files of men and boys carrying sticks and machetes. A fortunate few have old shotguns. As far back as late 1981, "General Benny" too had recognized the attraction of recruiting Indian peasants from the war-zone into a permanent military reserve force. Like the death squads which flourished in Zacapa and Izabal in the late 1960s, they could help legitimize the war, only this time on a vaster scale. Some in fact *were* existing death squads, dusted off and embellished with a new name, organized by ex-soldiers and conservative small property owners. Others, in more prosperous areas relatively untouched by the fighting, may have been more willing accomplices of the military. But the bulk of the patrols in the highlands were not given the luxury of choice. For all able-bodied man between the ages of 15 and 60, the patrols were obligatory. In mountain villages, it was not uncommon to see children of ten or eleven drilling with wooden rifles.

Divided into groups of between ten and 14 men, each patrol found itself obliged to serve one day out of three, guarding any local installations of strategic value — bridges or electric pylons — setting road-blocks or combing the surrounding hills in prolonged searches for suspicious characters. The best two performers in each patrol would be drafted into 30 months of military service in the regular Army. Control of local population was greatly enhanced by the patrols. "Now, when men want to migrate to the coast to pick cotton, they have to check in with the Army for permission to leave the Civil Defence Patrol," explained an Army captain in San José Poaquil, a medium-sized town in Chimaltenango. "That way, we always know where everyone is."[60] The reward for patrol members was food and partial deliverance from the repression; the penalty for refusal was to be considered a subversive. The same law applied to the civilian population at large. Villagers moving from place to place in areas of recent guerrilla activity — even if only carrying their produce to market — were obliged to carry the blue-and-white flag of Guatemala at all time, as a token of their loyalty. This is guns and beans.

The Civil Defence Patrols served as cannon-fodder; pitifully armed advance detachments for military depredations, shielding the regular troops from the line of fire, their casualties to be vaunted as civilian victims of communist terror. If they engaged in combat, they were "the people" defending their quiet, idyllic life against guerrillas. In the moral wasteland of the Army's making, everything became its opposite, and neutrality was not permissible.

By September 1982, the military was boasting that it had organized 40,000 Civil Defence Patrol members. Eventual strength, claimed Army public relations chief Colonel Pablo Nuíla Hub, would reach 300,000.[61] But could the patrols be trusted? The Army faced the same dilemma it faced with the evangelicals: joining the patrols, even turning them to the advantage of the Left, was another obvious survival technique for the threatened Indian population. That constant fear of infiltration, apart from any budgetary restraints, helped explain why the patrols carried sticks and machetes instead of M-16s.

So much for paramilitary organizations; similar rules governed the level of civilian planning. The old Indian parish councils were banned by the Army as a likely breeding ground for subversion, and in their place came the CIC. Their task was to plan and execute community activities: everything from granting permission to hold a dance and organizing villagers into forced "public works" labour gangs, to planning the introduction of new economic development programmes and distributing available resources — food, building materials and agricultural inputs — to the community in liaison with local military officers. And therein lies the key: far from being agencies for community decision-making, the CIC are rigidly under the control of the military. Each is answerable to the local garrison, its members are named by the local *comandante,* and the Army holds veto power over all CIC decisions.[62]

At a national level, the counterinsurgency state has tried for the first time to confront systematically the realities of an economic crisis, though its actual plans appeared only a partial solution. The existing economic model, dominated by traditional cash crops, has run into the ground; it cannot absorb the labour force. Landowners' old need for cheap plantation labour has peaked, as demand for crops subsides and scarce capital feeds mechanization, not more salaries. Only an arrant optimist would predict that the world market will again demand Guatemalan coffee, cotton, sugar and meat in the old quantities, at the old high prices. At the same time, the subsistence farms of the Indian peasantry are ever less viable, their poor soil declining and their acreage shrinking as each generation subdivides the land among its children. The old equation of survival — nine months on the family plot and three on the plantation — is collapsing. New sources of income must be created for those whose very starvation, in the absence of political channels of dissent, makes them a threat to the state.

Agrarian reform as a solution to the problem was explicitly denied from the outset by the Ríos Montt regime. For a time, rumours abounded — to the fury of the private sector — that the US Agency for International

Development (AID) was cajoling the government into agrarian reform. But the political message of an AID report of October 1982 was explicit enough, and it seems to mirror the bitter experience of promoting a land reform against the wishes of the Right in El Salvador. Since the Guatemalan military was unwilling to budge on the issue:

> We accept this limitation as a *given,* for reasons of both substance and prudence. The United States risks ineffectiveness and counter-productive relations with a host government by getting ahead of the latter, in effect finding itself in an out-front advocacy position, on sensitive domestic policy issues such as land reform.[63]

But the landowners had no need to fret: a new package of economic proposals conveyed to the private sector in October 1982 laid the ghost to rest. "The government has never thought about and will never think about carrying out an agrarian reform," declared Finance Minister Figueroa Villate. Ríos Montt himself was known to regard reforms as superfluous, not to say downright dangerous. For him, the cardinal error of the 1944-54 democratic revolution was its assault on private estates, above all those of the United Fruit Company.[64]

The watchword for the countryside would be transformation without reforms, with no significant change taking place in the first two years until the military situation had been brought under control.[65] Ríos Montt foresaw a three-phase programme, to be co-ordinated between the Army, the private sector and the evangelical Churches, the regime's staunchest point of liaison with the emergent structures of local military control. The first such programme, known as FUNDAPI, concentrated its efforts in the Ixil Triangle.

The initial phase would be of feeding those who remained after the *Plan Victoria 82* counterinsurgency sweeps. The second — called "predevelopment" — would put these survivors to work. These two phases were well underway by the end of the year. Maize, flour, oil and milk from the United Nations' World Food Programme — administered locally by regional military commanders, much to the UN's distaste — kept the rural poor from starvation. In return for elementary rations, and under the watchful eye of Army patrols, Indian forced labour gangs hacked out new rural access roads and carried out reforestation schemes. This virtual slave labour, as the regime boasted, created 60,000 "new jobs" building a new highland infrastructure, and would cost the impoverished regime scarcely a penny. The problem, however, was that it only addressed the consequences of counterinsurgency in the north-west mountains; there was no visible economic plan for the rest of the country.

In the highlands, these two phases would supposedly lay the groundwork for phase three, which the Army called "development". That was the gleam in the eye of National Reconstruction Committee planners; their emergent vision was of militarized model villages, where tamed Indian communities — no longer a political threat — would generate new income for themselves

149

and the tottering national economy by farming new cash crops. Colonel Eduardo Wohlers, head of the *Plan de Asistencia a las Areas de Conflicto* (Assistance Plan to Conflict Areas: PAAC), foresaw in 1983

> the definitive transformation of the face of the Guatemalan highlands. We foresee huge plantations of fruit and vegetables, with storage and processing facilities and refrigeration plants. We aim to put in the entire infrastructure for exporting frozen broccoli, Chinese cabbage, watermelons . . . a total of fifteen new crops.[66]

It sounded ambitious, but again there was both continuity and rupture here between Lucas García and Ríos Montt. Certainly Ríos Montt had brought more efficient technocratic planning and improved Army morale. Equally important, landowners with declining labour needs might accept social action programmes — and even co-operatives — in the *altiplano* more readily than they had five years earlier, especially if the experiment took place under the guarantee of tight military surveillance. But the plan for any wholesale remodelling of the highlands was as likely to be a pipe dream for Ríos Montt as for his predecessor. Presidential candidate Guevara had spoken in ambitious terms during his electoral campaign, promising that "we will attack forcefully with social and economic action the causes that can push a man into the ranks of the guerrillas." "Integral Development of Rural Communities" had been a watchword of Lucas' Third National Development Plan (1979-82), which had proposed 118 model settlements in areas affected by the guerrilla insurgency.[67] In 1980, there had even been extravagant promises of a multi-million dollar civic action and rural development scheme in the Ixil Triangle — the so-called *Plan Ixil.*[68]

Only large inflows of foreign aid could hope to keep a programme of this size afloat; internal resources alone could never underwrite it. Government allocations to the PAAC in 1982 were a scant $1 million, enough to attend to the basic needs of only 500 hamlets. Two decades ago, Venezuela eradicated a guerrilla movement and then launched a far-ranging programme of corrective social action. But the analogy stops there. First, Venezuela's guerrillas were never so pervasive, and second, Guatemala does not have Venezuela's booming oil economy: the money had to be sought elsewhere.[69]

A wide array of international actors had a stake in the outcome, from the United States and Mexico to Israel and the international banking community. But those who sought to aid Ríos Montt's stalwart anti-communism — above all in the Reagan Administration — were obliged to overcome human rights opponents and congressional restraints. In part they would resort to subterfuge; and in part they would channel dollars to Guatemala's authoritarian exterminism under the guise of humanitarian aid. After all, what could be touted as a greater advance from the "Two F's" — *fusiles y frijoles* — than the "Three Ts" which Ríos Montt announced as their successors — *techo, trabajo y tortillas?* From "guns and beans" to "roof, work and bread" — who would argue with that?

Notes

1. *Washington Post*, 10 March, 1982.
2. *Inforpress*, 11 March, 1982; *ALAI*, 26 March, 1982.
3. *Inforpress*, 1 October, 1981.
4. Economist Intelligence Unit, *Quarterly Economic Review of Guatemala, El Salvador, Honduras: 1st Quarter 1981.*
5. Cynthia Arnson and Flora Montealegre, *IPS Resource Update* (Washington DC) June 1982.
6. *Excélsior* (Mexico City), 31 July, 1981.
7. INCO Press Release, "Guatemalan Nickel Investment Revalued down by $220 Million", December 1981.
8. US Embassy Quarterly Report on Guatemala, January-March 1982.
9. *Business Latin America*, 10 November, 1981.
10. *Latin America Weekly Report*, 20 August, 1982.
11. *Unomásuno* (Mexico City), 22 January, 1982.
12. ANACAFE report, cited in *El Gráfico*, 16 June, 1981, and *Prensa Libre*, 10 June, 1981.
13. *Inforpress*, 26 November, 1981; *Latin America Regional Report: Mexico and Central America*, 12 February, 1982; *New York Times*, 14 March, 1982.
14. Arnson and Montealegre, *IPS Resource Update.*
15. *Washington Post*, 24 March, 1982.
16. *El Gráfico*, 29 December, 1975.
17. *Unomásuno*, 24 March, 1982.
18. *El Día* (Mexico City), 24 and 29 March, 1982; *Latin America Weekly Report*, 2 April, 1982.
19. *Latin America Regional Report: Mexico and Central America*, 10 June, 1982.
20. According to an interview with former Arbenz Foreign Minister Guillermo Toriello, citing the Mexico City dailies *Excélsior* and *Unomásuno*, Havana International Service, 0000 GMT, 11 May, 1982, in *Foreign Broadcast Information Service (FBIS)*, 12 May, 1982.
21. *Excélsior*, 8 May, 1982.
22. Panama City ACAN in Spanish, 2146 GMT, 23 March, 1982, in *FBIS*, 26 March, 1982; also NACLA interviews in Guatemala City, June 1982.
23. *Latin America Weekly Report*, 30 July, 1982.
24. *Latin America Weekly Report*, 18 June and 30 July, 1982; *Unomásuno*, 24 June, 1982.
25. Americas Watch Committee, "Human Rights in Guatemala: No Neutrals Allowed", (New York, November 1982), p.3.
26. *Latin America Weekly Report*, 2 April, 1982.
27. For a full theoretical discussion of the counterinsurgency state in Latin America, see Ruy Mauro Marini, "The Question of the State in the Latin American Class Struggle", *Contemporary Marxism* (San Francisco, California), no.1 (Spring 1980), pp.1-9.
28. *Prensa Libre*, 21 June, 1982.
29. *Unomásuno*, 25 June, 1982; see also *El Día*, 23 June, 1982 and *Washington Post*, 26 May, 1982.
30. Interviews in Guatemala City, August 1982 and March 1983.
31. Susanne Jonas, "The Guatemalan Counterinsurgency State: The Complicity of the U.S. Government and U.S. Capital in the Violation of Human Rights in Guatemala", paper presented to the Tribunal Permanente de los Pueblos, Madrid, Spain, January 1983, p.15.
32. *Diario de Centroamérica* (Guatemala City), 26 March, 1982.
33. Guatemala City *Cadena de Emisoras Unidas*, 0023 GMT, 25 March, 1982, in *FBIS*, 29 March, 1982; *Latin America*, 2 November, 1973.
34. *Latin America Weekly Report*, 2 April, 1982.
35. *Latin America Regional Report: Mexico and Central America*, 9 July, 1982.
36. See for example the comments of Assistant Secretary of State for Human Rights and Humanitarian Affairs Elliot Abrams, on the *McNeill–Lehrer Report*, PBS-TV, 11 January, 1983.
37. *This Week in Central America and Panama* (Guatemala City), 20 September, 1982; see also *Los Angeles Times*, 19 September, 1982.

38. *Latin America Regional Report: Mexico and Central America,* 24 September, 1982.
39. Antonio Cabral, in *Unomásuno,* 21 March, 1983.
40. Ríos Montt, weekly broadcast to the nation, reprinted in *El Gráfico,* 17 June, 1982.
41. Author's interview with Ríos Montt, Guatemala City, 23 August, 1982.
42. Radio Televisión Guatemala, 0400 GMT, 2 September, 1982, in *FBIS,* 7 September, 1982.
43. *Los Angeles Times,* 30 September, 1982.
44. Author's interview, Santa Cruz del Quiché military base, 24 August, 1982.
45. James D. Sexton, ed., *Son of Tecún Umán* (Tucson, University of Arizona Press, 1981), pp.139-41.
46. *Wall Street Journal,* 7 December, 1982.
47. See *This Week in Central America and Panama,* 6 September and 6 December, 1982; and Cor Bronson, "Guatemala's Coup — A Protestant Perspective", in Washington Office on Latin America (WOLA), *Guatemala Update,* no.5, 7 May, 1982.
48. *Prensa Libre,* 17 September, 1981.
49. *Washington Post,* 19 July, 1982.
50. Author's interviews with Guatemalan Army officers, August 1982; see also *New York Times,* 12 September, 1982.
51. According to testimony by Elías Barahona, reported in GNIB, September-October 1982; also *Latin America Regional Report: Mexico and Central America,* 4 June, 1982.
52. *El Gráfico,* 21 June, 1982.
53. Americas Watch Committee, "Creating a Desolation and Calling it Peace", April 1982 supplement to the human rights report on Guatemala.
54. *New York Times,* 12 October, 1982.
55. These groups call Amnesty International's figure of 2,600 dead by July 1982 "responsible and conservative". See for example, Americas Watch Committee, *Human Rights in Guatemala,* pp.10, 101-2.
56. See *Inforpress,* 19 August, 1982; *El Día,* 6 April, 1982.
57. Interview with Colonel Eduardo Wohlers, director of the PAAC, Guatemala City, 29 March, 1983.
58. *ENFOPRENSA* (Mexico City), No. 8, 10 June, 1983.
59. Sergio Aguayo, *Las posibilidades del fascismo guatemalteco, Unomásuno* 21 March, 1983.
60. Author's interview, San José Poaquil, March 1983.
61. *Los Angeles Times,* 19 September, 1983.
62. See three-part series by Antonio Cabral in *Unomásuno,* 21 March, 1983; and *Nexos* (Mexico City), July 1983.
63. United States Agency for International Development (AID), *Land and Labor in Guatemala* (October 1982), p.51.
64. *Die Tageszeitung* (Berlin and Frankfurt), 3 June, 1982.
65. *New York Times,* 12 September, 1982.
66. Interview with Colonel Eduardo Wohlers, March 1983; *Latin America Regional Report: Mexico and Central America,* 6 May, 1983.
67. *Miami Herald,* 4 December, 1981; *Inforpress,* 19 August, 1982.
68. Shelton Davis, "The Evangelical Holy War in El Quiche", *Anthropology Resource Center Newsletter* (Boston, Massachusetts), March 1983.
69. See the report of a National Council of Churches (NCC) delegation to Guatemala in *Christianity and Crisis,* 27 December, 1982. The NCC report was one of the first serious attempts to decipher the long-range economic logic behind the massacres.

7. Guatemala on the World Stage

"They just don't understand our needs" complained one Guatemalan field commander in an interview in the summer of 1982. He was referring to the United States; "Perhaps they will wake up to our reality when 80 million Mexicans have been enslaved under the Soviet boot."[1]

If only instinctively, the officer was in fact fighting on a decisive front of the war. No matter how limited the Guatemalan Army's margin for political and economic manoeuvre, and no matter how coherent and widely supported the opposition movement inside the country, the war will not ultimately be determined on the ground alone. Ultimately, it will turn also on which of the belligerent forces inside Guatemala can best capture the hearts, minds and purse-strings of the international powers that be. And today more than ever, it will hinge on the broader evolution of the regional conflict in Central America.

The commander, in his radical right-wing nationalism, was largely mistaken about Washington — if indeed his comment signified anything more than the petulant frustration that has characterized Guatemalan élite attitudes to the United States in recent years. For underneath the posturing, there is a shrewd and cynical recognition that the US will ultimately stand by Guatemala's rulers if they are seriously theatened.

Under Ronald Reagan, there may have been no more coherent a policy towards Guatemala than there was towards the rest of the region, but there was no lack of political will to come to the assistance of Ríos Montt. The Guatemalan Right has both ardent sympathizers and nail-hard, pragmatic supporters in Washington, who understand its needs only too well. For the most violent tendencies of the New Right, the issue is simple and self-defining: according to one characteristic analysis, "Guatemala is of strategic value to the United States because it is of strategic value to the

> "It is very difficult for any small country to withstand an assault supplied by training and matériel from one of the superpowers and its assistants without help from the other."
> US Deputy Assistant Secretary of State John Bushnell.

Jean-Marie Simon

Instruction for members of the kaibiles, Guatemala's crack counterinsurgency troops

Soviet proxies who threaten it."[2] For Administration officials, the language may be more calculated, but the logic is no less compelling. Defending a closer embrace of the Ríos Montt regime, Deputy Assistant Secretary of State John Bushnell declared that

> it is very difficult for any small country to withstand an assault supplied by training and matériel from one of the superpowers and its assistants without help from the other.

All of them believe that the Guatemalan conflict, like the broader Central American war, is abetted — if not inspired — by the Soviet Union and Cuba; all share a fear of creeping communism as if it were a disease with no known antidote which will flood the Rio Grande with millions of "foot people"; and all agree that Guatemala is of strategic significance and must be defended. But their selling line will depend on the milieu they represent, whether economic, military or political. And all know that they will have to surmount the opposition of a sceptical Congress.

It is not the big corporate lobbyists who crowd Washington corridors on behalf of the Guatemalan regime, though five of the *Fortune* top ten companies (Exxon, Texaco, IBM, ITT and Gulf Oil) have interests in the country.[3] Most of them would as happily do business in pro-socialist Mozambique as in anti-communist Guatemala, for multinational managers are notoriously pragmatic. The businessmen who stridently remind Washington of its responsibilities are an expatriate bunch, many of them participants in the 1954 CIA operation who settled in afterwards to enjoy the fruits of their labour. Grouped together in the American Chamber of Commerce (AMCHAM), they identify fiercely with the bunker mentality of their Guatemalan counterparts.

Then there are the Pentagon circles, which argue in the traditional discourse of strategy planning that two variables determine a country's strategic value — its geographical location in relation to vital transportation arteries and its deposits of raw materials. The rationale of sea lanes, oil transportation routes and contingency planning for use of the Caribbean in the event of a European war has become familiar as the basis of US policy in Central America. But the Pentagon makes a special argument for Guatemala — it has petroleum and nickel reserves, albeit on a modest scale, and access to both the Pacific and Caribbean coasts. With Honduras and Colombia, it is the most important site for "protecting" the Pacific Coast of Central America. Pentagon sources have also disclosed that Guatemala is the contingency site for a regional US military base. For the still unconvinced, the argument moves regional. Add Panama's canal, Mexico's oil-fields and Soviet boots poised on the Texas border, and Guatemala becomes a Pentagon nightmare of strategic import.

The State Department would likely add another dimension — that of ideology. Unlike the days of the Carter–Lucas García standoff, the economic and strategic arguments find resonance in a Reagan-sanitized

State Department. It is here that the Administration's bipolar view of the world reaches back in time to clasp hands with Guatemala's bitter cold war legacy. The ideological grip is firm enough to make the whole appear greater than the sum of the arguments. For it was draped in the 1954 myth of "salvation from communism" that Guatemala became the repository for US regional economic plans, investments and counterinsurgency techniques. When El Salvador and Nicaragua were still foreign policy backwaters, Guatemala was a regional guinea pig. In the new cold war, the chickens of Allen and John Foster Dulles have come home to roost.

1976-1980: Loosening the Grip

Upon receiving the State Department's damning human rights report in 1977, the Guatemalan regime retorted that it would reject in advance any military aid from a government which dared to impose conditions on matters it considered an internal affair. By 1980, Lucas was publicly denouncing Jimmy Carter as a communist; congressional delegations were being branded as "fellow travellers of the subversives"; and Carter's roving envoy William P. Bowdler could not even get a hearing from the Lucas government or the official right-wing parties. So perverse did Guatemala's animosity become that it would even send a team to the 1980 Moscow Olympics just to defy Carter's call for a boycott after the Soviet intervention in Afghanistan.[4]

Military aid had actually begun to decline in 1975, when Great Britain pressured President Ford to send Guatemala a warning to drop invasion plans against neighbouring Belize, then busy negotiating its independence from Britain. As a result, by the start of Carter's term, Guatemala was already buying Galil assault rifles and Arava counterinsurgency aircraft from its new supplier, Israel.

Carter's tactics were probably doomed to founder. His human rights policy, as applied to Guatemala, had been designed to press for normalized electoral democracy; instead, the Guatemalan military imposed its own candidate by fraud in the 1978 elections. Seeking to reinforce centrist forces, Carter only saw their influence eroded and their leaders assassinated. The arrogant response of the Guatemalan military was as effective as a blackmailer's note: play your foolish game, but you have no real alternatives; Guatemala's importance to the United States will prove decisive.

It was cruelly true: having boldly stepped into the vacuum at the centre of Guatemalan politics, the Carter Administration had nowhere to go. In desperation, State Department liberals and human rights activists exhorted him to broaden the search for acceptable alternatives. For most, this meant at least talking to the new, broadly-based FDCR coalition — even though the FDCR had never been designed as a force to parley with the US regime.

For the boldest minority, it even meant exploring the participation of the guerrillas in a settlement. But Carter, stung by accusations from the ascendant Right that he had "lost" Nicaragua, and lacking the kind of centrist options that still seemed present in El Salvador in 1979, declined to extend the spectrum of those who could be considered democrats.

Carter was in a cul-de-sac, stuck with the intransigence of Lucas and stuck with an arms embargo that was doubly ineffectual. Its existence permitted Lucas to firm up relations with new allies, while its loopholes allowed him to continue receiving a certain amount of US equipment.

Though Congress took a firm stand against a resumption of military sales, even denying a modest request from the Pentagon in 1980 for $250,000 in military training (IMET) funds, and though Carter blocked a Guatemalan government request for the purchase of six F-5 jet fighter aircraft, the US arms flow never entirely dried up. During the last half of Carter's term, more than $34 million worth of US military equipment wormed its way into Guatemala, mostly under contracts licensed by the Department of Commerce. The largest amount was a $20 million order for two Lockheed L-100-20 transport planes, updated versions of the Hercules paratroop-carrier.[5]

Even Friends Couldn't Do More

> "Hang in 'til we get there. We'll get in and then we'll give you help. Don't give up. Stay there and fight. I'll help you as soon as I get in." Ronald Reagan, speaking to Amigos del País envoy Eduardo Carrete, 1980.

With Reagan in the White House, the Guatemalans assumed that everything would change overnight. News of his election was greeted with firecrackers in Guatemala City. Their optimism seemed justified: after all, Reagan had seemed to display his enthusiasm — as well as his skill at talking in monosyllables — when meeting with *Amigos del País* envoy Eduardo Carrete in the pre-election period of 1980. "Hang in 'til we get there," Reagan had said, "We'll get in and then we'll give you help. Don't give up. Stay there and fight. I'll help you as soon as I get in."

Throughout Reagan's election campaign, the two-way lobbying had been intense, reflecting in large measure the rise of the New Right within the Reagan coalition. Policy advisers Roger Fontaine, General Vernon Walters and retired General Daniel O. Graham headed down to give positive signals to the Lucas regime. New Right and neo-conservative delegations swarmed over Guatemala City — from Young Americans for Freedom and the Heritage Foundation to the Coalition for Peace through Strength, the Moral Majority and the American Conservative Union.

In the opposite direction came delegates from *Amigos del Pais* and the Guatemalan Freedom Foundation, recruiting professional lobbyists and public relations firms like McKenzie-McCheyne, which had performed similar tasks for the Somoza regime in Nicaragua and the Salvadorean rightist politician Roberto D'Aubuisson.[6] Guatemalan business leaders reportedly pumped large illegal contributions into the Reagan campaign coffers. Their tentacles reached right into the core of the new administration through the lobbying activities of the Hannaford-Deaver law firm of White House troika member Michael Deaver. Within three days of the Republican victory, on 7 November, 1980, Hannaford-Deaver were busy arranging a Capitol Hill briefing for *Amigos del Pais.*

Yet Congressional resistance held, and the Administration faced stiff opposition to any normalization of relations. Joint hearings on 30 July, 1981 of the House Sub-committee on Inter-American Affairs and that of Human Rights and International Organizations confirmed that the situation was as wretched as ever. It was impossible for the Administration to defend Lucas in public, no matter what its private sympathies.

Like Carter before him, Reagan's initial overtures failed to discern the nature of the beast, and the extent to which the Guatemalans felt free to thumb their noses at the United States. He thought his envoys had come to a four-point "understanding" with the Lucas regime, under which the United States would resume arms deliveries, restart Pentagon training for the police and security forces, stay silent on death squad killings (a.k.a. "quiet diplomacy ") and hold open the possibility of direct US troop commitment in an emergency.[7] Lucas understood these terms well enough, but not as a trade-off for even cosmetic human rights improvements. Such a request was as unacceptable from the new team as from the old. Within eight months of the Reagan inauguration, the climate was so bad that a Guatemalan City daily newspaper could run the headline, "General Haig, ally of Dr Castro." There was almost no leverage for the United States, and Reagan's envoys returned from their meetings with Lucas with as little latitude as Carter's. The paramilitaries of the far Right were the only ones who felt they had leverage, and went about their grisly business with impunity, encouraged by Reagan's arrival. By the end of 1981, the State Department would lament to the *New York Times* that "we have no options in Guatemala".[8]

Around this time, the Administration would shift its line of attack. No longer trying to rehabilitate a lost cause, it shifted focus to Guatemala's insurgent "enemy" and its supposed Cuban–Soviet sponsorship. Assistant Secretary of State Thomas O. Enders elaborated on the super-plot. The recent agreement among Guatemala's revolutionary forces, he charged, "exemplifies Cuba's systematic efforts to unify, assist and advise Marxist-

Leninist guerrillas".[9] In one particularly bizarre flight of fancy, the State Department asserted that the Left's success in recruiting Indian peasants was due to the establishment in Cuba of secret language schools to teach Guatemalan communists their country's 22 indigenous languages. Nor did Nicaragua's Sandinistas — by this time becoming part of a supposed "Soviet–Cuban–Nicaraguan axis" — escape. They were alleged to be repeating their Salvadorean gun-running operation, channelling 50mm mortars, sub-machine-guns, rocket launchers and other weapons across Honduras into the Guatemalan countryside.[10]

But the Cuban smear failed to stick. The widespread discrediting of the White Paper on El Salvador in early 1981 had provoked general scepticism at a repeat performance, and many in Congress took pains to stress the indigenous nature of Guatemala's revolt. After all, when the Guatemalan revolution began, Fidel Castro had been a sixteen-year-old basketball star at a Jesuit high school.

> "The implications of a Marxist takeover in Guatemala are a lot more serious than in El Salvador . . . Congress does not realise the historic importance of the competition in Central America." General Wallace Nutting, commander of US forces in Panama.

Secretary of State Alexander Haig tried another approach. Guatemala was the next target on his infamous Soviet "hit list", "because of its size, population and raw materials, oil included . . . "[11] But that argument too wore thin as it emerged that the State Department had over-estimated the country's modest oil deposits by relying on inflated figures about Guatemala's proven reserves, supplied by Haig's special envoy, General Vernon Walters.[12] Walters had previously been employed as adviser to the Luxembourg-based Basic Resources Inc., which, with extensive drilling rights in northern Guatemala, had its own reasons for exaggerating the figures in the hope of forcing more favourable concessions from the Lucas regime. Congress still would not bite. Now, General Wallace P. Nutting, commander of United States forces in Panama, began to show real alarm at its refusal to accept the administration line. "The implications of a Marxist takeover in Guatemala," he declared, "are a lot more serious than in El Salvador . . . Congress does not recognise the historic importance of the competition in Central America."

By the time of the March 1982 elections, the Administration found itself in a blind alley, to which none of the presidential candidates offered a solution.

Lies and Loopholes

The United States Embassy in Guatemala City had been kept abreast of coup plans since January. Although there was no indication of direct US involvement in the coup, Ambassador Frederic Chapin leapt to embrace Ríos Montt's de facto regime with almost indecent haste and exuberance. Within three weeks of the coup, Chapin announced — with more satisfaction than substantiation — that "the government has come out of the darkness into the light."[13] In the State Department, the tone was equally euphoric: "political paralysis has ended", declared Deputy Assistant Secretary of State Bosworth to Congress.

A high gear public relations exercise, a veritable Big Lie campaign, sought to put as much distance as possible between the new dictator and the unsavoury memory of Lucas. The selling of Ríos Montt would make the impossible seem possible. But it meant building a propaganda drive around very slender resources. The defence of Ríos Montt rested on three things: the moral image of anti-corruption and evangelism, the promise of a democratic *apertura,* and the removal of the worst *urban* human rights violations. The first was a solid asset among the corresponding lobbies in the United States, but was a dubious one in Congress, which saw Ríos Montt as erratic and messianic. Even those who trusted his honesty doubted his longevity on the Guatemalan scene. The second quickly proved a threadbare promise, as the very centrist politicians who might have proved Washington's most reliable allies headed north to tell the State Department that there would be no return to constitutional rule as long as Ríos Montt remained in power. On the third count, Washington could point to a decrease in death squad activity in Guatemala City, but was left with the problem of covering for the excesses of a rural counterinsurgency programme — vigorously supported by the US Embassy — in which a high body count and the summary treatment of civilians were inevitable components. It was a demanding exercise in public relations, but the Administration was not deterred, and a new overt linkage between counterinsurgency and respect for human rights began to filter into its pronouncements.[14] According to Bosworth, "the Administration's objective is to make our security considerations and our human rights concerns mutually reinforcing, so that they can be pursued in tandem." Secretary Enders briefed the State Department on the contradiction. "In Guatemala," he said, "a coup has installed a new leader who has improved the human rights situation and has opened the way for a more effective counter-insurgency effort."[15]

The trouble was that Congress was not willing to buy the story. Nor, for the most part, was the press. The Administration would continue to push for legitimacy for its policies, but for the moment, subversion of opposition was to be the order of the day. Until the end of 1982, when Congress began to relent — taken in by the claims of military success made by Ríos Montt after *Plan Victoria 82* — Reagan's Guatemala policy was a text book case of circumventing restraints. Congressional restrictions, alarmed public opinion, even the law itself, were all systematically flouted. Not on a grand scale, it is true, but through a complex variety of channels assistance flowed to help Ríos Montt's military drive and to offer a lifeline to his sinking economy.

In January 1983, the State Department pushed a request through the House Foreign Affairs Committee for $6.3 million worth of military equipment. The aid package contained communications gear and earth-moving machinery. It also included $1.12 million in spare parts for the Guatemalan Air Force's A-37B "Dragonfly" counterinsurgency fighter aircraft. But its symbolic centrepiece, and the main source of grievance for the Guatemalan military during the Carter years, was $3.24 million in parts, accessories and reconditioning of Guatemala's small fleet of Bell UH-IH "Huey" helicopters, vital to the aerial war against the guerrillas.[16]

The move marked the end of a five-year hiatus in military aid and the culmination of a two-year propaganda blitz against Congress. In the interim, the Administration had resorted to indirect, semi-legal and downright illegal devices to help the Guatemalan military weather the cut-off. Although the Administration pleaded that the military aid package was setting no precedents, merely clearing up some messy unfinished business inherited from Carter, within a month it was clear that a continuing commitment was foreseen; under the foreign military assistance prog-ramme for Fiscal Year 1984, Guatemala was scheduled to receive a hefty increase in military aid.[17]

The tone had been set as early as May 1981, when the Administration side-stepped Congress by reclassifying military items and approving their sale through the Department of Commerce. A semantic subterfuge, changing "Crime Control and Detection" equipment to "Regional Stability Controls", allowed $3.2 million worth of Army trucks and jeeps to slip through the net.

In late 1982, 23 contracts on items approved before 1977 remained open and exempt from the arms sales embargo. Arms transfers from a decade before were still moving through the pipeline.[18] Documents captured by ORPA from a military helicopter brought down near Sololá indicated that spare parts for the Guatemalan Air Force were being shipped out surreptitiously from the US airbase at Homestead, Florida.[19] In the case, of helicopters supplied by the Bell Company, a coach and horses were driven through the gaping loopholes in the law.

One end of the tarmac at Guatemala City's La Aurora airport is crammed with helicopters: in the two years from 1980 to 1982, the Guatemalan helicopter fleet swelled from nine to 27 machines, all manufactured in the United States by Bell. The cost of the new machines exceeded $25 million; during the first year of Ríos Montt's rule, they were arriving at La Aurora at the rate of one a month.

In expanding their fleet, the Guatemalan armed forces broke through the five-year embargo on US arms sales on a scale inconceivable without the tacit approval of the Reagan Administration. By the end of 1982, the fleet

included:
* four Bell UH-1H "Hueys", updated version of the UH-1D. Under Lucas, Guatemala had listed its inventory as eight UH-1Ds; in early 1983 four were known to be out of service. The implication was that the other four had been illegally refitted during 1981 and 1982;
* three Bell 212s and 6 Bell 412s — sales approved by the Department of Commerce in 1980-1;
* eight Bell 206-Bs, known as the "Jetranger". Though nominally a civilian craft, 4,000 of the Jetrangers have been sold worldwide by Bell to military customers, and only 2,000 for civilian purposes. They are often to be seen flying military missions in Guatemala;
* six Bell 206-Ls. This model, known as the "Longranger", has double the capacity of the 206-B.

Bell employees and Guatemalan pilots confirmed that these latter machines had been fitted out with machine-guns for counterinsurgency use. Equipment had been removed from the unserviceable "Hueys" and refitted to the 412s.

From 11 January to 31 March, 1982 — both before and after the coup, in other words — more than 20 Guatemalan Air Force pilots received training at Bell Company facilities in Fort Worth, Texas. Flight training was also provided by Bell's Fort Worth neighbour, Flight Safety International Inc. The Dallas-based company Southwest Vert-All Inc. supplied sophisticated radio transmission equipment for all Bell models.[20]

Meanwhile, more direct security assistance continued to go through. The military assistance group at the US Embassy continued to give routine advice to their Guatemalan counterparts. In late 1982, it was revealed that two US active service officers were on duty in the country. One, Special Forces Captain Jesse Garcia, was teaching a range of skills — including counterinsurgency techniques — at the military's *Escuela Politécnica* (Polytechnic School), camouflaged as an English-language instructor; the other, Air Force Lieutenant-Colonel Benjamin Castro, was teaching Guatemalan pilots.[21] On the covert front, it was not known until April 1983, when a National Security Council paper was obtained by the *New York Times,* that an additional $2.5 million had been granted from Central Intelligence Agency contingency reserve funds for covert action in Guatemala. The ostensible purpose was the same as that for funding the anti-Sandinista *contras* in Nicaragua — an "arms interdiction programme".

Allies and Pariahs

Back in 1981, Lucas' presidential candidate, Defence Minister Guevara, was asked by a reporter how Guatemala had fared as the result of the US cold shoulder. Guevara asserted that things could be much worse; Guatemala was receiving military supplies from "countries who still believe in us", he said, citing trading partners as diverse as Argentina, Israel and Belgium.[22]

Guevara could have more than doubled that list. Western democracies, conservative or social democratic, even communist nations, tend to swallow political qualms quickly if export earnings or trading needs are at stake. These links may take the form of military hardware and know-how — Austria and Belgium have both given Guatemala advice on munitions manufacture, in line with the Army's plan to open its own arms factory; Yugoslavia supplied weapons, Switzerland fighter aircraft.[23] Or then again the links may be purely commercial — West Germany's largest regional investments are in Guatemala, while the People's Republic of China purchases more than 50% of Guatemala's cotton crop. Italy in 1982 promised to pump a possible $500 million in credits into hydroelectricity, railway modernization and port facilities.[24] Even Spain offered $61 million for tourist development, industry and transport — all to a country with which it had broken diplomatic relations two years earlier after the Spanish Embassy massacre. It is all part of the harsh world of *realpolitik*.

The regime's attempt to secure its international flanks depended on a web of alliances far beyond the reach of the Reagan Administration. There is no Washington-controlled super-plot here; though some countries act directly as surrogate forces, serving American ends, others — with foreign policy agendas of their own — may in fact operate counter to US interests.

Even at the immediate regional level, United States options are far from absolute. Since the fall of the Somoza regime in Nicaragua in 1979, Washington has sponsored successive attempts to build a new regional counterinsurgency bloc, and one of the main stumbling-blocks has been the incorporation of Guatemala. The first attempt, in August 1979, was the so-called Iron Triangle of El Salvador, Honduras and Guatemala; it faltered at that time for the dearth of *any* democratic credentials. Next came the "Strategic Triangle", in which more palatable countries — Costa Rica, the Dominican Republic and Colombia — were to be enlisted as pincer states, where US troops would come and go freely. As Congress lagged on allocating funds for upgrading airstrips in those three countries, a new idea was born: that of the Central American Democratic Community. By now, Honduras and El Salvador had been through the "laundering" process of elections, and the new grouping gathered to isolate revolutionary Nicaragua. But the Democratic Community quickly became moribund — not to mention a contradiction in terms — when the Administration urged the inclusion of Guatemala. Even the Community's key members could not agree among themselves on Guatemala's democratic credentials: though the Salvadorean Christian Democrats hailed the March 1982 coup as a step in the right direction, Costa Rica in particular was cool towards Ríos Montt. Newly elected President Luís Alberto Monge derided the coup as "failing to offer the Guatemalan people any way out of chaos".

With the Malvinas–Falklands war in the summer of 1982, US hopes of rehabilitating Guatemala took a further nose-dive. Guatemala, identifying with its own long-simmering claims to Belize, ardently took the Argentine side, placing 350 paratroopers and marines on standby to be flown to Port Stanley for combat duty if requested.[25]

The Argentine connection was nothing new: relationships with the Southern Cone dictatorships had long been a part of Guatemala's attempt to break out of international isolation by joining forces with other pariah nations. The London *Guardian* had reported the presence of Argentine and Chilean torture specialists in Guatemala under Lucas; others alleged that Guatemalan soldiers and police were taking courses, including interrogation techniques, from Southern Cone mentors — 200 in Argentina and a further 175 in Chile.[26] In the summer of 1981, sophisticated Argentine computer analysis methods (using Israeli hardware) had been crucial in detecting and breaking 27 guerrilla safe-houses in Guatemala City.[27] Under Ríos Montt, the Southern Cone connection only intensified, and Economy Minister Julio Matheu returned from a trip in October 1982 with extensive new trade agreements with both Argentina and Chile.

Other sympathetic members of the "Pariah International" have also rallied to the Guatemalan cause: South Africa has offered to send counterinsurgency troops, while Chairman of the Taiwanese Joint Chiefs of Staff, Admiral Chang Chi-Soong assured Guatemala that the US arms embargo would not be allowed to affect existing Taiwanese military assistance or officer training programmes.[28]

The Israeli Connection — Not Just Guns[29]

The tightest role is played by Israel, and in no other case does the independent foreign policy agenda of a Guatemalan ally dovetail so neatly with the role of a loyal US surrogate. In June 1982, Israeli armoured divisions invaded Lebanon. At once, the parallels resonated through Central American military circles. Defence Minister José Guillermo García of El Salvador spoke wistfully of making a pre-emptive strike at Managua of the same kind that Israel had launched against Beirut, frustrated that his hands were tied by Washington. The analogy between the Sandinistas and the Palestine Liberation Organization (PLO) were irresistible to the Right, the more so since State Department rationales for the "external" roots of the Central American crisis had dwelt so heavily on the small PLO presence in revolutionary Managua.

The Central American Right admired the Beirut summer on so many levels: to them, Israel appeared as a country that used decisive military force to resolve its contradictions, did so in open defiance of world opinion (particularly attractive to the chauvinistic Guatemalan military) and was able to bend Washington to its will. And behind the militarist posture was a solid-looking parliamentary democracy, with an agrarian sector that seemed both technologically efficient and socially visionary.

In Guatemala, the metaphor was stretched furthest. There, rightists spoke openly of the "Palestinianization" of the nation's rebellious Mayan Indians. By the end of *Plan Victoria 82,* with its accompanying talk of a new "integrated nationalism", the Indians — with up to 100,000 languishing in exile in Mexico and a further million displaced inside Guatemala — began to look very much like a people stripped of a homeland. Army planners, when considering long-range resettlement plans for the Indians, looked hard at Israeli agricultural settlements as a model for reworking the devastated rural highland economy.

Israeli penetration of Central America as a weapons supplier is by now fairly well-established: Defence Minister Ariel Sharon pays a lightning visit to Honduras in late 1982 with his Air Force chief; short take-off and landing Arava aircraft are the favourite choice of rural counterinsurgency strategists; Galil assault rifles and light, stubby Uzi sub-machine-guns are standard issue light arms. After the rout of PLO centres in Beirut, Sharon offered captured PLO weapons free to any Central American army willing to pay transportation costs.

Even with all this, Guatemalan–Israeli relations remain something of a special case, and touch areas well beyond arms supplies. The ties date back to 1948, when Guatemala provided one of three United Nations commissioners charged with overseeing the creation of the Jewish state. Jorge García Granados, later to be a close political associate of Lucas García, used his tenure as Guatemalan ambassador to the United Nations to strengthen the connection, and Guatemala has taken a loyal and dependable pro-Israel stance ever since in international forums.

Nowadays, Israel's role in Central America forms part of a concerted diplomatic offensive, which responds to Israel's need for foreign allies and the demands of an economy top-heavy with arms exports. In 1982, the number of Latin American military attachés in Israel doubled to a dozen. The Israelis are more than happy for these bilateral ties to serve the United States' geopolitical interests in the region. Israeli Minister of Economic Coordination Ya'acov Meridor told a gathering of Israeli businessmen in 1981 that "Israel coveted the job of top Washington proxy in Central America".

Arms remain the most visible and highly publicized evidence. Until the mid-1970s, Guatemala's military needs were supplied mainly by obsolete US war matériel. But in 1975, Israel stepped into the gap which opened with British pressure on the Ford Administration not to supply arms that might be used in an invasion of Belize and widened with the Carter era human rights policies. In 1975, it made its first delivery of Arava aircraft, and followed up with artillery and small arms, including 10 RBY armoured cars. With the Aravas came technicians and military advisers. After the US decision to suspend arms shipments in 1977, Israel became Guatemala's principal supplier. In 1980, the Army was fully re-equipped with Galil rifles at a cost of $6 million; in the same year, Guatemala began to make inquiries about acquiring the advanced Kfir jet fighter-bomber, though negotiations on the purchase were stalled because the Kfir — which uses an American-made engine — is thereby blocked by US legislation prohibiting the sale of Israeli weapons systems using US-manufactured components.

Agreements for large-scale police assistance, again designed to replace a defunct US programme, were sealed by the visit of Interior Minister Donaldo Alvarez Ruíz to Israel in March 1980. Since then, Israeli advisers have worked closely with Guatemalan police intelligence (G-2), and both the London *Guardian* and the Tel Aviv newspaper *Haolam Hazeh* reported in December 1981 that Israel was collaborating with Argentina in Guatemala on specialized electronic surveillance techniques, interrogation and even torture methods.

With the advice came the latest in electronic hardware. Star exhibit was the new Army Transmissions and Electronics School, opened in 1981 by President Lucas García. Designed, staffed and funded by Israelis, its sophisticated systems were unprecedented in Central America. At the school's opening ceremony, then Israeli Ambassador Moshe Dayan (no relation to the late Defence Minister) hailed Guatemala as "one of our best friends", and promised that further technical and scientific assistance programmes would follow.

> "Guatemala is one of our best friends."
> Israeli ambassador to Guatemala Moshe Dayan, 1981.

The adulation was reciprocal: on the military front, Defence Minister Benedicto Lucas García praised Israel for the "gigantic job" it was doing on behalf of the Guatemalan armed forces. Yet for all the ideological affinities between the rightist Begin and Lucas governments, the Israeli role became even more marked with the Ríos Montt coup. Tel Aviv newspapers reported that 300 Israeli advisers had been instrumental in the execution of the coup, and Ríos Montt himself paid homage to their role, acknowledging to an ABC reporter that the bloodless operation had gone off so smoothly "because many of our soldiers were trained by Israelis".

But military aid was only the tip of the iceberg. The new Israeli technology, for example, had civilian as well as military applications. The radar system at La Aurora international airport is run by Israeli technicians, while others instruct government bureaucrats in the use of computerized information and management systems. As Guatemala's economic crisis has bitten deeper, Israel has helped the military regime to ride out the recession. Soon after Ríos Montt's seizure of power, new Minister of Economy Matheu made a visit to Israel, and a new Trade and Economic Co-operation Agreement, one of his first priorities.

Guatemala also relied on Israel to revive its wilting tourist industry. Bilateral tourism agreements were signed in March 1982, and reports were that the Guatemalan tourist board INGUAT was targeting Jewish communities in New York City, Miami and Los Angeles for the promotion of tourism in Guatemala. In return, parallel cultural agreements have brought a regular flow of Israeli programmes to Guatemalan radio.

The Israeli national airline El Al, Guatemala's Aviateca, and Air Florida have held discussions on joint tourist promotion campaigns involving Guatemala City's Sheraton Hotel, locally owned by the Kong family, which has extensive links with the far-right MLN.

As a token of Guatemala's gratitude for this Israeli assistance, current Israeli Ambassador Elieser Armon is now the proud wearer of the highest honour awarded in Guatemala — the Order of the Quetzal (Grand Cross). At the award ceremony, Armon was lauded by his hosts for "boosting the programme under which Guatemalan grant-holders have gone to study on a wide range of specialized training courses which Israeli instructors have given here in a broad variety of productive activities."

The majority of these exchange study programmes have concentrated on the agrarian sector, and agriculture may well hold the key to Israel's current political role in Guatemala. The opposition URNG certainly sees it that way. In the rural areas, they identify an interlocking mosaic of assistance programmes — weapons to help the Guatemalan Army crush resistance and lay waste to the countryside, security and intelligence advice to control the civilian population and agrarian development models to construct on the ashes of the highlands.

This type of collaboration began under the 1974-8 regime of General Kjell Laugerud García, when the Guatemalan Army first displayed interest in co-operatives as a limited way of defusing social tensions in the countryside. Colonel Fernando Castillo Ramírez, director of the National Co-operative Institute (and at the same time an expert Arava pilot) travelled to Israel in 1977 and flew back much impressed with the kibbutz system. He was joined by Leonel Girón, in charge of land colonization programmes in the *Franja Transversal del Norte*. In return, Israeli advisers arrived in Guatemala to plan civic action programmes in the conflictive Ixcán area, heartland of support for the EGP, and scene of continual military repression of local co-operative members.

1978 saw the initiation of a two-year programme of grants for Guatemalan officials to study co-operativization and rural development under the auspices of the Israeli Foreign Ministry's International Co-operation Division. A steady stream of planners, economists and credit managers flowed from the National Agricultural Development Bank (BANDESA), the General Directorate of Agrarian Services (DIGESA) and the National Institute of Agrarian Transformation (INTA).

The Lucas regime proved particularly interested in Israel's Rehovot land settlement centre. Here were workable models of rural development which precluded the need for agrarian reform. Colonization projects in the occupied territories were carried out under strict military supervision, expressly designed to colonize and redevelop infertile lands, often clashing with the wishes of a hostile local population. Some elements of the Israeli kibbutz and the cash crop *moshav* found their way into Lucas' ill-fated Integral Plan of Rural Communities in 1979, a programme of agricultural development in highland zones of conflict.

Again, what developed unevenly under Lucas was magnified and systematized under Ríos Montt. Under the Plan of Assistance to Conflict Areas (PAAC), launched in August 1982, the Israeli agrarian model became more explicit. The Guatemalan military also acknowledges today that the PAAC is influenced by co-operatives in Taiwan and the agricultural communes of South Korea, two other staunch US allies that have provided object lessons in efficient land use in heavily militarized societies. PAAC Director Colonel Eduardo Wohlers admitted in 1983, however, that Israel remained the main inspiration:

> Many of our technicians are Israeli-trained. The model of the kibbutz and the moshav is planted firmly in their minds, and personally I think it would be fascinating to turn our highlands into that kind of system.

There are still deeper parallels between the actions of the Guatemalan military in the Indian highlands and Israeli tactics in the West Bank and other occupied territories. Armed village committees in Israeli settlements prefigure Guatemala's ubiquitous Civil Defence patrols. Like the Israelis, the Guatemalan Army has designated tame local mayors from indigenous communities. One Catholic priest interviewed in Guatemala City even suggested that the promotion of Catholic–evangelical factionalism in an effort to divide and conquer communities is the result of Israeli guidance, based on the successful exploitation of rivalries between Christian, Moslem and Druse communities in Lebanon.

Washington Dollars

The announcement in January 1983 that the Reagan Administration intended to send military assistance to Guatemala was far from the end of a running skirmish with Congress. It had taken the Administration the whole of its first year just to get Representatives Michael D. Barnes (Democrat–Maryland) and Stephen J. Solarz (Democrat–New York) to withdraw proposed legislation that would have formalized the ban on arms transfers in exchange for a "gentlemen's agreement" with Assistant Secretary of State Enders that Congress would be consulted for its approval in advance.[30]

Kicking off the Ríos Montt round of its propaganda onslaught, the Administration found itself countered by a stream of hostile reports to Congress from international human rights groups. The reports hammered home not only the Guatemalan armed forces' unequivocal responsibility for massacres but the fact that the political system which Ríos Montt was promoting was the antithesis of the vaunted "democratic opening". The Guatemalan regime had already been fighting its own battles against the human rights community — labelling the July 1982 Amnesty International report charging "massive extrajudicial executions" as "a horror story conceived by an insane writer". The United States Embassy now took up the charge with a vengeance. Attacking groups such as Americas Watch and the Washington Office on Latin America (WOLA), it reserved its greatest wrath for Amnesty, which received a five-page letter from Enders disputing its conclusions and accusing it of lacking professionalism and relying on biased sources.

As allies in the public relations fight, the Administration enlisted the support of a wide range of conservative lobbies — not only New Rightists within the coalition, but corporate groupings with economic interests in the region. Their role was both to apply direct pressure on Congress and to counteract mounting disquiet at closer links with Guatemala's military rulers.

Not surprisingly, all the leading lights of conservative evangelism and the "electronic church" rallied round Ríos Montt's cause, from Billy Graham and Jerry Falwell, to Bill Bright's Campus Crusade for Christ and the Christian Broadcasting Network. Soon after the coup, Ríos Montt was telling bewildered reporters that he expected a billion dollars from the evangelical connection. Scaling down the General's hyperbole only somewhat, evangelical leaders themselves reckoned that their "International Lovelift" could channel $10 million into Army redevelopment plans for the Indian highlands. Within a few months of the first offers, boats from California and the Gulf Coast ports began shipments of building and roofing materials for the new rural settlements. The Christian Broadcasting Network dispatched teams of agricultural and medical technicians to help design the "model villages".[31]

More importantly, the evangelicals flexed their muscles inside the Administration itself. Prominent born-again members of the Reagan team, including White House adviser Ed Meese, Deputy United Nations Ambassador William P. Middendorf and Interior Secretary James Watt, held enthusiastic meetings in Washington with top Ríos Montt aides.[32] The evangelical movement used its extensive media access and its highly mobilized mass base to help neutralize the impact on Congress of progressive Roman Catholic opinion and the socially oriented programmes of the Protestant National Council of Churches. For the US Embassy in Guatemala City, all these were vital services in combatting what it believed to be a "Communist-backed disinformation campaign".[33]

Finding ways to circumvent opposition from human rights organizations and Congress to military aid was only part of the story. That might help the Guatemalan government stave off military defeat, but the bullets alone would be useless without the commitment of hard cash to rescue Guatemala's tottering economy. And for the US Administration, that meant turning the clock back on economic as well as military aid sanctions.

In 1977, the Carter Administration's International Financial Institutions Act included Guatemala on a list of gross and consistent violators of human rights. That Act prevented US representatives from supporting multilateral loans to Guatemala through either the World Bank or the InterAmerican Development Bank (IDB) unless they demonstrably financed "basic human needs".

> "Improvement of communications in zones where the government is committing atrocities is a form of indirect military aid." Representative Jerry Patterson, chairman of the House Banking Subcommittee.

In November 1981, though abstaining from the final vote, the Reagan Administration had privately lobbied in favour of a $75 million IDB loan for hydroelectric energy. A month later, it tried to steamroller through the House of Representatives Banking Sub-Committee an $18 million IDB loan for a rural telephone network. When Chairman Jerry Patterson (Democrat–California) of this oversight committee protested that such a loan did not serve the basic human needs of the Indian highlands, the Administration backed down. Worse for them, Patterson angrily drew attention to the logic connecting economic and military assistance. "Improvement of communications in zones where the government is committing atrocities," he stressed, "is a form of indirect military aid."

By June 1982, three months after the coup, the Administration felt ready to test the waters again. This time, they re-submitted the telecommunications loan with the audacious argument that Guatemala was no longer a gross human rights violator — there was no further pretence that the loan would meet basic human needs. On 29 September, 1982, the Administration formally erased Guatemala from the list of human rights offenders. The policy change immediately affected six World Bank and IDB loans, worth a total of $170 million. Only strictly economic criteria would henceforth apply to loan requests; IDB applications would be considered case by case on their merits. A $71 million slice of IDB funds would now cover the rural telephone network, small industrial development and specialized rural education. The World Bank would weigh in with $100 million more.[34] The decision not only opened the door for multilateral finance, but for the extension of bilateral aid through the Agency for International Development (AID), previously subject to the same criteria; to OPIC guarantees for oil exploration and for Export–Import Bank credits. It also permitted the last-minute assignation of $11 million to Guatemala under Reagan's Caribbean Basin Initiative.[35]

Welcoming the coup, US Ambassador Chapin promised that his government would provide up to $50 million in economic assistance. Its primary goal was the war zone of the north-west, paying for small new agricultural production units and access roads in the Indian highlands. Further AID initiatives included a $20.1 million investment guarantee for low-cost housing as well as government-sponsored colonization and resettlement programmes in the northern lowlands.[36] As in the 1960s and 1970s, US aid strategies continue to centre on support for the export sector of the Guatemalan economy. But this time around, as well as going directly to traditional élites, the money for "development" around the strategic hamlets will be closely tied to the success of the counterinsurgency war.

What Friends for the Left?

The decline of US hegemony in Central America has of course opened up space for new actors such as Mexico, Venezuela and the European social democracies — none of whom has any vested stake in a military-ruled Guatemala — to play a role in determining the outcome of the crisis. A central goal of the revolutionary movement has been to raise the profile of the Guatemalan war in the international arena. In 1983, international sympathy for the plight of the Guatemalan people was simmering, and reports of widespread atrocities under Ríos Montt had gained worldwide notoriety, but the sympathy had not yet matured into tangible diplomatic terms. The Socialist International issued a denunciation of the military's systematic extermination of the Indian population, but pointedly refrained from any more active political initiative.[37] Above all, Mexico — the prime mover of diplomatic initiatives over El Salvador and Nicaragua — held its fire.

Asked in 1982 about the differences between his country's activist role in the Franco-Mexican declaration on El Salvador in 1981 and its caution over events in Guatemala, then Foreign Minister Jorge Castañeda noted that, "In the case of Guatemala, the right moment has not occurred in the international arena to allow us to take a similar step."[38] What steps any country might or could take requires a complex analysis of its own internal political balances, its international alliances, the role of its foreign policy in relation to its domestic policy and in relation to the United States and Central America. For Mexico, that means weighing elements such as its attitude towards Guatemalan refugees in Chiapas, the use of progressive Third World-oriented foreign policy rhetoric as a means of securing the continued "revolutionary" prestige of the ruling PRI at home, ongoing bilateral negotiations with the US on matters of trade and immigration. But, generally speaking, one can expect changes in the international balance of forces around Guatemala as Castañeda's "right moment" approaches.

Before this can happen, the Guatemalan Left must clearly pose itself as a force to be reckoned with. One aspect of this will be to push to higher levels of military capability, proving their bargaining power as a real political alternative and galvanising the support of many inside the country who fear the repercussions of premature exposure.

Guatemala's revolutionary movement faces peculiar difficulties here. It is the most genuinely indigenous of all the Central American movements, and its growth owes nothing to assistance from Cuba and the Soviet Union. This is not yet Nicaragua or El Salvador, and the struggle may not reach that pitch for some time to come. The regime, despite intense difficulties, has not yet been seriously threatened with overthrow; until that happens, potential international sympathizers with the Left will not risk overplaying their hand. In the polarization of Guatemala's political conflict, furthermore, moderate democratic allies have found few straws to grasp; conventional notions of a political centre were eliminated here long before they were in El

Salvador. Guatemala's Christian Democrats have firmly kept their distance from the revolutionary camp; its social democrats — represented by two parties, the PSD and the FUR — are weak inside the country. Though they will in due course have a significant role to play (as will the communist PGT) in determining international alliances, they are not yet sufficiently engaged in the unification process of the Left to have much impact.

All this implies that the Guatemalan revolutionaries achieve a more consolidated and operative degree of unity than they yet have. Part of the problem is the lingering unity problem on the ground; part of it is the concomitant difficulty of building a coherent diplomatic voice that can represent their fight abroad. Together with this, the revolutionary forces must convince sceptical foreign powers of their commitment to a revolution which is "democratic, pluralist and non-aligned". The Reagan Administration has worked overtime to paint the popular movement in Central America, and the Sandinista government in Nicaragua, as totalitarian puppets of the Soviet Union. But that effort, if directed against the Guatemalan Left, is likely to founder on the difficulty of depicting the status quo as democratic.

As the Somoza regime in Nicaragua began to crumble in early 1979, Mexico carefully engaged its diplomacy to ease out a military dictatorship while at the same time pressing for the moderation of the revolutionary transition that would inevitably follow. Panama, Costa Rica, Venezuela and others played their role too. "The region is living through its hour of change," said Mexican Foreign Minister Castañeda more than two years after the fall of Somoza, "and our nation must come to terms with that fact."[39] Reagan's response has been to set his back against the minute-hand. Yet, although briefly boosted by Reagan's declarations of support, the Guatemalan military otherwise did little under Ríos Montt to break out of the international isolation into which it sank under Lucas García. In the sphere of international diplomacy, it is the Left that has everything to play for.

Notes

1. Author's interview with local commander, El Quiché, 25 August, 1982.
2. Edward J. Walsh, "Strategic Guatemala: Next Red Plum in the Hemisphere?" in *National Defense: The Journal of the Defense Preparedness Association* (Arlington, Virginia) October 1981.
3. Antonio Cavalla Rojas, "Guatemala en la estrategia militar de los Estados Unidos", in *Cuadernos de Marcha* (November-December 1980).
4. *New York Times,* 1 June, 1980.
5. Institute for Policy Studies *Resource Update,* June 1982; *Washington Post,* 25 April, 1978.
6. Allan Nairn, "Controversial Reagan Campaign Links with Guatemalan Government and Private Sector Leaders", *COHA Research Memorandum,* 30 October, 1980.
7. Ibid.
8. *New York Times,* 16 December, 1981.

9. See, "Cuban Support for Terrorism and Insurgency in the Western Hemisphere", statement by Thomas O. Enders to the Senate Subcommittee on Security and Terrorism, 12 March, 1982; Statement of Deputy Assistant Secretary of State Stephen W. Bosworth before the Subcommittee on Human Rights and International Organisations and the Subcommittee on Inter-American Affairs of the House Foreign Affairs Committee, 30 July, 1981.

10. "Cuba's Renewed Support for Violence in Latin America", State Department, *Special Report,* No. 90, 14 December, 1981.

11. *Washington Post,* 18 April, 1982.

12. Nairn, "Controversial Campaign Links".

13. *Miami Herald,* 17 April, 1982.

14. The notion is cogently debunked by Allan Nairn in his opinion piece, "Guatemala Can't Take Two Roads", *New York Times,* 20 July, 1982.

15. *Latin America Weekly Report,* 27 August, 1982.

16. Institute for Policy Studies, *Resource Update,* March 1983, citing *Prensa Libre,* 8 January, 1983.

17. *New York Times,* 8 January and 5 February 1983.

18. *New York Times,* 19 December, 1982

19. *Latin America Regional Report,* 19 January, 1983.

20. Sources on the Bell helicopter sales include: *Washington Post,* 23 January, 1981; the *Guardian* (London), 3 January, 1983; *Fort Worth Star Telegram,* 15 December, 1982; International Institute for Strategic Studies (London), *The Military Balance 1982-83*; National Action/Research on the Military-Industrial Complex (NARMIC), *The Central American War: A Guide to the U.S. Military Build-Up,* Philadelphia, 1982.

21. *New York Times,* 19 December, 1982; *In These Times* (Chicago), 23-7 November, 1982.

22. *Excélsior,* 19 July, 1981.

23. Ibid, 23 October, 1982; Arnson and Montealegre, *IPS Update,* June 1982.

24. *Inforpress,* 1 July, 1982.

25. Paris AFP in Spanish, 1630 GMT, 3 June, 1982, in *FBIS,* 4 June, 1982.

26. The *Guardian* (London), 29 December, 1981; Testimony by former Interior Ministry Press Secretary Elías Barahona, in Guatemala News and Information Bureau (GNIB), *Guatemala* (Berkeley, California), November 1982.

27. *Latin America Political Report,* 6 November, 1981.

28. *IPS Resource Update,* June 1982.

29. The section on Israeli–Guatemalan relations is drawn from, *inter alia, Haolam Hazeh* (Tel Aviv), 12 April, 1982; *Miami Herald,* 13 December, 1982; The *Guardian,* 29 December, 1981; numerous issues of the Guatemalan government newspaper *El Diario de Centroamérica;* correspondence with Professor Benjamin Beit-Hallahmi of the University of Haifa, Israel, whose original research is gratefully acknowledged.

30. *Washington Post,* 23 January, 1982.

31. *New York Times,* 20 May, 1982.

32. CBS Television, "Guatemala", Special Report, 1 September, 1982.

33. Document received by congressional offices, Autumn 1982, cited in Jonas, "Counterinsurgency State", p.50.

34. Center for International Policy, *Aid Memo,* October 1982.

35. Ibid.

36. Arnson and Montealegre, *IPS Update,* June 1982.

37. See Gregorio Selser, "Presencia de la Internacional Socialista en América Latina y el Caribe", in CECADE–CIDE, *Centroamérica: Crisis y Política Internacional* (Mexico, 1982), pp.269-312.

38. *Unomásuno,* 23 June, 1982.

39. Interview with UPI, 24 November, 1981.

8. The War Goes On

23 March, 1983: in the leafy square outside the National Palace, the Army has built a monument to commemorate the first anniversary of the coup, a year of what Ríos Montt calls *"la nueva Guatemala"*. Even by Central American standards, it is an ugly memorial: merely a plain metal flagpole let into a crude concrete plinth.

The desultory crowd of curious passers-by is almost outnumbered by the armed ranks of camouflage-uniformed *kaibiles*. The keynote speaker, too, wears the maroon beret with the yellow flash of the *kaibil*. He is Lieutenant Héctor Mauricio López Bonilla, youngest and fieriest of the council of young officers who act as Ríos Montt's advisers. In the ring of dignitaries behind the podium, there is no sign of official delegations from the Catholic Church, the political parties who originally supported the coup or the private business federations. The parties are locked away in their headquarters preparing angry press statements condemning Ríos Montt's refusal to schedule elections. This is a government in deep trouble.

Even the Army is in bad shape. All week, the capital has buzzed with the latest in a series of coup rumours. The man tipped to take over this time is General Federico Fuentes Corado, a dapper young reformist who runs the National Reconstruction Committee. As the young lieutenant concludes his ringing appeal for a new military populism, a patter of applause runs through the crowd, barely loud enough to be picked up on the waiting television and radio microphones. His president claps noisily, but the rest of the Army high command stands stony-faced. In the barracks later, the talk is resentful. One former Defence Minister complains that "the Army is now being run by captains and little lieutenants". The upper echelons are especially nervous of López Bonilla; the young lieutenant reminds the old guard uncomfortably of a young and rebellious officer from an earlier generation — Luís Turcios Lima, who ended up leaving the Army and founding Guatemala's first ever guerrilla movement.

The Guatemalan Right has bought itself a little time, but at enormous political cost. It has emerged from the euphoric illusion of success which the scorched earth policies of 1982 briefly brought it, to recognise that none of its fundamental problems are solved, and its room for manoeuvre has shrunk. Political and economic setbacks, coupled with heavy military casualties in combat, made 1982 an arduous year for the regime, despite its veneer of self-confidence. The war is not over; Guatemala still has the most skewed distribution of wealth in all Central America, and reform is explicitly not on the agenda; the economic crisis has bitten deeper, hitting the mass of Guatemalans harder than ever. The objective reasons of revolt remain.

Worst of all for the bourgeoisie, the Ríos Montt offensive failed to wipe out the Left, even using the largest and best trained counterinsurgency force in Central America at full stretch. The core structures of the Left —rooted in 29 years of history — survived one of the most coherent, sustained and sanguinary counterinsurgency campaigns ever unleashed in Latin America. The country is militarized as never before, and class conflict has been polarized beyond easy repair. The essence of Ríos Montt's mandate was to win the war; without this, the ruling élites could not seriously begin to address their deep-rooted crisis of power.

The brutality of *Plan Victoria 82* was explicitly aimed at breaking the EGP, strongest of the four guerrilla groups, and military action was accordingly centred in huge sweeps through the highlands of El Quiché, Huehuetenango and other highland *departamentos*. The civilian base was battered and traumatized by the terror, but the EGP itself withdrew to its old strongholds, with its military forces in good order. Having swept through the north-west, the Army then moved on in the early months of 1983 to the ORPA-held areas of San Marcos on the Mexican border. There, the different nature of ORPA's organizing work dictated different Army tactics; instead of sweeping through villages —since ORPA did not aim to organize villages into formal support structures — the tendency was towards kidnappings, selective house-to-house raids and occasional aerial bombing and strafing. In El Petén in the north, areas of strong FAR influence too were hit by Army attacks, though these received much less publicity.

> "We simply cannot understand why a people must suffer so much to achieve their freedom." Rigoberta Menchú, Quiché woman whose father died in the Spanish Embassy massacre.

What did *Plan Victoria 82* actually achieve? It massacred anything from 5,000 to 10,000 unarmed *campesinos*. It uprooted perhaps a million more from their homes for several months. It drove tens of thousands more into exile in a straggle of camps in southern Mexico, and all available testimony shows that they blame the Army for their predicament. Large stretches of the highlands were left devastated; the local economy in turmoil.

At the most, the Army could argue that it had begun to control the population by creating the nation-wide network of Civil Defence Patrols designed to kill peasant morale and divide the communities. It could also

General Oscar Mejía Víctores   George Black

claim to have confused segments of the Guatemalan urban middle class
and the international community. But those are essentially pyrrhic
victories. Both were part of a larger political strategy — involving the
permanent mobilization of large sectors of the population — which quickly
ran out of steam. This kind of populism needs a backbone, and press-
ganged peasants and evangelical fanaticism are a poor substitute for a
political party or a trade union movement, especially when the Catholic
majority of Guatemalans mobilize in response. The huge turnouts for the
Papal visit in March 1983 were a stinging rebuff for Ríos Montt's spiritual
alternative, and the middle classes and business interests who once found
the general's televised Sunday homilies amusing — if not attractive — were
widely outraged by their sanctimonious unpredictability at the end of a
year. The conservative Bishops' Conference, too, awoke from its slumbers to
deliver an outspoken condemnation of Ríos Montt's "fanatical sectarian-
ism", fearing — as did some military officers — that the promotion of
evangelical sects could get out of hand and even lay the basis for a religious
war.

The Evolving Military Situation

After a year of fierce fighting, the Army faced an acute dilemma. It was run ragged trying to control the population, supervise the untrustworthy Civil Defence Patrols and guard the strategic hamlets. Perhaps two-thirds of its total troop strength in early 1983 was tied up in securing El Quiché and Huehuetenango; whole areas where the Left was relatively strong — such as the *bocacosta* and the plantation areas — were seriously neglected by the Army, much to the disgust of local landowners. Military casualty levels in all areas of combat were alarmingly high.

To move beyond the holding operation of 1982 and 1983, the armed forces had little alternative but to increase their absolute size and firepower. The military budget for 1983 soared by 62% to $142 million, but as El Salvador has

General Efraín Ríos Montt

amply demonstrated, a guerrilla war cannot be won by throwing money at it. Increasing the Army's size and effectiveness is fraught with political complications. The Guatemalan officer corps is by and large more professional than its Salvadorean counterpart, but its teenage Indian recruits are poorly disciplined and morale is low. Recruitment becomes ever harder. There are real limits to the speed with which such an Army can absorb new training and matériel; again, the poor performance and low re-enlistment rates in special US-trained battalions in El Salvador illustrate the problem. And if these strictly military considerations were not enough, there was also increasing political fragmentation at the command level after a year of Ríos Montt.

Though helpful surrogates such as Israel and Argentina may continue to play their part, the scale of expansion which the Guatemalan Army will need can only ultimately come with large infusions of US assistance. But can the Guatemalans boost their strength and win the war without again repeating the monstrous level of human rights violations that made Congress so mulish and tied Reagan's hands?

Nor was there any sign that the Army could follow its 1982 sweeps, as military logic demanded, with direct assaults on the strategic military forces of the Left. The breathtaking savagery of Ríos Montt's first months had found the Left unprepared. Though confident that it had learned the lessons of the 1960s, and would no longer expose its civilian supporters to military terror, the guerrilla infrastructure in 1982 was still inadequate in many communities to withstand such an unprecedented onslaught. In other areas, political work had far outstripped military preparedness. The Left now traces these weaknesses back to the over-optimism which set in after the Sandinista victory in Nicaragua in 1979 — that same "triumphalism" that had led the FMLN in El Salvador to over-estimate its strength in the January 1981 "general offensive". The Guatemalan conjuncture had seemed so favourable: with Lucas in the saddle, polarizing society so fast and so clumsily, victory seemed only a matter of time.

This triumphalism had been spurred by — and in turn fuelled — massive support among the predominantly Indian population. Some parts of the north-west had come close to spontaneous insurrection, with peasants anxious to besiege military garrisons with only their own home-made weapons. The net effect had been to spread the movement's strength too thin — the most enthusiatic peasant supporters do not make a regular people's army overnight. It had been a boon under Lucas for the left to disperse its resources, keeping the Army off balance and shredding its morale; but under Ríos Montt it became a liability, as the Army concentrated its forces under new political camouflage and directed them at unarmed civilians the Left could not protect.

For the Left, the period of early 1983 was a time of taking stock of the previous year's setbacks, a time to devise new modes of operation, revamp logistics and rethink military tactics. After the premature fervour of 1981, the movement retrenched into its strongholds in a mood of soberness.

Those "strategic rearguards" — the Ixcán and northern Huehuetenango for the EGP, San Marcos for ORPA and the Petén for the FAR — proved impossible nuts for the Army to crack. Their geography, much wilder than anything to be found in El Salvador, is vastly favourable to the guerrilla forces, and largely obviates the need for a second country to act as rearguard territory.

From these fastnesses, a new stage in the continuing war was launched. It was marked by continual harassment of the Army, designed to wear down troop morale. The kind of guerrilla activity which took place even in the heart of military-occupied areas of the highlands would have been hard to mount without continued civilian backing.[2] At the same time, the country as a whole has now been touched by the war. In the highlands, the military offensives of 1982 sucked into the conflict entire stretches which the Left had never penetrated.

If the harassment tactics against the Army proved successful, they would be followed — according to plan — by an escalation of the military level of the war. Columns would grow larger, combat more fierce, with vital stocks of weapons fed by successful encounters with government forces. This phase of *aniquilamiento y recuperación* — annihiliation and recovery (of arms) — would aim primarily at offsetting the Left's deficiencies in weaponry. If the re-escalation of the war worked, it would hope to be accompanied by increasing rank-and-file pressure to push ahead with the creation of a unified political front for the mass movement.[3]

The young and fragile unity of the Left was severely tested by the setbacks of 1982, but the original unitary agreements remained in force, and by early 1983 the process was once again underway. The signs of renewed unity began to show by the spring of 1983, on the military as well as the political level, with joint columns of fighters from more than one organization — under the single banner of the URNG — starting to conduct major actions.

The Narrowing Space for Manoeuvre

Where would the military regime turn next? It had exhausted much of its margin for manoeuvre in the fruitless search for a rapid victory in the field. The crisis of 1982 forced the ruling sectors to abandon their last fragile layer of legitimacy — elections. The pattern of presidential succession, controlled by a cabal of senior officers, was now broken.

In the process, it became impossible to conceal that there were now deep fissures within the military itself, within the civilian opposition and private sector, and between the two. The national economy, already stumbling, was further disrupted by the war effort. As the economic crisis worsened, further rifts opened between the armed forces and the businessmen of CACIF.

Whatever benefit of the doubt the civilian parties had given to the military evaporated at the coup anniversary celebrations on 23 March, 1983.

Politicians reacted with a mixture of anger and disillusionment to the much-vaunted package of three electoral laws unveiled that day by Ríos Montt. Their main expectation and demand had been an electoral timetable; but they were given no hint of a date. The far-right MLN derided the laws as "a mockery of the people ... [the new laws] aim only to put back the date of elections and allow the *de facto* government to remain in power indefinitely." Well might the MLN have complained: its supporters had, after all, drawn up the existing electoral register, which was believed to contain the names of 500,000 dead people whose identity cards were in the party's files.[4]

Two of the three new laws looked like delaying tactics. One proposed laborious and time-consuming machinery to appoint a Supreme Electoral Tribunal. A second — the Law of Registration of Citizens — called for issuing the population with new identity documents. Those who believed that the latter law was really designed to enhance the surveillance capacity of the security forces were hardly surprised that the documentation procedure — or *cedulación* — was placed in the hands of Colonel Jaime Rabanales, a fierce right-wing officer and close confidante of Lucas García.

But most controversial was the new law governing the formation of political organizations, whose purpose appeared to be to weaken the power of the traditional parties of the oligarchy and replace them with a party system of the Army's choosing. For a year after the coup, all party activity had been suspended. Parties were now required to re-register as "pro-party committees". Under previous legislation, they had required the signatures of 50,000 adherents to qualify for registration. Ríos Montt now lowered that figure to only 4,000, and new parties began to spring up on all sides.

In just two months, 16 new political parties — in addition to the eight "traditional" parties — applied for registration. Some of the new groupings were little more than personal vehicles for ambitious local politicians. The *Coordinadora Nacional Democrática* backed General Angel Aníbal Guevara; the *Fuerza Democrática Popular* was headed by Francisco Reyes Ixcamey, defence lawyer for prisoners brought before the secret military tribunals until death threats forced him to step down. Other parties, with bizarre titles such as the *Movimiento Emergente de Concordia* and the *Partido Equicrático de Conciliación Nacional,* only demonstrated how far civilian politics had been reduced to an irrelevance. Of the 24 parties, the centrist Christian Democrats remained the furthest to the left on the political spectrum; they — like four other "traditional" parties — were by now split into warring factions.

By the spring of 1983, many had begun to speculate that the Army's eventual goal was to instal a carefully groomed civilian president at the head of a new official party, once the political system had been made watertight. The obvious historical parallel was with the tenure of Julio César Méndez Montenegro, the civilian figurehead for military rule between 1966 and 1970. But the second time around, the plan was rather more sophisticated, for it depended both on creating a new party apparatus from a vacuum and at the same time atomizing the traditional parties of the Right. The clearest clue to the military's intentions was the newly registered *Partido Social Cristiano* (Social Christian Party: PSC). Not to be confused with the rival Christian Democrats, the PSC put itself forward as a multi-class, populist party, an expression of the Ríos Montt mélange of quasi-developmentalist civilians and docile Indians, technocrats and evangel-icals. Insistent rumours in Guatemala City predicted that the eventual military–PSC presidential candidate would be Jorge Serrano Elías, the born-again evangelical named by Ríos Montt to be president of the Council of State. Another emerging early leader of the PSC was Carlos Gehlert Matta, one of a group of disaffected Christian Democrats who hoped to recruit middle-class support and wean it away from the divided ranks of their former party. In late May, Félix Zarazúa Patzán, one of the ten indigenous representatives on the Council of State, announced that he would "provide a group of Indian leaders for the ranks of the PSC".

But Zarazúa enjoyed no measurable support among the Indian communities; Gehlert and Serrano Elías represented no perceptible social base. Business looked sceptically at a party with no semblance of an economic programme and no contact with the entrenched agrarian and business élites. The Army's ambitious design to build a new institutional framework and a populist base seemed destined by mid-1983 to run aground, no matter how much leeway the military might seem to derive from its absolute monopoly of coercive power. Opponents of every political stripe recognized that if the elaborate goal of creating a façade of democratic civilian rule were to prove beyond the military's grasp, its centralization of power under Ríos Montt and the far-reaching institutional changes underway could equally well signify the foundations for a sustained period of open military dictatorship.

Battles with the Private Sector

The perilous state of the Guatemalan economy, however, remained the weakest link in the military's plan. The slump of 1980-1 only worsened in 1982-3. During 1982, 185 businesses went into liquidation; though most were small, even a number of multinational giants such as Nestlé, Sears-Roebuck and Kerns pulled out of Guatemala. Publicly owned corporations such as the merchant marine company FLOMERCA and the railway enterprise FEGUA, slid into bankruptcy, and the government could find no private investors willing to risk taking them over.[5] Investment confidence remained low, and the heavy flight of capital continued through 1982 and 1983 despite tight exchange controls. By the end of 1982, the current account deficit stood at $124 million.[6] In a May 1983 report, the Guatemalan Managers Association (AGG) characterized the period from 1979-82 as "crisis with well-being": 1982 onwards, they declared, had seen Guatemala enter an unprecedented phase of "crisis with instability".[7]

Yet the Army showed no clearer sign under Ríos Montt than it had under Lucas García that it had a coherent economic recovery policy. Nor did it seem any more willing to mend the rupture between the military and the civilian private sector over who controlled the direction of economic policy. Ríos Montt's advisers still resisted giving the business federation CACIF any major say in economic planning. Though CACIF won two cabinet positions, it was otherwise often side-stepped. A major package of economic proposals unveiled in October 1982 was presented neither to CACIF nor to any of its individual member chambers, but to a grouping of prominent individual capitalists known as the "Honourable 14", whose identity was kept a closely guarded secret.[8] CACIF voiced its resentment at this exclusion in the most strident terms, accusing the governmental team of economists and technocrats of inexperience and incompetence — a charge that bore more than a grain of truth. Import controls, declared CACIF, were "absurd". Moves against speculators, in line with the president's new moral order, constituted "a dictatorial threat to two million Guatemalan traders".[9] A fierce credit squeeze and high interest rates drove CACIF's blood pressure to the danger point.

The paradox is that there are few fundamental conflicts of economic objective. But history has decreed mutual bitterness and distrust between those who were once natural allies. In some broad areas of policy, of course, that congruence of interests will still show through. CACIF was in basic agreement for example — how could it not be? — with Ríos Montt's stated goal of reviving production and easing the foreign exchange crisis by placing the burden of austerity on the poor, as the IMF had demanded. In 1983, health, education and public works would be the worst casualties of an 11.3% budget cut. Nor did CACIF have many qualms about Ríos Montt's vigorous campaign to promote fresh foreign investment, including a revised petroleum code easing many of the former restrictions on drilling rights. When trade delegations from the United States, Israel and Taiwan poured into Guatemala during the summer of 1982 asking to set up assembly plants, the government rewarded them with a package of incentive legislation which included the tax-free import of raw materials and semi-finished goods.[10] Domestic private enterprise had no major conflict of interest with these new runaway shops.

Elsewhere, though, the picture changed to one of unremitting hostility. "Never before," the AGG report continued, "has the [state of] the economy been so deplorable."[11] Their complaints were directed at much more than just the imported effects of world recession and the export–import imbalance common to all the Central American economies. CACIF recommendations, above all from the strongest member fractions —the Chamber of Commerce and the modernized agro-industrialists — were ultra-liberalizing, in favour of a total unbridling of international trade. As such, they were diametrically opposed to what they saw as a state-interventionist — even dangerously left-wing — set of policies from Ríos

Montt, which would close up the Guatemalan economy and rob the private sector of many of its traditional prerogatives.

CACIF's main running battle with the government was over monetary policy: while agreeing that monetary stabilization was a key short-term objective, CACIF argued vehemently for a devaluation of the quetzal. Long pegged to the US dollar, by early 1983 it had lost 40% of its value on the parallel market. The private sector's prime target was Central Bank President Jorge González del Valle, a leading protagonist of import controls as a means of conserving scarce currency and a firm opponent of devaluation. Powerful agro-exporters promoted devaluation not only because it would make their thus-cheapened products more competitive on the international market; but also because it would help to ease their domestic indebtedness, since their swollen overseas dollar accounts would pay off more debts in quetzales than the prevailing exchange rate allowed.

Blocking devaluation as well as resisting the clamour for a moratorium on agricultural debt repayments, González de Valle instead offered the agro-exporters a $50 million credit line to roll over their obligations with the Central Bank.[12] CACIF, however, was not satisfied, and eventually the pressure told, forcing González del Valle to tender his resignation on 23 December. With his removal, Ríos Montt forfeited one of the few people on his team respected for both his professional talents and his moderate political views. At the same time, a joint CACIF–government advisory council was set up, giving the private sector a greater role in economic legislation. Business delegates on the Council of State continued to harangue government economic policies. CACIF began to win further concessions for its members. For the industrialists, it got foreign exchange controls on capital goods imports relaxed for spare parts, tools and pharmaceutical inputs; for the agrarian oligarchy, the guarantee that land tenure patterns in place since 1954 would not be touched. The government was unable, then, to neutralize CACIF's influence; but the continuing conflict between the two guaranteed only further economic and political turmoil.

By the spring of 1983, remaining currency reserves were only sufficient to pay for two weeks worth of imports. The expensive rural pacification programme was draining resources at a vertiginous rate. This was not just a problem of diverting available funds — including foreign loans — to the war effort rather than the productive sector; it was also a problem of targetting the north-west *altiplano* at the expense of the rest of the country. Given Guatemala's history of extreme fiscal conservatism and the political unfeasibility of a progressive fiscal reform, low tax revenues could not be expected to underwrite the war effort. Instead, the Army would ask the upper echelons of private enterprise for a $60 million "voluntary" war tax. This proposal, involving contributions of $24 million from commerce, $15 million from industry, $12 million from bankers and $9 million from agriculturalists, was immediately decried by CACIF as "harebrained". The war would also mean a further curtailment of public expenditure and a decline in urban services — steps already in line with successive agreements with the IMF. These cutbacks, of course, falling heavily on transportation and higher education, would hit the urban middle classes — supposedly a bastion of support for the regime.

It seemed — and was — a Catch-22. Any break in the economic paralysis could only alienate the military's likeliest allies. Ultimately, the only road to economic recovery appeared to be through massive inflows of foreign aid and borrowing on foreign capital markets: to keep alive any hopes of an upturn in the Guatemalan economy over two to three years, upwards of $1 billion might be needed. Already, this has produced a substantial rise in Guatemala's traditionally low external debt; but that in turn generated yet another trap for the military. Historically afflicted with the isolationist desire to go it alone and damn the world, Guatemalan regimes have relied less heavily on foreign borrowing than other Central American republics. That chauvinism has led them to disregard the international repercussions of their monstrous human rights abuses. And today, the continuation of those abuses represents the largest obstacle to the needed inflow of foreign dollars, especially from those most disposed to help — the United States under Ronald Reagan.

The War Goes On

As the crisis intensifies in El Salvador and Nicaragua, the Reagan Administration will necessarily plunge deeper into the Guatemalan mire. The $10 million in US military assistance designated for Fiscal Year 1984 was a token that the Administration had the political will to stay the course; but the political hurdles would not go away.

The irony is that Washington's strongest regional protégé is a defiant pariah, with a deep-seated resentment against its historic mentor. Even Reagan's extravagant personal endorsement of Ríos Montt failed to bring a *rapprochement*. Within a month of the two men's meeting, the United States lifted the five-year military sales embargo, but Ríos Montt promptly declared he had no funds to meet the Americans' terms of cash on delivery; relations grew tenser. In March, Washington registered its complaint at Guatemala's secret tribunals, and Ambassador Frederic Chapin was briefly summoned home for consultations. A month later, Army Chief of Staff, General Mario López Fuentes scornfully dismissed US special envoy

> "Ríos Montt is as tough and murderous as the rest of them when you get underneath that veneer of piety."
> Representative Clarence Long, chairman of the House Appropriations Subcommittee on Foreign Operations.

Richard Stone — once a paid lobbyist for the Lucas García regime — as "a proconsul". Congress continued to be treated with equal contempt, and set its face against further aid. When Congressman Clarence D. Long, Democratic Chairman of the influential House Appropriations Sub-committee on Foreign Operations, visited Guatemala on a fact-finding mission, he was treated to the full wrath of Defence Minister Mejía Víctores, who accused him of speaking like an emissasry of the EGP and Amnesty International (the latter, if anything, a worse insult). Long, never one to mince words, returned home to declare that

> If the committee does anything for El Salvador it would be on the condition that Guatemala doesn't get a penny . . . Ríos Montt is as tough and murderous as the rest of them when you get underneath that veneer of piety."[13]

Can Reagan dare to continue selling the "new" Guatemala — whether under Ríos Montt or any plausible successor — as a democracy that must be defended? The US people have been dragged down that road before in El Salvador, only this time the options are even narrower. As in El Salvador, the commitment of the United States is primarily to form rather than to substance; in El Salvador, constituent assembly and presidential elections can be called unilaterally by Washington to satisfy the demand for political legitimacy — that is part of the "leverage" that accrues to the US as it takes over more and more directly the military conduct of the war. But in Guatemala there is no leverage. While international consumption demands democracy in Guatemala, the internal logic of political events there suggests its negation. Even the US Administration has found it impossible to sustain the fallacy: speaking before the General Assembly of the Organization of American States, Secretary of State Shultz lauded the hemispheric trend towards democracy, that illusion which Jeane Kirk-patrick gave to the world that authoritarian regimes could be democratised. El Salvador, of course, was the star turn. Even the dictatorships of Argentina and Uruguay, Shultz enthused, were examples of "democratic trans-formation". But Guatemala, pointedly, was no longer on his list.[14]

The summer months of 1983 saw the steady crumbling of the young officers' Promised Land. Ríos Montt's early promises of "no more bodies by the roadside" gave way once more to a steady resurgence of death squad victims in the main towns, kidnappings, disappearances, killings of university teachers and Christian Democratic politicians. Police corrup-tion and extortion took on an old, familiar look; one after another, old *luquista* faces began to creep back into public life. On 5 June, Guatemala's highest ranking Army General, Guillermo Echeverría Vielman, was cashiered for daring to demand prompt elections and an end to the military's monopoly — and abuse — of power. The hand of the MLN, ex-president Arana's CAN and the United States Embassy was variously detected behind the general's call. Three weeks later, amid the most serious threat so far of a coup, from former junta member Colonel Francisco

Gordillo and perennial MLN plotter Leonel Sisniega Otero, the clamour for a political opening became deafening.

Ríos Montt was a leader of great political astuteness, but by now he looked cornered. The Army gave him a week to defuse the crisis, and he responded with a package of crucial concessions, which guaranteed his temporary survival but eroded his power base. Ríos Montt offered elections for a Constituent Assembly on 29 July, 1984, to be followed by the drafting of a new constitution and presidential elections — these perhaps in 1985. In an even more surprising step, he sacked the key advisory council of young officers, who by this time appeared to have lost their ascendancy within the military. The fragile coalition around Ríos Montt had all but collapsed and he remained in power largely by virtue of his ability to divide and rule. The Ríos Montt experiment had always had the look of a wild card; if that desperate — though ambitious — last resort had now been played out, the utter fragmentation of the Guatemalan Right and its incapacity to resolve the challenge posed by the Left made it hard to discern any more viable alternative.

After 20 years of power with scarcely a coup, the Guatemalan Army had lost much of the cohesion that was bred within the hermetic confines of the *Escuela Politécnica.* The options for a post-Ríos Montt era were bewildering; which option would win out? The alternatives included:
1. a return to full-blooded right-wing militarism, headed by key figures from the Lucas era;
2. the creeping "Bolivianization" of the Guatemalan military, with one unstable fraction after another displacing each other through coup and counter-coup;
3. a bold US attempt to create a civilian reformist illusion, perhaps around Christian Democratic leader Vinicio Cerezo, to be immediately backed with large infusions of aid;
4. a US effort to keep Ríos Montt in the saddle against all odds until Constituent Assembly elections, when he could be substituted with an interim "president" akin to El Salvador's Alvaro Magaña.

No likely scenario carried real conviction. The dilemma for the United States is in many respects more complex than in El Salvador. In Guatemala, the political centre has withered and died; the military is not responsive to Washington, which is burdened with the monster it did so much to create. The Guatemalan bourgeoisie has a rare head-in-the-sand quality to it. Its domestic conflicts appear insoluble, but it refuses to recognize that reality. The durability of the Left; the real limits of the local military; the institutional weaknesses and schisms of the Right — all suggest that a protracted war of attrition, broken by nervous stand-offs, is the best that this ostrich-like élite can look forward to. Inevitably, Washington will be drawn into more direct management of the Guatemalan crisis.

In mid-1983, Washington still maintained a watchful distance. But a higher imperative than any qualms about human rights violations, or any anti-American nationalism in the local military, is that the United States had not yet *needed* to become directly enmeshed in Guatemalan politics in recent years. It will do so only when all other avenues are closed. This happened once in 1954, and again in 1967-8. Such a moment now seems set to recur, but this time in the context of an explosive regional war. The rhythm of that war is likely to overtake the slower rhythm with which Guatemala's long internal conflict can play itself out. Ríos Montt — even though he proved to be an historically ephemeral figure — set the scene for Guatemala to be sucked into a war without frontiers. "Central America," he announced in a televised Sunday homily in April 1983,

> is the backyard of the United States, so it is natural the owner of the house is concerned about regional security . . . And why shouldn't the owner of the house be the United States? When one considers that the distance between Guatemala and Los Angeles is much less than between Los Angeles and New York. This means that with missiles based in Guatemala, Russia could destroy Los Angeles at any time.

But the fact is that it will be neither Efraín Ríos Montt nor Ronald Reagan who thrusts Guatemala on to the East– West chessboard; it has been there since 1954, when the CIA installed a sleazy dictator named Colonel Carlos Castillo Armas in the National Palace. Guatemala's current crisis is the child of the first cold war. Indeed, along with Iran and Greece, it offered a cardinal definition of what the cold war was all about. Reagan's explicit resurrection of the Truman Doctrine in 1983 leaves little doubt that, in the new cold war, the renewed "defence" of Guatemala will again be considered ineluctable.

The murderous and unmediated war in Guatemala is far from over; it has lasted three decades already. On the larger backdrop of a Central American war in the 1980s, it has scarcely begun.

Notes

1. Conferencia Episcopal de Guatemala, *Confirmados en la fé*, May 1983.
2. *Inforpress,* 27 January, 1983.
3. NACLA interviews with opposition leaders in Mexico City, Autumn 1982.
4. *Latin America Weekly Report,* 1 July, 1983.
5. *El Día,* 22 May, 1983.
6. *Enfoprensa* (Mexico City), 31 January, 1983.
7. *Enfoprensa,* 15 May, 1983.
8. *Inforpress,* 11 November, 1982.
9. Guatemalan press reports, August 1982; *Inforpress,* 18 November, 1982.
10. *Business Latin America,* 7 July, 1982; *Inforpress,* 7 October, 1982.
11. *Enfoprensa,* 15 May, 1983.
12. *Inforpress,* 16 December, 1982.
13. Council on Hemispheric Affairs, *Washington Report on the Hemisphere,* 19 April, 1983.
14. George Shultz, "Reflections Among Neighbours", speech delivered to the General Assembly of the Organization of American States, Washington DC, 17 November, 1982.

Appendixes

Appendix 1
Strategy of the Guatemalan Army

The closest approximation to a political manifesto issued by the Ríos Montt regime was its 14-point outline of "Current National Objectives", issued on the day of the coup. Details of how this 14-point plan, and the accompanying counterinsurgency campaign "*Victoria 82*", would work, were contained in a series of confidential army memoranda and a *Plan Nacional de Seguridad y Desarrollo* (National Plan of Security and Development) dated 1 April, 1982. The following are extracts from these documents.

National Plan of Security and Development
PNSD-01-82
GUATEMALA CITY CEM 01ABR82
RLHGCC-82

. . . .

CURRENT NATIONAL OBJECTIVES

1. To make citizens feel that authority is at the service of the people and not that people are at the service of authority.
2. To achieve the reconciliation of the Guatemalan family in order to favour national peace and harmony.
3. To bring about individual security and tranquillity on the basis of absolute respect for human rights.
4. To recover individual and national dignity.
5. To establish a nationalistic spirit and to lay the foundations for the participation and integration of the different ethnic groups which make up our nationality.
6. To achieve economic recovery within the system of free enterprise in accordance with those controls made necessary by the prevailing national situation.
7. To restructure the judiciary with the participation of the legal profession, to have it meet the demands of the current situation and guarantee its ethical, moral and juridical functions.
8. To eradicate administrative corruption and to encourage among state employees a genuine spirit of public service to act as the basis of a national government.
9. To stimulate among the various pressure groups which represent the activity of the nation a new way of thinking, developmentalist, reformist and nationalist.
10. To strengthen national integration, taking effective advantage of cooperation with

other countries and international bodies, at the same time as projecting the problems of the Guatemalan state abroad.

11. To improve the standard of living of the population in order to diminish existing contradictions.

12. To restructure the electoral system so that, as the fruits of a genuine democracy, there will be respect for political participation and avoidance of frustration among the people.

13. To reorganize public administration, with the goal of dynamizing the execution of government programmes, making them efficient, regulating their operation and avoiding administrative anarchy.

14. To re-establish constitutional rule in the country as a matter of urgency, in order that Guatemala may know and demand their duties and obligations with the free play of the democratic process.

E. BASIC STRATEGIC CONCEPT

1. *Statement of Intent:*

Guatemala will promote and undertake, in the short and medium term, administrative, functional and juridical reforms of the structure and functioning of the organs of the state, employing the relevant branches of public authority, and will co-ordinate and integrate anti-subversive programmes at the level of all political bodies of the nation; this action will be supported, assuring the optimum working of economic structures and activities and giving attention to the priority economic problems of the people; guaranteeing the implementation of programmes designed to shape and maintain a concept of nationalism compatible with the traditions of the country; assuring the improvement of the structures and functioning of the Army of Guatemala and the internal security forces in order to confront and successfully fight subversive movements and groups. Programmes will be put into effect which aim to improve living conditions for the dispossessed classes. Finally, efforts will be made to improve the image of Guatemala abroad, based on clearly defined and aggressive diplomatic actions.

2. Suppositions:

A. Any changes made to the basic structures of the state will be minimal.

B. Russia and Cuba will maintain and increase their support to the subversive groups operating in the country.

C. Subversion will continue to menace the internal order of the nations of Central America.

D. The eventual fall of the Republic of El Salvador into the hands of international communism would aggravate the situation of Guatemala.

RECOMMENDATIONS

. . . .

4. *Military Sphere*

To maintain and improve, in accordance with the situation, the organization of the Army and the internal security forces, to confront successfully the subversive movements and groups and perfect all bodies and training systems in this area.

To promote meetings, conferences and seminars within the Army and at the inter-army level regionally, allowing for the exchange of anti-subversive experiences, and to encourage the efficient distribution of their findings, studies and conclusions.

To propose the signing of international agreements, both multilateral and bilateral, to assure an efficient interchange of intelligence and assistance among countries of the region in subversive matters of mutual interest.

To optimise the organization of intelligence headquarters, enhance its methods, modernize its systems and extend its action to cover every corner of the country as well as internationally, in order to detect in all fields and in all areas the conditions which may give rise to subversive movements or may help them to flourish.

To locate and identify subversive groups, their essential characteristics and activities.

To determine those countries, institutions and bodies that promote and support subversive movements and groups.

To compile information on successful anti-subversive methods and actions employed in other countries.

. . . .

ARMY GENERAL STAFF
NATIONAL PALACE — GUATEMALA
160800JUL82
LEMG — 1800
APPENDIX "H" (STANDING ORDERS FOR THE DEVELOPMENT OF
ANTI-SUBVERSIVE OPERATIONS) TO THE "*VICTORIA 82*"
PLAN OF CAMPAIGN

. . . .

1. GENERAL OBSERVATIONS
The responsibilities of the Army in the war against subversion are many and varied. At every level, at all ranks and in every sphere of military activity, the Army Officer plans, co-ordinates and executes this type of operation.

Subversion exists because a small group of people support it and a large number of people tolerate it, either out of fear or because there are causes which give rise to it.

The war must be fought on all fronts: military, political, but above all socio-economic. *The minds* of the population are our main target.

. . . .

B. Military Strategy
To increase the size of the Army, especially of commands in conflict areas, as well as relying on the support of the Civil Defence Units, and working in co-ordination with other security forces in the country and other instances of Public Administration, and with appropriate legislation to:

a) deny the subversives access to the population who constitute their social and political support base.

b) win back as many members of the Irregular Local Forces (FIL) as possible and at the same time eliminate those subversives who refuse to lay down their arms.

c) annihilate the Clandestine Local Committees (CCL) and the Permanent Military Units (UMP) of the enemy.

. . . .

Jointly with Military Operations, Psychological Operations will be carried out in order to:
 a) win the support of the population.
 b) obtain information to allow continued operations.
 c) permit the normal economic development and progress of the nation.
 d) forge closer links between the people and the Army.
 e) exploit to the maximum the Army's successes in anti-subversive operations.
 f) organize Civil Defence Patrols in the most conflictive areas, suitably supervised and
  controlled by the local army command

D. Tactics to be Employed

1. *Trick them:* Subversion must be fought with its own methods and techniques. A Plan of Disinformation must be in effect at all times.
2. *Find them:* The biggest problem is always to locate the guerrilla military units which, from the very nature of their methods of combat, remain hidden. Use local intelligence and saturate the area with patrols.
3. *Attack them:* When you have succeeded in locating a guerrilla force, maintain contact at all costs and immediately inform your command so that a larger unit can support you and annihilate the enemy.
4. *Annihilate them:* Destruction of guerrilla forces is your mission. Control of territory is a means towards the achievement of this goal but never an end in itself.

. . . .

H. Code of Conduct Towards the Civilian Population

 1. Take nothing from the civilian population, not even a pin.
 2. Do not make sexual advances or take liberties with local women.
 3. Protect and do not damage the crops.
 4. Pay a fair price for what you purchase. If in doubt, pay a little more.
 5. Return all objects loaned and be sure to pay compensation for any property damaged.
 6. Be polite and talk to all local people. Show particular affection and respect for old people and children. Remember that old people influence local opinion and that children may be valuable informers.
 7. Welcome in a friendly and polite manner all persons who wish to speak with you and greet them whenever you meet on the road or on footpaths.
 8. Respect the population's customs and traditions, as well as their civil and religious authorities.
 9. Respect the tombs, sepulchres, churches and other buildings which the community respects.
10. Yield right of way on all roads unless this places at risk the safety of the troops.
11. Accept no gifts or flattery.
12. Do not abuse the hospitality of country people.

 (Signed)
 López Fuentes   **Mendoza García**
 Army Chief of Staff   G-3 Army General Staff

Appendix 2
Witnesses of Indian Massacres, 1982

In October 1982, the Washington Office on Latin America (WOLA) collected testimony of massacres committed in the Indian highlands of Guatemala under the Ríos Montt regime, between March and September of that year. Their findings were presented at a conference on Human Rights in Guatemala, organized by WOLA and the Johns Hopkins University School for Advanced International Studies (SAIS). The following are taken from the total of 58 separate massacre testimonies submitted by WOLA, and are reprinted with their kind permission.

Date: April 5-8, 1982
Department: El Quiché
Municipality: Ixcán
Village: La Unión
Witness: Unidentified
Source: Christian Solidarity Committee, San Cristóbal de las Casas diocese, Chiapas, Mexico.

I was there when the massacre began, in a sector called La Unión. There, they killed 400 people inside the church, a big church, and they didn't let anyone out. If they came out, they made them go back in — men, women, children, old people. They left them there and threw three grenades. But they didn't all die and so they shot them. Four hundred died there. Outside, in the marketplace, they killed even more. Those weren't counted; who knows how many? The soldiers had a plane and a helicopter and they landed on the road. There were about 400.

Then, they went to another sector and killed the people they found. But there were others outside the place. I was one and I heard the massacre begin and left with my children. After that they came on April 5th to kill people and they finished on April 8th, in Holy Week. They took five young girls and raped them, then made them prepare food. They killed small animals, livestock and chickens and made the girls cook their food. They did what they wanted with the girls, but they didn't let them go. After they finished eating, they killed them.

Little girls, little boys — ones that didn't think yet and didn't run — they threw them in the fire or the ashes or the hot water. Then they grabbed the adults, but they didn't shoot them. They put them all in the Evangelical church, tortured them and stuck them with needles, stuck needles in their eyes, bashed their heads and cut them with machetes. Some they hung with ropes. They burned the animals. Many people were thrown into a bathroom, a large bathroom in the church. Many, many. They stuck them with needles. Everybody — old men and women, young boys and girls. And then they killed them. They carried chairs and benches, tables, all the furnishings of the church which they used to make the fire.

Date: May 26, 1982
Department: San Marcos
Witness: Female, name withheld
Source: Father Luís Gurriarán, Chiapas, Mexico

Yesterday, 25 of us from the same village arrived here and many others are coming behind us, also fleeing. We fled because we thought they would kill us. It took three days to get here because we walked slowly, by night, carrying the small children. They cried because they were tired; but it is better to be tired and alive.

They threatened us. They told us that after this month they were going to kill all the Indians — all of them — and burn their villages. They told us they were going to come and kill us. They have already killed many and taken the men away. They took my husband and they killed by brother on the spot and told us, "We are going to finish off all the Indians." So we fled. It is not possible to live in Guatemala. They have killed many people — the children, the women, it doesn't matter who. They are killing everybody. They say that we are all guerrillas and that is why they are killing us. Just take this example: there was one family that took some brush from the woods and used it for fertiliser in the cornfield. The army came and said that the place where they had cleared the brush was a guerrilla camp where the guerrillas trained and that this family had fed them. So they carried off the man and later came back and took about 80 people, including my husband and my brother. They took them to the school and asked them who the guerrillas were. They didn't know. So they grabbed my brother and hung him from a rafter and began hitting him and asking him who the guerrillas were in the village. But he didn't say anything because he hadn't seen anything and he didn't know anything. So they cut him with a knife all over his body. They cut away little pieces until they killed him. Then they threw him a a truck with 15 others including my husband. There were two trucks full of soldiers. They threw my brother off a cliff and took the rest to the barracks in Huehuetenango. The ones who took them away were those who are called "kaibiles", dressed in camouflage uniforms. They were all armed. At this time we don't know what happened to those who were taken away. Maybe they are alive, maybe they are dead. They were never seen again.

Date: July 2
Department: Huehuetenango
Municipality: San Mateo Ixtatán
Source: Ronald Hennessey, Maryknoll Missioner

On July 2, 1982, the army came to San Mateo Ixtatán to organise the Civil Defence. They read out the list of the names of several men and one woman, saying that these have been picked to be the leaders of the Civil Defence organization. Ten men from the list reported to the military. They were advised that it was necessary that they be taken to the military base in Barillas for special training to fulfil the leadership positions. About half way there, at the village of Nuca, the soldiers cut the throats of the ten men and dumped their bodies off the road.

Date: July 18
Department: Baja Verapaz
Municipality: Rabinal
Village: Concul
Source: Justice and Peace Committee

For our people, July 18 was a day made horrible from the suffering of so many families returning from buying and selling in the market. On the way, about 3.30, they met the army. A young girl who is a survivor told me that she was with her mother and grandmother, with five members of her family when they saw the army on the road to the village of Concul. They were in uniform and carried arms which is the clearest sign that they were soldiers. They told the mother to go to their house and for the young girl to stay with them. They told all the adults to go to a house and they gathered up about 200 people. Some soldiers were stopping people who passed by in the road. Others got people out of their houses and took them to the same spot. Some people, for example those from the village of Raxul which is along the same road, were able to flee.

They took the young girls to another, more distant house and when it was getting dark, a soldier came and asked them what they were going to give them. Then they began raping, beginning with the youngest who were about twelve years old. When the soldier went off with some of the girls, this girl escaped and got into the woods in the dark. In the morning, she didn't see anyone and went to the house to look for her mother and found that everyone had been burned. The houses were burned and so were the people. She found her mother's body, only half burned and she heard an old lady cry out, "kill me once and for all". She was so afraid that she ran off and passed the house where the young girls had been and saw them spilled in the bush and on the road and around the house. She went on to her own house, which is near, but not part of Rabinal — about two hours away. She told her brother what had happened and he went to Rabinal and saw the bodies and estimated that there were about 250. Some of them weren't dead from burning, but from asphyxiation from being piled on top of each other. One girl was sitting up with her jaw broken and he went and told her family. Then he went to Rabinal to report to the authorities and they gave him permission to get his mother's body.

Appendix 3
Unity Agreement of the URNG

TODAY THE FLAME of the People's Revolutionary War is burning strong in all parts of the country. In the West, North, South, East and center, and in the capital city, there are victorious guerrilla operations every day, and mass sabotage and propaganda support activities. The revolutionary forces maintain a constant siege in the border areas, in the plantations, the oil zones, highways, tourist centres and the slums in the capital. Nearly all of the Indian groups have joined the People's Revolutionary War, and together with the ladino population they support thousands and thousands of guerrillas. In 1981, the guerrilla organizations moved from occupying villages and plantations to the occupation of municipal and departmental capitals, and from propaganda actions to generalized military harassment operations. We are now beginning to systematize operations which directly destroy the enemy forces. In 1981, we caused approximately 3,200 enemy casualties, including soldiers, police agents and members of the local repressive power in the countryside and in the city. Our guerrilla units have begun to recover enemy weapons, destroy military transport, and to down planes and helicopters. We have moved from operating with small units to using larger ones, and have managed, despite important blows, to completely defeat the offensives launched by the enemy in 1981 against the strongholds of the revolution in the city and the countryside. The People's Revolutionary War is spreading to more parts of the country; it is deepening its mass support and is increasing its offensive capacity. The exploited, oppressed and discriminated Guatemalan Indians have risen up and through their integration into the People's Revolutionary War, together with the masses of ladino workers, have already decided the outcome of the war . . .

The Revolutionary, Patriotic, Popular and Democratic Government that we will construct in Guatemala commits itself to the Guatemalan people and to the international community to fulfill the following five fundamental programmatic points:

1. *The Revolution will eliminate once and for all the repression against our people and will guarantee to all citizens, the supreme rights of life and peace.*

Life and peace are supreme human rights. The Revolution will end our people's repression and the political regime that has given itself the right to assassinate its opposition to remain in power. Since 1954, the government of the rich exploiters and repressors has killed thousands of Guatemalans for political reasons. Their blood represents for the Revolution, a commitment to freedom, peace and respect for life.

II. *The Revolution will set down the foundations for resolving the basic needs of the great majority of our people by eliminating the political domination of the repressive rich, both national and foreign, who rule Guatemala.*

The Revolution will put an end to this domination, and guarantees that those who produce with their own creative effort will benefit from the product of their labor. The properties of the very rich will be taken over by the Revolutionary government, which will see to it that this wealth is used to resolve the needs of the working people. The Revolution will guarantee a true agrarian reform, giving land to those who work in an individual, collective or cooperative fashion. The Revolution will guarantee small and medium-sized agricultural properties, and will distribute to those who work the land with their own hands those properties now held by the military hierarchy and the corrupt, greedy and repressive functionaries and businessmen. The Revolution will guarantee small and medium-sized commerce and stimulate the creation and development of a national industry which Guatemala needs to be able to develop. The Revolution will guarantee an effective price control to benefit the great majority and will at the same time, allow reasonable profits as long as they do not hurt the people.

The Revolution will wrest power from the very rich, both national and foreign, and thus create jobs and guarantee decent salaries to all workers in the countryside and the city. Once the people have power, we will have a base to begin to resolve the great problems of health, housing and illiteracy which afflict the vast majority of the population.

III. *The Revolution will guarantee equality between Indians and ladinos, and will end cultural oppression and discrimination.*

The domination by the rich is the root cause of the cultural oppression and discrimination which the Indian population suffers in Guatemala. The first step towards eliminating cultural oppression and discrimination is to enable Indians, who are an integral part of the Guatemalan people, to participate in political power. The participation of the Indian population in political power, together with the ladino population, will allow us to meet Indians' needs for land, work, salary, health, housing and general welfare. Meeting these needs is the first condition toward achieving equality between Indians and ladinos. The second condition toward guaranteeing this equality is respect for their culture and recognition of their rights to maintain their own identity. The development of a culture which gathers and integrates our people's historic roots is one of the great objectives of the Revolution. Indians and ladinos in power will freely decide Guatemala's future contours.

IV. *The Revolution will guarantee the creation of a New Society, in which all patriotic, popular and democratic sectors will be represented in the government.*

The Revolution will respect the people's rights to elect their local, municipal and national representatives. All those citizens who with their work, skills or capital, are willing and able to help Guatemala overcome its poverty, backwardness and dependence will have a place in the New Society. Patriotic businessmen who are willing to contribute to the achievement of this great objective will have full rights, without conditions, except that they respect the interests of the working people. The Revolution will guarantee freedom of expression and of religious belief, as a way of facilitating the contribution of all citizens to the construction of a New Society. The Revolution will be severe in its judgment of the most repressive among the enemy, and of the clique of highranking military officers and their accomplices who have planned and directed the repression against our people. The Revolution will be flexible in its judgment of those who have refused orders to repress our people. The Revolution will eliminate forced conscription for military service, a practice which discriminates against the Indians. All patriotic officers and soldiers who have not stained their hands with the blood of our people will be able to participate in the new People's Revolutionary Army which the Guatemalan people will build to guarantee the security and defense of the country.

In the New Society, women will have the same rights as men, since they share the same obligations as men and even greater ones in their role as mothers. Children and the aged will enjoy the protection they deserve for the contribution they will make or have made to the production of social wealth.

The Revolution recognizes the Christian population as one of the pillars of the New Society, since they have placed their beliefs and faith at the service of the struggle for the freedom of all Guatemalans.

V. *Based in the principle of self-determination the Revolution will guarantee a policy of nonalignment and international cooperation which poor countries need in order to develop in the modern world.*

In today's complex and interdependent world, it is necessary to maintain a position of nonalignment with the great powers and of international cooperation.

Poor countries need foreign investment and this must be agreed upon on the basis of respect for each country's national sovereignty, taking into account both the needs of the poor countries and reasonable returns on foreign investments. Political stability is in this respect indispensable, as without it there can be no international cooperation. International cooperation is possible between nations which are different ideologically, and have different forms of government as long as there is respect for each country's right to self-determination.

Select Bibliography

Books on Central America

Anderson, Thomas P. (1983) *Politics in Central America.* New York, Praeger.

Barry, Tom, Deb Preusch and Beth Wood (1983) *Dollars and Dictators.* London, Zed Press.

CECADE-CIDE (1982) *Centroamérica: Crisis y Política Internacional.* Mexico City, Siglo XXI.

Debray, Régis (1977) *A Critique of Arms.* Harmondsworth, Penguin Books.

— *The Revolution on Trial.* Harmondsworth, Penguin Books.

Diskin, Martin, ed. (1984) *Trouble in our Backyard: Central America and the United States in the Eighties.* New York, Pantheon.

Fagen, Richard and Olga Pellicer, eds. (1983) *The Future of Central America: Policy Choices for the U.S. and Mexico.* Stanford, California, Stanford University Press.

Feinberg, Richard, ed. (1982) *Central America: International Dimensions of the Crisis.* New York, Holmes and Meier.

Gott, Richard (1970) *Guerrilla Movements in Latin America.* London, Thomas Nelson.

Pearce, Jenny (1981) *Under the Eagle: U.S. Intervention in Central America and the Caribbean.* London, Latin America Bureau.

Stanford Central America Action Network (SCAAN) eds. (1983) *Revolution in Central America.* Boulder, Colorado, Westview Press.

Torres-Rivas, Edelberto (1971) *Interpretación del desarrollo social centroamericano.* San José, Costa Rica, EDUCA.

— (1981) *Crisis del poder en Centroamérica.* San José, Costa Rica, EDUCA.

— and Julio César Pinto (1983) *Problemas de la formación del estado nacional.* San José, Costa Rica, ICAP.

Books on Guatemala

Adams, Richard N. (1970) *Crucifixion by Power: Essays on Guatemalan National Social Structure 1944-1966.* Austin, University of Texas Press.

Agency for International Development (AID) (1982) *Land and Labor in Guatemala: An Assessment.* Guatemala City, Ediciones Papiro.

Andersen, Nicolás (1982) *Guatemala, Escuela revolucionaria de nuevos hombres.* Mexico City, Editorial Nuestro Tiempo.

Arévalo, Juan José (1963) *Anti-Kommunism in Latin America.* New York, Lyle Stuart.

— (1963) *The Shark and the Sardines.* New York, Lyle Stuart.

Burgos, Elisabeth (1983) *Moi, Rigoberta Menchú: Une vie et une voix, la révolution au Guatémala.* Paris, Gallimard.

Cardoza y Aragón, Luis (1956) *La Revolución Guatemalteca.* Montevideo, Uruguay, Ediciones Pueblos Unidos.

Cook, Blanche (1981) *The Declassified Eisenhower.* Garden City, New York, Doubleday & Co.

Falla, Ricardo (1978) *Quiché Rebelde.* Guatemala City, Editorial Universitaria.

Fried, Jonathan L. et al., eds. (1983) *Guatemala in Rebellion: Unfinished History.* New York, Grove Press.

Galeano, Eduardo (1969) *Guatemala: Occupied Country.* New York, Monthly Review Press.

González, José and Antonio Campos (1983) *Guatemala: Un pueblo en lucha.* Madrid, Editorial Revolución.

Guzmán Böckler, Carlos and Jean-Loup Hébert (1970) *Guatemala: Una interpretación histórico-social.* Mexico City, Siglo XXI.

IEPALA (1982) *Guatemala: Un futuro próximo.* Madrid, IEPALA.

Immerman, Richard H. (1982) *The CIA in Guatemala: The Foreign Policy of Intervention.* Austin, University of Texas Press.

Jonas, Susanne (1981) *Guatemala: Una historia inmediata.* Mexico City, Siglo XXI.

— and David Tobis, eds. (1974) *Guatemala.* Berkeley, California, NACLA

Kinzer, Stephen and Stephen Schlesinger (1981) *Bitter Fruit: The Untold Story of the American Coup in Guatemala.* Garden City, New York, Doubleday & Co.

López Larrave, Mario (1979) *Breve historia del movimiento sindical guatemalteca.* Guatemala City, Editorial Universitaria.

Martínez Peláez, Severo (1976) *La Patria del Criollo.* San José, Costa Rica, EDUCA.

Melville, Thomas and Marjorie (1971) *Guatemala: Another Vietnam?* Harmondsworth, Penguin Books.

Payeras, Mario (1983) *Days of the Jungle.* New York, Monthly Review Press.

Plant, Roger (1978) *Guatemala: Unnatural Disaster.*
London, Latin America Bureau.

Poitevin, René (1977) *El proceso de industrialización en Guatemala.*
San José, Costa Rica, EDUCA.

Schneider, Ronald (1958) *Communism in Guatemala 1944-1954.*
New York, Praeger.

Toriello, Guillermo (1955) *La batalla de Guatemala.* Mexico City,
Ediciones Cuadernos Americanos.

Ydígoras Fuentes, Miguel (1963) *My War with Communism.*
Englewood Cliffs, New Jersey, Prentice Hall.

Articles, Reports and Monographs

Aguilera, Gabriel (1979) The massacre at Panzós and capitalist
development in Guatemala. *Monthly Review,* Vol. 31 no.7, pp.13-23.

Amnesty International (1981) *Guatemala: A Government Programme of
Political Murder.* London, AI Publications.

Arnson, Cynthia, Delia Miller and Roland Seeman (1981) *Background
Information on Guatemala, the Armed Forces and U.S. Military Assistance.*
Washington DC, Institute for Policy Studies.

— and Flora Montealegre (1982) *Background Information on
Guatemala, Human Rights and U.S. Military Assistance.* Washington
DC, Institute for Policy Studies.

Black, George (1982) Central America: Crisis in the Backyard.
New Left Review, no.135, pp.5-34.

— (1983) Guatemala's Silent War. *Monthly Review,*
Vol. 35, no.3, pp.3-17.

— with Milton Jamail and Norma Stoltz Chinchilla (1983)
Garrison Guatemala. *NACLA Report on the Americas,* Vol. XVII,
no.1.

— (1983) Guatemala: The War is not Over. *NACLA Report on the
Americas,* Vol. XVII, no.2.

CIDAMO (1980) The Workers Movement in Guatemala. *NACLA Report
on the Americas,* Vol. XIV, no.1, pp.28-33.

Davis, Shelton H. and Julie Hodson (1982) *Witnesses to Political
Violence in Guatemala: The Suppression of a Rural Development
Program.* Boston, Oxfam America.

El Parcial (1980) *Guatemala: El laboratorio de la contrarrevolucion
centroamericano.* Hamburg, El Parcial.

— (1982) Guatemala: *Fusiles y frijoles contra el avance del movimiento
popular.* Hamburg, El Parcial.

Gilly, Adolfo (1965) The Guerrilla Movement in Guatemala.
Monthly Review, Vol. 17, no.1, pp.9-40 and Vol. 17, no.2, pp.7-41.

Gleijeses, Piero (1981) *Perspectives of a Regime's Transformation in*

Guatemala. Bonn, Friedrich Ebert Stiftung.
— (1982) *Guatemala: Crisis and Response.* (unpublished Ms.)
— (1982) *Tilting at Windmills: Reagan in Central America.*
Washington D.C., Johns Hopkins University, School of Advanced
International Studies (SAIS).
Gordon, Max (1971) A Case History of U.S. Subversion:
Guatemala 1954. Science and Society, Vol. XXXV.
Jenkins, Brian, Caesar D. Sereseres and Luigi Einaudi (1974)
U.S. Military Aid and Guatemalan Politics. Los Angeles, Arms Control
and Foreign Policy Seminar.
National Lawyers Guild and La Raza Legal Alliance (1980)
Guatemala: Repression and Resistance. New York, National Lawyers
Guild.
Organization of American States (1981) *Informe de la Comisión
Interamericana de Derechos Humanos sobre la Situación de los Derechos
Humanos en la República de Guatemala.* Washington DC, OAS.
Shenk, Janet and Judy Butler (1981) Central America: No Road Back.
NACLA Report on the Americas, Vol. XV, no.3.
Simons, Marlise (1981) Guatemala: The Coming Danger. *Foreign
Policy,* no.43, pp.93-103.
Stoltz Chinchilla, Norma et al., (1980) Central America: The Strongmen
are Shaking. *Latin American Perspectives,* nos.24-5.
Torres-Rivas, Edelberto (1980) Guatemala: Crisis and Political Violence.
NACLA Report on the Americas, Vol. XIV, no.1, pp.16-27.

nacla
report on the americas

NACLA — the North American Congress on Latin America — is an independent, non-profit research and publishing institute founded in 1966. Its work focuses on in-depth reporting and analysis of the political economy of Latin America and the foreign policy of the United States.

NACLA's bi-monthly magazine, *Report on the Americas,* presents the results of NACLA's in-house research and also publishes the work of prominent outside journalists, academics and other observers of Latin American affairs. Each issue of the *Report* treats in depth a single topic of central concern to U.S.-Latin American relations and offers a selection of shorter feature articles on current political and economic developments, all illustrated by the work of outstanding photographers.

The *Report on the Americas* are widely used in classrooms and study groups, and by journalists, church leaders, trade unionists, human rights activists and concerned citizens in the United States and in over 60 countries around the world.

NACLA, 151 West 19th Street, 9th Floor, New York, NY 10011, USA.

LATIN AMERICAN TITLES FROM ZED PRESS

POLITICAL ECONOMY

DONALD HODGES AND ROSS GANDY
Mexico 1910–1982:
Reform or Revolution?
(New, updated edition)
Hb and Pb

GEORGE BECKFORD AND MICHAEL WITTER
Small Garden, Bitter Weed:
Struggle and Change in Jamaica
Hb and Pb

LIISA NORTH
Bitter Grounds:
Roots of Revolt in El Salvador
Pb

RONALDO MUNCK
Politics and Dependency in the Third World:
The Case of Latin America
Hb and Pb

GEORGE BECKFORD
Persistent Poverty
Pb

TOM BARRY, BETH WOOD and DEB PREUSCH
Dollars and Dictators:
A Guide to Central America
Hb and Pb

CONTEMPORARY HISTORY/REVOLUTIONARY STRUGGLES

GEORGE BLACK
Triumph of the People:
The Sandinista Revolution in Nicaragua
Hb and Pb

CEDRIC ROBINSON
Black Marxism:
The Making of the Black Radical Tradition
Hb and Pb

TEOFILO CABASTRERO
Ministers of God, Ministers of the People
Hb and Pb

WOMEN

LATIN AMERICAN AND CARIBBEAN WOMEN'S COLLECTIVE
Slaves of Slaves:
The Challenge of Latin American Women
Hb and Pb

MIRANDA DAVIES
Third World — Second Sex:
Women's Struggles and National Liberation
Hb and Pb

MARGARET RANDALL
Sandino's Daughters:
Testimonies of Nicaraguan Women in Struggle
Pb

BONNIE MASS
Population Target:
The Political Economy of Population Control in Latin America
Pb

JUNE NASH AND HELEN ICKEN SAFA (EDITORS)
Sex and Class in Latin America:
Women's Perspectives on Politics, Economics and the Family in the Third
World
Pb

INTERNATIONAL RELATIONS/IMPERIALISM

DAVID STOLL
Fishers of Men or Founders of Empire:
The Wycliffe Bible Translators in Latin America
Hb and Pb

JAMES PETRAS ET AL
Class, State and Power in the Third World
With Case Studies of Class Conflict in Latin America
Hb

WOMEN IN THE THIRD WORLD: TITLES FROM ZED PRESS

BOBBY SIU
Women of China:
Imperialism and Women's Resistance, 1900-1949
Hb and Pb

INGELA BENDT AND JAMES DOWNING
We Shall Return:
Women of Palestine
Hb and Pb

MIRANDA DAVIES (EDITOR)
Third World — Second Sex:
Women's Struggles and National Liberation
Hb and Pb

JULIETTE MINCES
The House of Obedience:
Women in Arab Society
Hb and Pb

MARGARET RANDALL
Sandino's Daughters:
Testimonies of Nicaraguan Women in Struggle
Pb

MARIA MIES
The Lacemakers of Narsapur:
Indian Housewives Produce for the World Market
Pb

ASMA EL DAREER
Woman, Why do you Weep?
Circumcision and Its Consequences
Hb and Pb

RAQIYA HAJI DUALEH ABDALLA
Sisters in Affliction:
Circumcision and Infibulation of Women in Africa
Hb and Pb

MARIA ROSE CUTRUFELLI
Women of Africa:
Roots of Oppression
Hb and Pb

AZAR TABARI AND NAHID YEGANEH
In the Shadow of Islam:
The Women's Movement in Iran
Hb and Pb

BONNIE MASS
Population Target:
The Political Economy of Population Control in Latin America
Pb

NAWAL EL SAADAWI
The Hidden Face of Eve:
Women in the Arab World
Hb and Pb

ELSE SKJONSBERG
A Special Caste?
Tamil Women in Sri Lanka
Pb

PATRICIA JEFFREY
Frogs in a Well:
Indian Women in Purdah
Hb and Pb

JUNE NASH AND HELEN ICKEN SAFA (EDITORS)
Sex and Class in Latin America:
Women's Perspectives on Politics, Economics and the Family in the Third World
Pb

LATIN AMERICAN AND CARIBBEAN WOMEN'S COLLECTIVE
Slaves of Slaves: The Challenge of Latin American Women
Hb and Pb

CHRISTINE OBBO
African Women:
Their Struggle for Economic Independence
Pb

GAIL OMVEDT
We Will Smash this Prison!
Indian Women in Struggle
Hb and Pb

AGNES SMEDLEY
Portraits of Chinese Women in Revolution
Pb

RAYMONDA TAWIL
My Home, My Prison
Pb

NAWAL EL SAADAWI
Woman at Zero Point
Hb and Pb

ELISABETH CROLL
Chinese Women
Hb and Pb

ARLENE EISEN
Women in the New Vietnam
Hb and Pb

Zed press titles cover Africa, Asia, Latin America and the Middle East, as well as general issues affecting the Third World's relations with the rest of the world. Our Series embrace: Imperialism, Women, Political Economy, History, Labour, Voices of Struggle, Human Rights and other areas pertinent to the Third World.

You can order Zed titles direct from Zed Press, 57 Caledonian Road, London, N1 9DN, U.K.